Advance Praise for
Hills, Hawgs & Ho Chi Minh

Don Kardong is our wittiest writer about the sport of distance running. If you don't believe me, read Hills, Hawgs & Ho Chi Minh. I promise you'll be laughing hard. When you hit a low spot with your workouts, read "Le Grizz" or another hilarious chapter in this book, and you'll begin a swift recovery.
Bill Rodgers, four-time Boston Marathon champion

Reading this book is like going on a long run with a treasured training partner. The time passes almost unnoticed while you're regaled with some of the most entertaining, witty and cogent running writing around. Given the quality of the camaraderie, you'll hardly believe the ground you've covered by the time you're done.
Scott Douglas, editor of *Running Times*

It's better to be known by what you do now than what you did once. Don Kardong did a lot as a young runner, including almost winning a medal in an Olympic Marathon. That was twenty years ago. We know him now as the writer that runners most enjoy reading. His stories — the best of which he brings to this book — make even the most serious of us laugh at ourselves.
**Joe Henderson, columnist for *Runner's World* and
editor of *Running Commentary***

In Hills, Hawgs & Ho Chi Minh, Kardong proves once again that he's the most gullible runner alive. He'll run anywhere — or so it seems. And neither grizzly bears nor urban skyscrapers nor too much mid-marathon wine will slow him down. Every story is a delight, filled with mystery, adventure and an unflagging appreciation for the absurdity lurking around the next bend.
Amby Burfoot, executive director of *Runner's World*

Don's numerous contributions to the sport have more than likely benefitted all of us in one way or another. Hills, Hawgs & Ho Chi Minh is just another example of one of his great contributions. Sit back, relax and let Don set the pace.
**Joan Benoit Samuelson, American female record
holder in the marathon**

Hills, Hawgs

& Ho Chi Minh

more tales of a wayward runner

DON KARDONG

Keokee Co.

PUBLISHING

SANDPOINT, IDAHO

"The Ultimate Runner" (1985), "Is There Life After World Class?" (1985), and "All that Jazz" (1986) appeared first in *The Runner* magazine. "Trials and Tribulations" was published in *New York Running News* in 1988. Except for "Blooms," the rest of the stories were originally published in *Runner's World*.

Keokee Co. Publishing, Inc.
P.O. Box 722
Sandpoint, ID 83864
Phone: (208) 263-3573

Printed on recycled paper

Printed in the United States of America
10 9 8 7 6 5 4 3 2 1

Library of Congress Cataloging-in-Publication Data
Kardong, Don.
Hills, hawgs & Ho Chi Minh : more tales of a wayward runner / Don Kardong.
    p.   cm.
ISBN 1-879628-12-0   (pbk. : alk. paper)
1. Kardong, Don. 2. Runners (Sports)—United States—Biography. I. Title.
GV1061.15.K37A3   1996
796.42'092—dc20
[B]   95-45039
                      CIP

CONTENTS

INTRODUCTION

This is my second collection of stories. Ten years ago, in the epilog of my first book, *Thirty Phone Booths to Boston: Tales of a Wayward Runner*, I reminisced about the tremendous changes that had occurred in my favorite sport from 1975 to 1985, many of which I had written about: the running boom, the 1980 Olympic boycott, the birth of professional running. Wondering what the next ten years would bring, I wrote: "I feel certain of only one thing. Ten years from now, I will find myself puffing up a hill somewhere, running a course that I've run many times before. And I will be enjoying myself immensely."

Amazingly, that is, in fact, where I find myself these days, ten years down the road. Puffing a bit more than I'd like, to be sure, but still enjoying the challenge of cresting the next hill on one familiar course or another. Sometimes, I guess, you guess right.

To be honest, though, it's been the unfamiliar "hills" — Pikes Peak, the Empire State Building, the ascent from the Colorado River to the rim of the Grand Canyon — that have really marked these last ten years in my life. Adventure runs in these and other locations have occupied a fair amount of my time, and they represent a number of the stories in this collection.

The topic of aging also surfaces fairly frequently in these writings. Turning 40 will do that to you. With or without birthdays to mark the years, though, it hasn't escaped my attention that I run slower, tire sooner and injure easier these days. For some odd reason, too, events that used to seem like ancient history — the Civil War, the Pilgrims landing at Plymouth Rock, Marco Polo's travels — seem more and more recent. For a 10-year-old, I suppose, the Wright Brothers' flight occurred over nine lifetimes ago. For me, less than two lifetimes, and getting closer all the time.

But I digress. The point is, I've noticed those ten years passing, and I'm just glad they haven't totally consumed my legs, at least not yet. As long as I can still get out with friends for two hours of running once a week, which I generally can, I haven't earned the right to whine about old age. For this I give thanks.

Speaking of thanks, I'd like to express my appreciation to a number of people for their help with this book. Claire Kowalchik, Managing Editor at *Runner's World* magazine, was responsible for numerous suggestions, recommendations and general editing, often for the second time around. When Claire marks "rambling" in the margin next to three or four paragraphs of text, I pay attention. I also discovered that Claire doesn't care for certain words: pretty, perhaps, seems. It seems to me she pretty much dislikes indecisiveness, but perhaps I'm wrong. I do know we have some differences about commas, a fact that doesn't at all diminish my appreciation for her help.

I also want to thank Chris Bessler, Stephen Drinkard and my other new friends at Keokee Publishing for helping bring this book to fruition. I've appreciated their input, feedback and diligence. They say there are disadvantages to working with a small publisher. I've yet to discover any.

Most of all, I'd like to thank my family — Bridgid, Kaitlin and Catherine — for their tolerance and support of this and other running and writing projects. This stuff can consume a lot of family time, weekends especially, and the three women in my household have been good sports about my absences, even when I haven't insisted I'm simply racking up frequent flyer miles for the next family vacation.

Speaking of vacations, there's no doubt we could all use one. From the time this book project began until now, Bridgid has fought and won a battle with cancer. Her struggle, more than anything, has put life and its blessings in perspective. Even a 100-mile run seems light-hearted in comparison.

That makes it reasonable that I would dedicate this book to Bridgid, but I made a deal. It's time to begin that novel I keep promising to write and dedicate to her. After ten years, some things don't change, and procrastinating on that particular project is one of them.

For now, then, I'd like to dedicate this book to my daughters, Kaitlin and Catherine, characters in several of these stories as well as in everyday life. Thanks for being great travelers, and for sharing a few adventures with your aging father. We'll do more soon, just as soon as I rack up a few more miles in the air.

And finally, to you readers out there, thanks for breaking away from the telly and online services often enough to keep the printed word alive. I found the individuals and events on which these stories are based to be inspiring, and I hope you do, too. God knows, we all need an occasional bit of inspiration to get us to the top of that next hill. So lean forward, lift those legs, breathe deep.

And enjoy yourself immensely.

DON KARDONG
SPOKANE, WASHINGTON

To Kaitlin and Catherine

Hills, Hawgs & Ho Chi Minh

more tales of a wayward runner

September 1985

THE ULTIMATE RUNNER

*What can you say about the marathon? On the best
of days, it hurts. On the worst, it burns. Run
quickly, it screams. Run slowly, it tortures. And it
sits waiting at the end of the Ultimate Runner — a
grinning, sardonic vulture.*

FOR ONCE, 6:45 A.M. DIDN'T SEEM SO EARLY. When the phone
rang, I had been awake for an hour and a half, stewing, and I was glad
to get on with it. I was tired of the questions.

Should I eat before the 10K or not? Was a 4:32 mile too fast or too
slow? Was I going to snap my hamstring during the 100? Should I go for
prize money or simple survival? Was I really ready to handle more than
33 1/2 miles of racing in one day? Should I eat between track events? Eat
what? And above all, the most basic question: Why had I agreed to do
this?

Race mornings are always riddled with uncertainty and fear, self-
doubt and introspection. In the midst of anxiety, one wonders about the
motivation for submitting to such tests. Why not run for fun and fitness?
Why put oneself through the race, where failure becomes a possibility?

These are common thoughts on race mornings, so common I've
learned to sleep through them. This time, though, the test would be
more brutal: 10K in the morning, three sprint races midday, a marathon
in the afternoon.

That's right: 10 kilometers, 400 meters, 100 meters, a mile and — take a deep breath now — the marathon. A pentathlon of running events, from the shortest to the longest, with points awarded for each. A test not just of endurance, not just of speed, but of the full range of running abilities. This was the "Ultimate Runner," an event hatched and nurtured in Jackson, Michigan. Somewhere along the line I had agreed to run the thing.

I knew it was going to hurt. A lot.

I headed downstairs. The cafe in the hotel wasn't scheduled to open until 8 o'clock, so groups of soon-to-be Ultimate Runners were approaching the front desk, seeking directions to the nearest carbohydrate filling station. The clerk gave depressing news. Nothing, she said, was open within two miles.

Survival, though, demands that at least one bee from the hive locate the nearest source of honey, then pass the information on to the rest of the brood. Word spread fast. I had soon joined a line of runners heading through the darkened streets of downtown Jackson to the B-Z-B Cafe, two blocks away.

The B-Z-B was swarming with runners making their final decisions about breakfast. Regular customers slunk in the background, smoking cigarettes and sneaking looks at us. What was going on here anyway?

Coffee? Pancakes? Juice? Bananas? What do you eat (if anything) on a morning when you're expecting to be doing more than 33 1/2 miles of racing, some of it at top speed, and all of it scheduled without sufficient time for digestion?

I ate oatmeal with milk and sugar. A cup of coffee. It seemed like the right blend of carbohydrates and enthusiasm, and there also seemed to be an outside chance that it might be out of my stomach before the 10K started. Still, I had never had a bowl of oatmeal before a road race, and I couldn't help but worry.

"Why should you be any different than the rest of us?" quipped 60-year-old Wally Ympa of Jenison, Michigan, when I complained of my indecision. "I've read every article written about what to eat before a race, and I still haven't figured it out."

I told him about the oatmeal.

"Yeah, I tried oatmeal one time," he responded dryly, "and I felt like I was running with a brick in my stomach."

My guts twitched. It was going to be a long day.

In truth, it had always been destined to be a long day, ever since that fateful moment in 1982 when two runners from the Jackson area, Mike McGlynn and Charlie Kuntzleman, first dreamed up the multi-race event that I would soon be grappling with.

McGlynn is an associate professor in the Health and Fitness Department of Jackson Community College, a running enthusiast and dedicated race director. Kuntzleman is a fitness consultant and author, a nationally recognized authority on children's fitness, and the source of at least one really outrageous, very painful idea — namely the Ultimate Runner.

"One day Charlie and I were out on a run," McGlynn tells me, sounding a little sheepish about the whole thing, "and I'd been thinking about running events, about how we needed to do something different. Everybody was doing the same thing — road races and marathons."

While they ran, McGlynn and Kuntzleman began sharing ideas about offbeat events. The conversation eventually focused on Kuntzleman's notion for a kind of Iron Man for runners, something that would test the gamut of running skills, from the sprints to the marathon. The collection would include the most glamorous foot events on road and track — the 100, 400, mile, 10K and marathon — events that physiologically demanded different skills.

"I guess the endorphins were flowing," says McGlynn in explanation. "We were running longer and longer, and it was sounding better and better, and we thought people were going to be breaking down our doors to get to it. We finished our run, and the next day I woke up and thought, 'What are we, nuts?' "

The notion might have ended there, one more fantastic idea that fails the test of postrun scrutiny, except that Kuntzleman got a little excited during a radio interview and told the announcer all about it.

"He went and shot his mouth off on the radio," says McGlynn. He was as good-natured as might be expected for the guy who got stuck with the detail work. "Charlie said, 'Yeah, we're going to do this in Jackson.' Of course Charlie is great with ideas."

And McGlynn is great at organizing. In no time flat, he was directing the first Ultimate Runner, held in the fall of 1983.

"We weren't sure if anyone could actually do it," says McGlynn, "so we decided to keep it local and not advertise it."

Twenty-four entered, twenty-two finished, and feedback from everyone involved was enthusiastic, even rhapsodic. Perhaps deranged.

"And nobody died," says McGlynn, who tends to worry about that kind of thing.

Prize money and an expanded national ad campaign drew more runners — even a few from overseas. By this particular year, entries passed 100 — a mark organizers like McGlynn feel, given the logistics of the event, represents a full house.

In ohe sense, a 100 seems like a small turnout. But then as McGlynn points out in obvious understatement, "This event is not for everyone."

Even so, once a runner hears about the Ultimate Runner, the imagination spins. A better measure of the event's success than the number of entries might be the fascination it engenders in any runner who hears about it.

Why the fascination?

"Partly because it's *so* challenging," speculates McGlynn. "And partly because, for many runners, their roots are on the track. A lot of people have been into road racing for a few years, and they're really curious to see what they can do now on the track compared to what they used to do. Not only that, but they wonder what they can do after a 10K and before a marathon."

The uniqueness of trying to sandwich top track times between two tough endurance events represents the heart of the dilemma; there is the contradiction and the challenge of the Ultimate Runner.

Strategy varies from individual to individual. Middle-distance runners, who have dominated the top few places in the Ultimate Runner over the years, use their speed to early advantage, racking up points, then just surviving the marathon. Ultramarathoners, in turn, rely on their endurance, hoping the young track runners underestimate the fatigue, hunger and dehydration that build throughout the competition, and thus prove vulnerable to a strong marathon performance.

"Some of the marathoners give up," says McGlynn. "Well, they don't really give up, but they say, 'I've just got to get through the track stuff.' Other guys, like Charlie Trayer, who was ranked third in the ultramarathon last year, give it everything they've got on the track. Charlie doesn't hold back. He knows he's not fast, but he's sure there's just a little more speed in those legs than he's gotten out of them."

In the end, in fact, whatever leg speed one can muster is crucial.

"The guys with speed can always run long," says McGlynn, "but the guys that can go long can't always go fast."

Still, as one's speed begins to wane, one hopes to use wisdom and trickery to advantage. I speak from personal experience here. And that brings us back to the question of diet. Could a clever ingestion of food and fluids before and during the competition make enough difference to offset a dearth of speed?

At least it ought to help. Charlie Trayer, for example, used both his ultrarunning background and one of the newest round of replacement drinks to reach the start of last year's marathon sporting a certain degree of smugness.

"Charlie just put up with the other four events," says McGlynn, "but he had a smile on his face at the start of the marathon."

Trayer's background brought him through last year's marathon in 2:30:58, a victory by nearly a mile. Clearly, the lessons of fluid and energy replacement that ultramarathoners thrive on served him well. There would be tables full of food options to choose from during the competition, and I hoped to outwit a few people there. As important as fluid and fuel would be, though, the peculiar demands of this event would offer little in terms of clear dietary direction.

"Some people go for the pasta," says McGlynn. "Others just suck down candy bars. For others it's cookies, and some don't eat at all, they just drink."

I, in my wisdom, had begun the day with oatmeal. But as I rode the bus to the start of the 10K that morning, I kept thinking of bricks.

8:30 A.M. — 10K
GOAL: 32:30

"The thing I worry about the most," McGlynn had said, "is the guys who come in here and don't respect that first event. My heart goes out to them at thirteen miles in the marathon."

Figuring my current 10K capability — fast course, cool weather, no bricks — at 31 minutes, I set my Ultimate Runner goal at 32:30. With the temperature in the low 60s and humidity close to 100 percent, I elected to do an abbreviated warm-up to avoid dehydration.

In a few minutes we were off and running. After 100 yards, the surprising leader was ultramarathoner Charlie Trayer, who when standing still looks like a cross between a leprechaun and Yosemite Sam, but who now looked mostly like a 10K runner. Though his goal was to win the marathon, Trayer wasn't sandbagging. This was his third Ultimate Runner, and he wanted to score a personal-best point total. Later, when someone suggested jokingly, "I don't think you went out fast enough in the 10K, Charlie," he agreed, not smiling. He would finish ninth in 33:20.

The lead soon went to Roger Soler, a Peruvian runner who had just graduated from the University of Texas at San Antonio and was one of the favorites in the Ultimate Runner. Mark Smith, a recent graduate of Eastern Michigan University, whose credits include multiple Mid-America Conference titles and an 8:30 steeplechase, was right with him. Smith, McGlynn's pre-event pick, went on to win in 30:38, followed by Soler, Ed LeBair of Mayville, Michigan, and Tim Mylin of Carmel, Indiana. Those four, it turned out, were to battle for the Ultimate Runner title throughout the afternoon.

For my part, after opening in 5:01, I settled into a pace closer to my 32:30 goal, slowed in part by the muggy conditions and partly by caution. I was thankful the oatmeal remained pacific.

Near the 5-mile mark, Barney Klecker, an accomplished ultramarathoner, went past. I managed to quell reflexes that nearly shot me forth in hot pursuit, putting stock in a conservative 10K.

A mile later I saw Hal Higdon, a friend and colleague, standing on the side of the road. Hal had originally planned to enter the competition but was sidelined with an injury. Now, he was giving unusual encouragement.

"Slow down," he shouted, "you've got four more races left."

I cruised in for a 32:20, seven seconds behind Klecker and sixth overall, then headed directly for the provisions at the Jackson Community College field house. Hal showed up shortly after.

"Start eating," he ordered, "even though you don't feel like it. Bananas and cookies are fine, maybe fruit. Don't eat any peanuts."

In the Ultimate Runner, anxiety leads to trust. You implicitly believe anyone who offers a strong opinion. Though I had originally considered waiting until after the last track event before eating, I heeded Hal's order and began peeling bananas.

10 A.M. — 400 METERS
GOAL: 58 SECONDS

"The pain only lasts one lap," said Marie Smythe. "Don't you just love it?"

Marie is an ultramarathoner from Allegan, Michigan, one of eleven women in this year's competition. She has unbounded energy and a loud ghetto blaster. In 1984 she ran the first open 400-meter run of her life during the Ultimate Runner. She loved it, but I wasn't so sure the 400 deserved that particular emotion.

One lap around the track can be a severe lesson in the limitations of personal performance. If you misjudge your reserves, you'll end up dead-legged. "Rigor mortis," it's been called. That fate, a symptom of excessive lactic acid in the muscles, would be even more dangerous in today's competition.

"There was a guy two years ago who was way ahead after the 10K," said McGlynn, "but as he came around the turn in the 400, the bear just jumped right on his back. He did okay, but in the mile he should have been right up front, and he was fifth or sixth. He never finished the marathon. That 400 ruined him."

Determined not to suffer a similar fate, I ran a few windsprints, put on my spikes, and went to the line repeating my mantra: "Relax 'n' fast, relax 'n' fast, relax 'n' fast ... "

The gun fired and I was on my way. Bill Stewart, age 42 and world record holder in the masters indoor mile, was in the lane to my left; 23-year-old Mark Smith was on my right. By halfway, the three of us were together, Stewart having made up the stagger on me, and both of us having caught Smith.

The closeness of the battle was short-lived, though, as Smith exploded around the turn and raced to a 55.2 clocking, followed by myself at 57.2. Masters runner David Oropeza of Phoenix, Arizona, was a hair behind me at 57.3, and Stewart came in at 57.5. In the second heat, Ed LeBair and Roger Soler were a tick apart at 54.2 and 54.3, the two best times of the day. After two events, the top three men were only 20 points apart.

I jogged to the field house for more bananas and cookies.

Later, I watched Trayer and another ultrarunner, Dan Brannen, run their heat, which Trayer won in 62.0. Brannen hit 64.5, the fastest time ever run by a human being without lifting the knees. How'd it feel?

"Absolutely ridiculous," laughed Brannen.

10:45 A.M. — 100 METERS
GOAL: UNDER 13 SECONDS

There is not much time during the Ultimate Runner to sit and think. The events come bang-bang-bang, like gunfire in a bad cowboy movie. Electronic timing of the 400, though, put us slightly behind schedule, so there I sat in the infield, waiting for the 100 to roll around, wondering about the hamstring I'd been nursing back to health all summer.

"Last year I got to the marathon," said Barney Klecker, "and I realized I had a chance to win the whole thing. 'I gotta run 2:20, 2:21,' I told McGlynn. Jeez, I felt good through about 15 miles. When I got to 18 though, I started to hurt. At 20 I was dog-tired. At 23 my hamstring cramped. I ended up running 2:45:30. I never fell apart like that in a race."

I massaged my hamstring and wondered if maybe I should have eaten another banana.

"Usually when I'm lying on the infield with my feet up like this," offered Dan Brannen, "I'm getting ready to get back on the track to run six hours. This time I'm going out there for 14 seconds, and I'm dreading it more."

Finally it was time to warm up, and as I did so I experienced tightness in my calves and hamstrings, especially the one I had injured. I stretched as best I could while I watched the women's leader, Ella Willis of Detroit, win the women's 400 in 64.6, more than 5 seconds ahead of the next woman. Willis was undefeated in two previous Ultimate Runners — undefeated overall and undefeated at every distance, from the 100 to the marathon. One year she won the Ultimate Runner on Saturday, a road race on Sunday, then finished second in the Detroit Marathon the following weekend.

The sun broke through the haze as I settled into what would have been starting blocks, except I wasn't using any. The accepted wisdom of the Ultimate Runner is that one shouldn't pretend to be a world class sprinter, settling into starting blocks, unless one has either practiced doing so for a few months or has an interest in falling on one's face, as marathoner Sy Mah did in 1983.

I started without them, ran flailing down the stretch with the veins in my neck popping and my hamstring singing and leaned into a 13.01. Electronic timing didn't care about my goal of breaking 13 seconds.

I went for more bananas.

The field house was looking more and more like a disaster relief station. Marge Munich, presiding mom-like over the assorted vittles on the food tables, was working hard with the rest of her crew to satisfy an increasingly morose band of runners. Like all of the more than 400 race-day volunteers needed to ensure safety and relative comfort for the runners, she performed her task with pride and honor. One of the most amazing things about this event, in fact, is the depth of support of the Jackson community. Every runner has both a sponsor and a "personal jogger" who tags along all day, supplying cool drinks and encouraging words at just the right times.

I saw Soler, who was encouraged by closing in on Smith in overall points. He expressed confidence.

"Great," I said, heading back to the track, peeling another banana. "I'll talk to you later."

Soler broke out in a big smile, remembering the monkey of a marathon sitting on his and everyone else's back.

11:15 A.M. — MILE RUN
GOAL: 4:32

The mile is just a mile, right? Not that long, not that fast. By the time it rolled around on the schedule, though, I had seriously fatigued every muscle I needed to get through it.

"My hamstring is beginning to hurt," I told a friend as I stood at the track watching the final heats of the 100.

"Shhhhhh ... " someone close by whispered in mock horror. "Don't say that word."

The runners took off, and I left to try warming up. By now, though, I was getting punchy. When I finally made it to the line, it was after one windsprint and a couple of half-hearted stretches.

The first lap was an apt reflection of my warm-up. Instead of a smooth and relaxed 68 seconds, I rattled through in 70. Going into the next lap, though, 1972 Olympian Jeff Galloway passed me, providing the inspiration a friendly rivalry always does. I hung on, began to loosen up, passed halfway in 2:18, passed Galloway and finally kicked to a 4:35.3, a couple of seconds ahead of Jeff.

The real mile race, though, was up ahead, where Mark Smith, who went out in 61 seconds, slipped back during the final lap as Roger Soler, whose first split was 65, passed Smith in the homestretch to win in 4:19.3, almost a second ahead of Smith. I saw Soler later in the field house, and he knew he was close to Smith in total points with just one event remaining. Suddenly his face lit up.

"You know what I just realized?" he beamed. "Today is my birthday. I'm 26."

We celebrated with rice, electrolyte fluids and more bananas. Then I went and lay down on my cot.

2 P.M. — MARATHON
GOAL: 2:40

What can you say about the marathon? On the best of days, it hurts. On the worst, it burns. Run quickly, it screams. Run slowly, it tortures.

And it sits waiting at the end of the Ultimate Runner — a grinning, sardonic vulture.

We all dragged ourselves to the track for the start, trying to grin back.

"The line is over there," shouted the starter as nicely as possible, pointing to the other end of the track.

"Is there a bus to get us there?" someone asked.

Lining up, I remembered the words of 41-year-old Ralph Abramowitz of Flanders, New Jersey, spoken the night before. "I don't know what I'm doing here," he said, whining moderately. "I should have listened to my wife."

But now it was too late. We were off and running.

After all the bananas, oatmeal, rice, candy, fluids and molasses cookies, specially provided by Marge, it's no wonder I had trouble. The bricks finally settled, and my stomach cramped as I tried to relax at a 6-minute pace. Up ahead, I watched Smith, a novice marathoner who has a 2:18 to his credit, shadow Soler for two miles before getting impatient and running ahead. Tim Mylin, the fastest 100-meter runner of the day, stayed with Soler until nine miles, then fell back. I passed him. I passed Smith at 13 miles, then Ed LeBair at 15. With three out of the four leaders behind me, it was clear that Soler would take the cake on this, his birthday.

In the midst of the anguish that descended around 17 miles, as the insects hummed their humid tunes, I chanted my new mantra: "Training run, training run, training run ... "

I was running with my friend Steve at this point, who brought me fluids and tried to lift my spirits as the remaining miles telescoped into the distance. I rewarded myself at each mile point after twenty with a brief walk and a drink. On the final stretch back to Jackson Community College, I passed David Oropeza, who was on his way to winning the masters division of the Ultimate Runner. With two miles to go I passed a dead raccoon — its eyes glazed, its legs stiff, its body a mess.

"Can you relate to that?" asked Steve.

I could, though the roadkill looked better than I felt.

And then I was back, sitting on my cot. Eating ice cream bars and drinking Mountain Dew. Water. The rest of my cookies. A few candy bars. Some more bananas.

Barney Klecker was sitting nearby, speculating on whether his 2:39:09

had been good enough to push his point total past mine. It hadn't. My 2:43:03 placed me fifth overall, just ahead of him. Charlie Trayer's 2:32:02 marathon victory moved him to seventh.

Claudia Ciavarella finished later, the first woman to beat Ella Willis in any of the five events during three years of competition.

"I started to cramp at six miles," she said, "and I told my personal jogger, 'I'm not going to make it.' "

As the clock neared 4 hours, Mark Smith sprinted the final meters of the marathon and nose-dived to the ground.

"I learned a hard lesson," he said later, after dropping from first to fourth overall with a 3:57:04.

Later that evening, sharing beer and experiences, we all recovered enough to put this Ultimate Runner thing in perspective. But sitting there in the gym at the end of the marathon, blood sugar still low, the pain of those last few miles of the marathon still fresh in my mind, and an ultimate exhaustion gripping my leg muscles, it was shocking to hear the question.

"Are you going to come back?" they asked.

Come back? To this? Dog-tired as I was, though, I knew the answer was "Yes."

Why? For all the usual reasons, none of which really make much sense.

And when? With marathons, I use the rule of toe to answer the question: I won't run another until the black toenails are gone. This time, though, the profound fatigue required more caution.

I determined to wait even longer this time. I decided to wait until I could stand the sight of bananas and oatmeal again.

September 1985

IS THERE LIFE AFTER WORLD CLASS?

In the midst of bloated unfitness, we remember the glory days, the hard workouts, and that unforgettable feeling of breaking free from the crowd, out into the clear, into the territory ahead of the rest.

SO THERE I WAS, about to begin a precarious descent down a trail of questionable footing. Around me, other runners huffed and puffed in the chill fall air and maneuvered for position, sensing the risks involved in this kind of cross country race on this kind of course: the narrow paths, sharp hills and rough ground of the Whitworth back-forty encourage serious self-examination.

Was this worth it?

A year earlier, at 35, I entered this same event, the Pelluer Invitational Cross Country Meet, on this same course.

"You're too old for this stuff, Kardong!" a college coach shouted at me happily, poignantly, as I warmed up.

In fact, I began to miss it — this stuff. The 11 o'clock call to action on Saturday mornings in the fall. The prerace ritual of jogging around paths where leaves were falling and teams of runners plotted strategy. ("We've got to get out fast before this hill or we'll get buried," he said passionately. "And pull out all stops on the downhill. The soft sand will cushion your fall.") And the adrenaline pumping into the bloodstream.

Racing always releases certain emotions — fear, elation, nostalgia, pride, despair. But I race so infrequently in cross country events these days that, when I do, feelings are heightened, and the experience becomes monumental somehow. (This is another episode in the racing life of Don Kardong. This is what he's done nearly every autumn since high school, when he was 15 years old and had acne.)

The experience has been repeated for over twenty years now. There is a comfort in repeating it and in knowing it can be repeated. Like Christmas, it is an island of refuge and stillness in a fast-moving, chaotic river. One has been here before, with friends.

And these days, except for a few tight, creaky spots in the old body, it feels the same as it always has. The mind in particular.

There is another thing about this race today, though. A year earlier, I had won it. The leader had gone off course late in the race, and some of the competition wasn't quite in shape, but all that seemed less than important in the final analysis. At age 35, competing in a crowd composed largely of collegiate runners, I had finished first.

And not only that. In winning it, I had beaten Mike Brady, a 24-year-old. Mike is a good friend, a training partner, and the manager of the running store I own — three compelling reasons why I relished, beyond words, beating him. Merrily and mercilessly, I had been reminding him of my victory at least once a week for an entire year. As Mike continued on the upswing of his competitive career, winning races and setting personal bests, and as I struggled to slow the progress of my own slide from world-class status, I took every opportunity to rub it in.

"You may have won the Ten-Miler," I conceded gleefully during a run a few days before the rematch, "but I'm going to kick your ass again at Whitworth."

Mike just smiled and picked up the pace.

In fact, I knew I was in trouble. Mike had been training ferociously, well beyond my level. In the spring, he had announced innocently one day that he had begun training twice a day, and I groaned. In the summer, as I began getting into better shape, Mike stayed well ahead of me, setting personal bests, winning local races, and leaving me in the dust on days we ran speedwork. I cursed him through gritted teeth.

That morning at Whitworth, as I raced through the first mile next to him, defending the fragile hope that I might somehow deny the inevitable, I knew I would have to run beyond expectations, take considerable risks, and flirt with injury to have any chance at all. For a moment, perched on the brink of the first drastic downhill, we seemed suspended in time. A decision was at hand.

Was it worth it?

There is a point at which one must admit to the inexorable. Time, wearing sharpened spikes, races on. The runner, once fast, slows down. World-class drops a notch to merely fast. Lofty goals, like becoming the fastest human being ever at a particular distance, become more modest — like beating your training partner.

All this is certainly part of the rhythm of the sport. Eventually, every world-class runner faces the situation. Training to stay ahead of the rest becomes difficult, dangerous, or simply unpalatable. Ultimately, it becomes impossible.

Common wisdom used to argue that this happened rather early on the age spectrum — that a runner's peak years were in the mid-to-late 20s, depending on the distance. During the past ten years, though, as opportunities for competition have expanded, the frontier of aging has been pushed back.

When 36-year-old Carlos Lopes became the Olympic marathon champion, he gave a lot of older runners a double shot of hope, and researchers something to chew on. Still, very little is really known about the exact timetable of aging as it relates to world-class running.

"The available evidence, which is almost entirely cross-sectional, would indicate that speed starts to decline sometime in the mid-20s, maybe even earlier than that for pure speed," says Russ Pate, once one of this country's top marathoners, now Director of the Human Performance Laboratory at the University of South Carolina. "The problem is that you're looking at all kinds of behavioral as well as genetically determined physiological factors."

A loss of speed may be offset for a while by an increase in strength and endurance in longer distance races, while in an event like the mile, where speed is crucial, loss of speed severely inhibits performance. Even in the mile, though, the promise of world-class, or at least near-world-class performances well into a runner's 30s and early 40s, seems reasonable. A sub-4-minute masters mile someday? Perhaps.

But as Pate suggests, the main reason that world-class performances wane has as much to do with behavioral as with physiological factors. Most top runners concur.

"Once you get up near the top, people start offering you a lot of other things to do with your time," says 1980 Olympian Benji Durden. "You get distracted, and being a top runner requires a certain amount of monomania."

Research indicates that world-class runners seem to be able to focus on their task better than other runners. That ability to "associate" rather than "dissociate" from bodily signals during a race seems to carry over to training as well. Concentration is essential, both in training and in racing, and as the runner ages, nonathletic concerns sneak to the top of the priority list. The runner looks at world-class goals and realizes they may no longer be feasible.

"Two factors have entered the picture," says 1972 Olympian Jeff Galloway, "a family and a business."

"More and more I'm caught up in the business side of the sport," says Bill Rodgers. "I like it, but it does seem to knock my training back."

Making a living is one thing. Waking up three times in the middle of the night to comfort a restless child is another. During peak years, a world-class runner learns to be selfish with time, both during the day and at night, and when the luxury of selfishness is gone, focus slips.

"It isn't just training," says Frank Shorter. "It's rest and recovery — ten hours' sleep and having time to recover."

And then, of course, there are injuries. The feeling of strength, power, and invincibility a world-class runner comes to associate with his own identity is suddenly shattered.

"Aren't you Frank Shorter?" a young runner asked the Olympic champion after Frank had suffered through a 10K on an injured foot.

"No," Frank replied, "but I used to be."

As the runner gets older, injuries increase.

"I have problems now every time I get up to 70 miles per week," says former Pan American gold medalist Mike Manley.

"Injuries pop up at annoying times," adds Jim Ryun. "Minor

problems interrupt the continuing progress you need to move to a new level of achievement."

Perhaps it isn't much worse at 40 than it was at 20. There is an oft-told story, after all, of the 60-year-old runner who visits his doctor about a sore knee.

"Of course it hurts," scolds the doctor. "After all, that knee is 60 years old."

"The other knee is 60, too, doc," the runner responds, "And it feels fine."

Whether it's injuries, lack of focus or diminished capabilities, and whether it occurs at 30, 40, 45 or 50, eventually the runner notices the change.

"I've fallen back, even in the marathon," notes Bill Rodgers. "At New York I went out in 1:04:36, and the leaders went out at 1:03:10 or something, and that's a long way for someone to be ahead of you. It throws off your pacing, and it's very discouraging."

Generally, the runner struggles to regain that old feeling.

"All my levels changed," says five-time world cross country champion Doris Brown Heritage, who tried to regain form after breaking her foot in the 1972 Olympics. "I don't know if it was because of age or what, but my iron levels never went up to where they were, my endurance never came back, I never had the strength. Everything just changed."

At that point, the runner may decide to make a clean break, leave running behind. But most who do find that something is missing.

"When I took a year off and wasn't competing," says three-time Olympic steeplechaser Doug Brown, "I found I was playing tennis and golf, and I would play with a *mission*." Now a successful coach at the University of Tennessee, Brown has found his job helps satisfy those old competitive instincts.

"Coaching at the level I'm at," he says, "is very satisfying and rewarding in filling that void."

And how much interest does the runner have in racing again?

"None," says Brown. "Zero."

Most world-class runners, though, don't find it so easy to replace the smell of the greasepaint and the roar of the crowd. Former world-class runners-turned-coaches like Heritage and Manley still yearn to race.

"I still have the urge to compete," says Manley. "My problem is that I like to compete at a high level, and the transition is almost impossible. I get myself injured every time."

To avoid injuries, to adjust to a less pliable body, and to fit the training in with the rest of life's concerns, goals must change. Expectations must shrink some. One must come to terms with one's changing body.

"The transition isn't difficult if you really enjoy what you're doing," says Ryun. "I feel frustrated at times, but I recognize I'm not training as hard as I once was; I'm not running a distance I was once good at, and I'm aging a little bit. If I'm going to enjoy what I'm doing, I have to recognize that I'm going to run a little slower."

And the goal becomes?

"Maybe just staying alive and making it to the next plane," laughs Ryun.

"I've been very goal-oriented my whole career," adds former marathon world record holder Jacqueline Hansen, "but my goals have always been centered on race times. I enjoy setting goals and beating them, not beating people. In the mid-70s, my personal goals correlated with world records. Now, if I run a 2:36 marathon, no one's going to notice, but I'll be happy."

"Every day is good when you're working toward a goal," contends Heritage. "It isn't that you're viciously competitive. It's a matter of setting goals and training to compete."

And for those looking for new goals, of course, there is masters competition.

"I've really started to think about competing with people 40 and older," says 38-year-old Bill Rodgers, "I'm motivated to go for the masters world record in the marathon. I think, with the possible exception of Carlos Lopes, I have a chance of being the best masters marathoner in the world."

The stage is set, in fact, for a dramatic influx of world-class runners into the ranks of the masters. Not just runners starting to compete again after a ten- or twenty-year layoff, but runners, like Rodgers and Shorter, who have never stopped, who have always maintained racing fitness.

When Mike Manley turned 40 in 1982, for example, the former steeplechase specialist immediately revolutionized masters competition.

He broke 30 minutes for 10K and ran 2:17:10 in the marathon — times well beyond the established level of competition for the division. Similarly, veteran U.S. competitor Barry Brown's 40th birthday was followed by a string of record-setting performances, including a 2:15:15 in the Twin Cities Marathon, a U.S. masters record. Does this new level of masters racing discourage those who are currently faring well in this age-group? Yes and no.

"Obviously, as top runners like Barry Brown turn 40, there's no way I can be competitive," says 44-year-old Kirk Randall, who has won the national masters cross country championship three times since his return to competition after a layoff of more than ten years. "But I'm still a runner, and I can justify my own progress because I can keep improving my PRs."

The influx of runners into the masters division with competitive backgrounds that extend more or less uninterrupted back to high school is certainly making competition in this age-group tougher. But it is also leading to more and more visibility and credibility for masters competition overall. No matter how fast runners like Carlos Lopes and Steve Jones may have run, first and foremost in the minds of the American public will always be Shorter and Rodgers. And their progression toward age 40 should be good news for those who want to see masters competition thrive.

Rodgers, in fact, is one of many people now looking toward the creation of a masters road race circuit, something similar to the Seniors Golf Tournament that brought Arnold Palmer back squarely into the public eye.

"I'm excited about the masters thing," says Rodgers, "and I do believe it's going to happen. We'll have the runners, we just need the organization."

Whether it's masters competition or something else, in fact, and whether it's world-class goals or something more pedestrian, it seems that most of us, once bitten by the bug of fastness, have trouble getting over it. In the midst of bloated unfitness, we remember the glory days, the hard workouts, and that unforgettable feeling of breaking free from the crowd, out into the clear, into the territory ahead of the rest. We want it, or at least some of it, back.

"Does a runner ever stop coming back?" asks Ryun.

"I don't see why those of us who have been in tremendous condition," adds Heritage, "should ever give it up."

We search out our old haunts, we resurrect old training schemes, we renew acquaintances with ovals and courses we used to travel in fitter days.

"I had a route back in 1964 that ran from Coach Timmons's rental house in town out to a huge old tree in the country," says Ryun. "It was an old gravel road. I still, on occasion, go out that way with the team. Now it's a four-lane street with heavy traffic, and the tree has aged and lost a few limbs."

No matter. We're older now, too, and have lost a few things we used to have. But not that connection with the past.

"I still spend all year training for cross country," says Heritage. "It's funny, but if I'm running down the street and see a good grass strip, I hop up on the grass and say to myself, 'This could be the grass strip that makes me a better cross country runner.'"

Ah, yes, cross country.

So there I was, perched on the brink, about to begin the descent. Clearly, racing the downhill on this course would be risky. Uneven ground, sandy shoulders and narrow passages lay ahead, while a pack of eager, pubescent-looking cross country runners were elbowing to take advantage of any opening. Only a fool would chance injury in this, a contest of no special merit. Brady accelerated, took the lead, and sped down the incline.

Was it worth the risk?

"Hell, yes," I thought, as I went careening down the hill after him.

July 1986

ALL THAT JAZZ

There is reason to smile, to laugh, to shout, to finally feel good about things. There is appreciation for struggle and perseverance, and the appreciation is vocal. And the runners who challenge this hilly course every year are the beneficiaries.

THE CITY OF DAVENPORT SITS QUIETLY, unpretentiously, in eastern Iowa, with its feet dangling in the Mississippi River. Next door is Bettendorf, and across the River in Illinois one notices Moline and Rock Island. Folks call this gathering of Midwest Mississippi towns the "Quad Cities."

The first bridge across the Mississippi River was built here in 1853, making Davenport a regional center of agriculture and trade. It grew to become the third largest city in Iowa. Riverboats steamed into port, bringing prosperity and a little pizzaz. A few people became wealthy, at least when corn was high and prices reasonable.

In 1903, Leon Beiderbecke entered the world here in Davenport. The Beiderbeckes were respectable, well-to-do German-American citizens with a musical bent. When son Leon, later nicknamed "Bix," showed an interest in music like his father and brother, they encouraged him. When that interest failed to harmonize with tradition, they worried. When his inclinations led him to buy a cornet and practice a decidedly low-brow musical form called "jazz" that had migrated from the seedy side of New Orleans, they cringed. And by the time he had gained an international reputation for his talent, it was too late. Bix Beiderbecke died in the far-off land of New York, a victim of alcohol and exhaustion, at age 28.

Today, though, in the town that failed to appreciate him while he lived, people have gathered to honor Bix Beiderbecke. This July marks the fifteenth edition of the Bix Fest, held annually in Davenport to celebrate the man and the music he loved.

"Bix Lives" say the signs, and the music floating across the still night air bears that assertion out. The Dixieland sound goes down easily in this crowd of Bix aficionados gathered around the bandshell next to the Mississippi. People sit quietly in lawn chairs, sipping lemonade and beer. Feet tap. A few couples, old enough to have heard this music when it was hatched, dance slowly, lightly, between groups of listeners. They're just a little tipsy.

And outside the enclosure, next to one of the old river boats that will soon be refurbished to become a source of pride and income for the area, a man in running shoes and running shorts is talking about the Bix 7 to some locals.

"You see," he explains, "the Bix 7 comes a long time after the Boston Marathon and far enough before the New York and Chicago Marathons, and the course is challenging but not too challenging, and that's why we're able to get world-class runners like Bill Rodgers and Jan Benoit here."

Well, what the heck? Whether it's Jan or Joan, Benoit or Samuelson, the message is clear. This year's Bix 7 will once again feature some of the best runners in the world, come to Iowa in the middle of summer to sweat, strain and generally enjoy themselves. And like the man in shorts who is now explaining this all so intently, runners from throughout the Midwest will participate, anxious to "Run With the Best" in Davenport's midsummer road-racing phenomenon.

Tomorrow will be warm and humid, facts of Midwest life that will fail to discourage more than 9,000 runners from testing themselves on the rolling hills of Davenport. Like the Bix Fest, the Bix 7 has become part of life here, and every year more and more people have been eager to join the fun.

It hasn't always been like this in Davenport, for either running or music. The Bix Fest has only been around since 1971, when a couple of visiting bands met at Bix's gravesite for a little informal jam session. A good time was had, the idea seemed worth repeating the next year and the year after, and soon the Bix Fest had become part of the summer landscape, drawing bands and fans from all over the country.

Running wasn't far behind. In 1975, local Davenport runner John Huedtz and the Cornbelt Running Club asked for permission to hold a road race ("Say what?") through the streets of town in conjunction with the Bix festival. Reluctantly, city fathers gave their permission, and seventy-four people signed up.

By 1979, entries in the Bix 7 grew to nearly a thousand, but the event still got little respect around town. That's when the event's present director, 39-year-old Ed Froehlich, joined the race committee and convinced them to gear up their recruitment of name runners.

"We wanted to make the Bix 7 a race everybody in the community knew about," says Froehlich.

Beginning with Bill Rodgers and later including luminaries like Frank Shorter, Rob de Castella, Joan (not "Jan") Benoit and Greg Meyer, Froehlich launched his campaign to develop a star-studded reputation for the Bix 7. Bringing name runners to a race to build credibility wasn't a new idea, and it didn't always pay dividends. At Bix, though, it worked wonders. In 1982 entrants had grown to more than 4,000. And last year, while many events around the country were suffering from declining numbers, the Bix field jumped to more than 7,000.

Fame, though, is not made by name alone. While the race among the stars drew attention to the event, Froehlich and his committee made sure that care and attention were paid to the growing numbers of less-than-elite runners, and that the festive nature of the road race was nurtured. Runners fast and slow began talking about the special ambiance of the Bix 7.

That ambience has a lot to do with Dixieland jazz, which winds its way in and out of hotels, restaurants, streets and alleyways all weekend, coloring the town in bright hues. And it has a lot to do with costumes: many non-serious entrants have embraced Bix as Davenport's answer to Mardi Gras. More than anything, though, the Bix ambience derives from the crowds along the way.

"I've never been to a race where there are as many people and where the crowds are as enthusiastic," said John Wellerding, a local runner who now ranks among the sport's top competitors. "They help you get over the hills."

"That's what separates Bix from a lot of races I've been in," added Phil Coppess, the top-ranked American marathoner last year, who lives a few miles upriver in Clinton, Iowa. "They make so much noise it carries you. It's great."

Great it is for invited runners like Wellerding and Coppess. Great it is, too, for local runners and visitors from Minneapolis, Chicago, St. Louis, and from throughout the region and around the country. And great it is for those in the throng who run dressed as superheroes and six-packs of beer and running shoes and animals and all that.

Bix is an out-and-back course, giving folks along the mostly residential streets plenty of opportunities to enjoy the spectacle. These are the sort of people who tell you, "Well, I'm from Iowa," with a chuckle when trying to explain their supposed shortcomings (mostly having to do with a lack of ostentation). But these same reserved Iowans have no trouble getting into the spirit of celebration on Bix weekend.

These have not been good years for the economy of the region, and these people have felt the bite. They know the vagaries of farm economics, in which a year of high yields, as this one will be, is not necessarily good news. And they know what happens when farmers have to tighten their belts and stop buying things. Especially farm machinery, a booming industry in the Quad Cities until a few years ago, when companies like John Deere, International Harvester, I.H. Case and Caterpillar began scaling down, cutting back and just plain shutting down. People here have felt the bite.

And so when something good happens, as it does on Bix weekend, there is more than the usual reason to celebrate. There is reason to smile, to laugh, to shout, to finally feel good about things. There is appreciation for struggle and perseverance, and the appreciation is vocal. And the runners who challenge this hilly course every year are the beneficiaries.

On the evening before all this, though, there is no shouting or cheering. Instead, there is the quiet of the slow-moving Mississippi, boats bobbing up and down at their moorings, fireflies and stars dotting the clear sky, and the warm music of local bad-boy-turned-hero Bix Beiderbecke drifting out across the river, filling the sky with sweetness.

It is one of the sad ironies of small-town life that a man like Bix must so often leave home, uproot himself from his native soil in order to find a place to express thoughts and feelings developed there. For Bix, jazz became a pathway that allowed the deep yearnings of his soul to reach the light of day. When he lived, his feelings flowed through his music. And when he died, so far removed from home, something seemed amiss in the world.

Tonight, though, his fans listen to his music, calmly assured that things are right again between Bix and Davenport. And so they sit quietly, enjoying the Bix Fest.

And there are people in running shoes and shorts and T-shirts enjoying all this, thinking about those hills they'll face tomorrow, anxious to run with world-renowned runners, and hoping those celebrated Bix spectators will be on hand to pull them through the ordeal.

Expecting to step into the steamy air of a midwestern midsummer, I walk out of the Blackhawk Hotel on the morning of the Bix 7 and am actually a little surprised. This is heat? Sure it's warm, but mid-70s at most. Humid? Try Atlanta on the Fourth of July.

Summer in Davenport, Iowa, or anywhere else in the U.S. heartland, is not what most people would call pleasant. When the sky is white with haze and you walk outside into intense glare, your eyes ache, your pores gasp, and your head turns to cement. Soon, you begin to notice that your clothes are sticking to your body like cotton candy.

But all that is later in the day. At 7 on this Saturday morning, conditions feel pretty comfortable, even for a hilly seven-mile race. Or so it seems, standing in front of the hotel.

Bill Rodgers is warming up on a side street. It is his seventh Bix 7, and "Bix Billy," as they call him here, has won twice. Last year, at 37, Rodgers gave winner Mark Curp a good scare before ending up second. This year, suffering from too much travel and business, Bill will have a tougher time of it, finishing twelfth.

Curp is back, too, to defend his title against the likes of Geoff Smith, Phil Coppess, John Wellerding and Alberto Salazar, who will run Bix as his first race outside Oregon in over a year, a test of his recovery from hamstring surgery.

Joan Benoit Samuelson is also looking at this year's race as a test of fitness after surgery. Samuelson, who has won here twice, has made steady progress from an operation on her heels, but she's still wary. She will run a controlled race, with this year's TAC 10,000-meter champion Nan Doak, an Iowa native, as her only competition.

As zero hour approaches, I squeeze into the pack of 9,000, which stretches back several blocks to the Mississippi. The road is wide, but it will take 10minutes for the last starter to cross the point where I stand. As the countdown begins, I look ahead.

The Brady Street Hill is as ominous a start as ever graced a road race, a good half-mile climb to the top, where the world-famous Palmer College of Chiropractic sits. About 2,000 students are enrolled at the school ("From New York and a lot of other foreign countries," according to one Cornbelt Running Club member), but now over four times that number are steaming toward it at the start of the 1986 Bix 7.

"The hill wouldn't be so bad," offers Geoff Smith later, "if you didn't start at the bottom of it. If it came after a mile, you'd have a chance to get into a rhythm. Instead, it's ..." And Smith puffs out his cheeks and pumps his arms, a parody of a runner in hill agony.

If Smith suffers much, though, it isn't apparent. By the top of the hill, he and Mark Curp have broken away and are looking strong, the only two runners in real contention for the victory.

Farther back, I struggle up the hill with the rest of the crowd, not exactly enjoying myself, and beginning to realize I have underestimated the humidity. By the mile point, I am beginning to cook.

As promised, the crowds are loud and enthusiastic. I know this because I hear them shouting for Samuelson, who is right behind me. By the time she passes, at about 3 miles, she is 7 seconds ahead of Nan Doak. And though she is clearly racing to win, Samuelson has time to think about her Athletics West teammate, Alberto Salazar. When she finds herself catching me, she thinks for a minute it's Salazar, having an extremely bad day.

"I know how hard the last year has been for him," Samuelson tells me later, referring to Salazar's long climb back to fitness after surgery. "And last night I dreamed I passed him in the race. When I saw you, I thought it was him, and I thought, 'Oh, no, my dream is coming true.' "

Not to worry, Joan. It's only me, eating my words about the heat and humidity, and fighting a hamstring problem of my own. Up ahead the real Salazar is having better luck, running about a minute behind the leaders. He has had a couple of close brushes with heatstroke over the years, and the Bix run has him a little worried.

"Usually, if I know I'm going to be running in a humid race I try to get to town a week or so ahead of time to get acclimated," says Salazar later. "So I was worried coming here directly from Eugene. At five miles I thought, 'Oh-oh, this feels like trouble.' "

The trouble abates, though, and Salazar finishes tenth, not quite world-class but at least a solid step in that direction. Later, at the awards ceremony, he will marvel publicly about the crowd support.

"There's only one other race I know of that compares," says Salazar, "and that's Falmouth. And I really think the support here is better."

Crowd enthusiasm is extended to everyone, but a few are lucky enough to get a little extra. Former mile-great Jim Ryun, for example, who has become a credible road racer in recent years, passes me at about six miles, running with that wonderful head-rolling, arm-pumping style that used to demolish opposing track racers. He is well known in this part of the world, and draws the frequent, "Go, Ryun!" and "Get 'em, Jim!" from the vocal locals.

"I don't normally respond to any comments when I'm racing," Ryun says later, "but the crowd was so good here I very uncharacteristically gave a big wave at the end."

Ryun has passed me on the return journey on Kirkwood Boulevard, a divided roadway through residential Davenport that has been paved a few days earlier in anticipation of the run. Here, among beautiful Victorian houses, fans are enjoying the second annual Bix Sit, whose organizers charge $10 for breakfast and a T-shirt, encouraging those who can't "run with the best" to "sit with the rest." Most can't stand to sit for long, though. The magic of Bix draws them to the curb to watch.

They shout for the leaders streaking toward the finish, and they yell for the plodders, who need the encouragement even more.

"Don't let your mom beat you," an old-timer encourages a 2-year-old riding in a stroller. The toddler stares ahead, befuddled by all the commotion.

Two women run along, dressed as running shoes. "Your laces are untied, and your tongue is hanging out," someone in the crowd shouts to them. The shoes continue along Kirkwood, the runners inside their costume certainly hotter than the rest of us.

It's all a little odd, this display of exuberance and revelry on the part of Iowans, runners and spectators alike. But then, of course, Bix Beiderbecke was considered a little odd too, and this, after all, is his weekend.

After Kirkwood, the course makes a sharp left to head back down the Brady Street Hill. Up front, the race between Smith and Curp is getting interesting.

Throughout the race, the leaders have waged their two-man battle; Curp surging, Smith responding, racing side by side. Smith runs with his head bobbing, squinting in the bright sunshine, arms pumping high. Curp runs powerfully, intense lines of concentration on his face, arms held low.

It is Curp's strength versus Smith's impending speed, and as they near the finish line, Smith is ready to strike. Turning onto Brady Street, Smith suddenly bursts ahead, gains 10 meters, and sprints wildly down the hill. Curp responds, trying to rally his forces and catch back up, but he can't quite do it. Smith crosses the line in 33:16, 3 seconds ahead of Curp. Jerrold Wynia of Worthington, Minnesota, finishes a surprising third, a minute behind the winner and just ahead of Wellerding and Coppess.

A few minutes later Samuelson crosses the line, almost a minute ahead of Doak. Still, it has not been an easy victory for the three-time Bix champion, and it is her slowest winning time.

"I never felt like I was in my fluid stride," says Samuelson, and later she admits that her heels are bothering her again. All in all it has been a bit frustrating, for her and for a few other runners. But I hear few complaints.

The two fastest Bix-ers, in fact, seem to be enjoying themselves immensely now, as they stand just past the finish chutes sipping water and rehashing the race.

"I tried to push it three different times," says Mark Curp, smiling at the man he tried to waste, "but I couldn't lose you."

"I think if you'd held it a little longer that last time," rejoins Geoff Smith, smiling even bigger, "I would've broken."

It is evening now in Davenport, and the heat of the day is beginning to fade into memory. So, too, is the heat of the race, and whatever pain and frustrations went with it. The special moments, though, have become more vivid. I remember that view up Brady Street at the start, the fans along Kirkwood, the shouts for Samuelson and Ryun, and the good humor of everyone involved with this event.

Now, though, most of the runners have gone home, leaving Davenport in the custody of Bix Beiderbecke and his music. At the bandshell on the Mississippi, they are beginning the evening session, the finale of the Bix Fest weekend.

Davenport is often described as a quintessential Midwest town. People greet each other warmly and openly. Visitors are welcomed. There's little here that threatens the stability of family life. The hard edges have been absorbed into one's view of life. People have trust in the land and faith in the future.

And now, sitting by the river listening to Dixieland jazz, I begin to feel connected to this, and can understand why a native like Bix Beiderbecke might feel disoriented living anywhere else. Much as he yearned for other things, he must have felt uprooted, too, traveling to Chicago, St. Louis, New York and elsewhere, searching for something. Bix is often described as being quiet, reserved and agreeable. A quintessential Iowan, I think.

I remember my first night in Davenport, when I was discussing Beiderbecke with a local barfly, a jazz fan who "knew some guys who knew Bix."

"Bix would've liked all this," he insisted.

"Really?" I said, wondering if the quiet jazzman could actually have related to his home town's new claim to fame — a hot, hilly run of seven miles, with participants dressed up like fire trucks and beer cans, and fans lining the roadway to shout encouragement. "Why do you say that?"

"Because," he answered, as if the answer were too obvious, "jazz is about emotion."

START ME UP

I would keep my psychic distance and avoid lecturing as I watched the transformation. "You don't wear shorts over lycra tights," I pronounced one day. I feel strongly about that. Otherwise, I didn't interfere.

EACH OF US CAN RECALL THE TIME when we started running. We took our first steps as a runner or jogger (or perhaps asking for no title at all, thank you), struggling with soft muscles and self-doubt. Others, we knew, could run long distances seemingly with ease. But would we ever be up to it? We would see.

In time, we found that we were. Our breathing evened out. Our hearts stopped thumping wildly against our rib cages. Our schedules adjusted to accommodate our new interest. We talked enthusiastically (our non-running friends would say incessantly, or worse) about new-found fitness, improved performances, sore knees and a re-awakened appreciation for the changing seasons, heightened by our one-on-one contact or conflict with them. A new world had unfolded, step-by-step, before our eyes.

We began with trepidation. Eventually, though, we ran with confidence, year-round.

In my own case, those first steps were taken in preparation for a high school cross country season. Truly, I didn't know what I was getting into, or why. As a sophomore, though, I was eager to prove myself, so when the coach sent me on a 3-mile run to the nearest track, I went. When he directed me to run five repeat miles with the other, better-trained team members, I did my best. And when, finally, he sent me back those three miles to school, I hobbled, then I walked. What was this nuttiness anyway?

By the next week, though, I was running more smoothly. By the end of the season, I was running with conviction. Now, twenty-two years later, I'm still at it.

Years after I ran my own first steps, I helped with a beginning running class at the local YMCA. Men and women who, on their first day out, could not jog 50 yards without stopping and gasping were able in ten weeks to raise their conditioning to a level where a steady 7.5-mile run was possible — the miracle of physical redemption!

And such stories they told along the way. Tales of struggle and aching calves and loss of heart — faith, that is, not that great leaping beast in the chest. And those little revelations about the relationship of the runner to the world: "Really, it was like that car was *trying* to hit me. Why would they do such a thing?" Then, at long last, that moment arrived when the implausible became fact. Seven and a half miles, without stopping! Pride blossomed. Life would never be the same.

One day very recently, my wife became a runner. And the sun stood still in the sky, the seas parted, and ducks began speaking French. Miracles!

Bridgid had always been an active swimmer. When we first dated, she would spend nearly as much time in the pool as I did on the roads. A competitive swimmer in her teens, she could speak every bit as rapturously about a powerful armstroke as I could about a flowing stride. When it came to aerobic preference, we were at an impasse, but neither of us minded.

After we were married, people introduced to Bridgid would ask, "Do you run, too?" And she would wrinkle up her nose and let them know what she thought about running.

"Bridgid's a swimmer," I would sometimes mention, until it began to seem like an excuse rather than an observation.

Even in those days, though, Bridgid would sometimes give in, not to my insistence — there was none, honest — but to the convenience of running or the chance to socialize with her sister Sally or the yearly spirit of the massive Lilac Bloomsday Run in Spokane. But she could always justify it.

"I only run Bloomsday," she used to say.

Then, "Well I run a little, but just because I don't have time to swim," she said later, when our two kids were raising havoc with our free time. "And I still don't like it."

And then, after an auto accident made it impossible for her to swim vigorously, it was, "You know I still don't like running, but I have to admit that it improves my disposition."

Then Bridgid entered the observation phase.

"You know," she offered after her first evening run, "when a car comes toward you at night, it blinds you for a few seconds."

"Wearing that visor," she admitted another day, after running in her first snowfall, "really kept the snow out of my eyes."

And so on. I would keep my psychic distance and avoid lecturing as I watched the transformation. "You don't wear shorts over lycra tights," I pronounced one day. I feel strongly about that. Otherwise, I didn't interfere.

One Sunday, pressed for time, Bridgid needed to cut back on her running time. When she returned, she was smiling.

"You're not going to believe this," she said, "and I really can't believe it myself. But as Sally and I got back to the house, we realized we had a few more minutes, so we decided to go around the block again. We actually *wanted* to run more."

There was a time, I think, when each of us who runs experienced a similar transformation. And there was a time when we encouraged others to stick around long enough to enjoy the change. These days, when running seems commonplace, we need to renew our appreciation of what goes on in the body and mind of a novice runner. More than that, perhaps, we need to remember the magic of change itself.

"Is that you, Mom?" our 3-year-old daughter asked my formerly non-running wife the other day. She was looking at a magazine cover showing Lesley Welch, one of the fastest females on this planet.

July 1987

SEOUL '88

"I don't know about the rest of you," Butts said, his voice powerful with indignation, "but I came here to jump." His eyes gleamed. "And I'm gonna jump."

AS POLITICAL TURMOIL RATTLES ever louder in Seoul these days, sounding very much like political turmoil elsewhere and always, I find myself once again struggling against pre-Olympic depression. Will politics gain the upper hand in the Olympics again? Must we go through this show every four years, battling the odds for a few weeks worth of international athletic competition?

The issues that disrupt the Olympic stage every four years are real ones: tyranny, brutality, oppression, freedom. The location varies, from Germany to Mexico City to South Africa to Afghanistan. And whatever the sin in whatever locale, in the midst of the strife one wants to be fair, listening to the wronged.

Above all this, though, one — at least *this* one — wants a few weeks of peace to enjoy the spectacle of human beings running, jumping and throwing. When the fire of competition burns, human differences seem insignificant for a few moments, long enough to matter. And that, for those who care, is what the Olympics is about.

I take the intrusion of politics in sport personally. In 1976, after achieving my dream of making the Olympic team, I was at the U.S. training camp in Plattsburgh, New York, when news of an Olympic boycott by African nations hit like a slap in the face.

The issue was a series of rugby games played between New Zealand and South Africa, an exchange that ignored the prevailing policy that excluded South Africa from most international athletic competition. This, it was argued, meant New Zealand should not be welcome in the Olympic fold, even though rugby was not part of the Olympic menu and the New Zealand government was not involved in the exchange. If New Zealand were not excluded from Montreal, the boycott organizers insisted, African nations would leave.

Like many athletes, I heard this in disbelief. Were African nations really ready to frustrate the Olympic dreams of their top athletes for such a tenuous political principle? This was still in the days, of course, when we Americans believed ourselves above the muck of politics and sport. Other nations might bicker and strut about boycotts. Not us.

Imagine our dismay, then, to hear that organizers of the boycott had approached black members of the U.S. team to ask them to join their protest. Would U.S. blacks see this as a legitimate attempt to express outrage against oppression in South Africa? Would our team be divided, black and white, on this question?

The problem of dealing with the issue fell to Dr. LeRoy Walker, our head coach, the first African-American to be selected for that honor. Dr. Walker immediately called a team meeting.

We gathered that evening, nearly a hundred of us, in the lobby of one of the dorms at the training camp. People were everywhere: on chairs, couches, tables and on the floor. Some stood leaning against the walls while Dr. Walker addressed us. He began by stating what we all knew, that black members of our team had been asked to join the boycott. This, he said, was a divisive and unacceptable approach.

"We're all on the same team," said Walker, "and we're going to decide what to do as a team."

Not far from anyone's mind, I'm certain, was an earlier political statement, the black-gloved salute of John Carlos and Tommy Smith in Mexico City in 1968. The racial anger of the '60s had manifested itself then on the victory stand. Would race once again become an issue for the U.S. team? Would the inability of white team members to understand the experience of blacks once again cause a division along racial lines? No one wanted that, and so the first opinions ventured in our crowded, charged meeting were carefully diplomatic, cautiously offered.

Wasn't the issue, someone noted, of a New Zealand rugby team a little remote from the Olympics? Were the needs of Africans really served by this boycott? Wasn't the ethic, peaceful competition, worth preserving?

The arguments were abstractions appealing to logic, as detached from emotion as their proponents could make them. This seemed to be the best way to tread on the thin ice of an issue that involved the relationship of one race with another. And yet, devoid of emotion, they inevitably missed the point.

Then James Butts spoke.

I had first met Butts, a triple jumper from Southern California, during a track and field trip to Brazil. I knew him to be likable and yet fierce, someone whose intensity burned when he stood at the head of the runway, sparks in his eyes. Like all competitors at the international level, he hated to lose.

Butts, so the story went, had worked his way out of a rough life in L.A. and established himself as a world-class triple jumper through hard work and desire. He was holding down three jobs and supporting his mother and family, while somewhere finding the time and determination to train for the Olympics. Now he was a contender for the gold medal, on the brink of a dream.

"I don't know about the rest of you," Butts said, his voice powerful with indignation, "but I came here to jump." His eyes gleamed. "And I'm gonna *jump*."

The last word hit like the thud of a fist. The room was silent. He had said it simply, defiantly, piercing to the heart of the only real issue. One had trained, dreamed and sacrificed. Now one must be allowed to compete. It was an athlete's perspective, and we athletes who heard it relaxed, laughed, realized we had heard our own feelings voiced. Nothing else needed to be said.

A few days later, Butts battled his Soviet rival, Victor Saneyev, in the triple jump. Watching from high up in the stands, I imagined that spark in the man's eyes as he stood at the top of the runway. He lost that duel, at least in terms of who finished first, Saneyev, and who was second, Butts. But he won the silver medal in a fair fight, one that drew human beings, those who competed and those who watched, closer together.

A few days earlier, I had seen the great Kenyan 800-meter runner

Mike Boit sitting in the stands, his eyes reflecting the sadness of a man bereft of a dream. Kenya was not participating in the Olympics. Now, Boit's experience seemed a tragic counterpoint to that of Butts.

Ironically, those seeking to disrupt Olympic Games and those athletes whose Olympic Games are disrupted are generally looking for much the same thing — unfettered self-expression, a chance to pursue their deepest yearnings. In 1976, that desire was crystalized in the words of a triple jumper:

"I came here to jump," he said. "And I'm gonna *jump*."

When I get depressed about the pre-Olympic political show, I remember those words. Now and then, the world listens.

September 1987

FITTEST TO GOVERN

"On one day of the year," muses Darman, "the power in Washington lies with me. The high and mighty are all standing there in their shorts waiting for me to tell them it's time to move."

IN SOME WAYS, THE SCENE IS TYPICAL of many road races. The sun rises over the city, streaking pink fingers through patches of cloud. Runners gather and begin jogging, stretching, chatting with friends. Trucks full of food, water, ropes and banners are unloaded. Officials scurry here and there, sharing anxious concerns over walkie-talkies.

And then one notices. At the far end of the action, where runners file into porta-potties for the prerace constitutional, the units are marked not with "Men" and "Women" but "Senate," "House," "Executive (Policy Makers)," "Executive (Workers)," "Media," "Judges" and "Grassroots." Perhaps, one muses, "Shakers" and "Movers" would have sufficed.

And then one hears: "Good morning, and welcome to the seventh annual Nike Capital Challenge. In this 200th anniversary of the ratification of the Constitution of the United States of America, I would like to start with a special preamble." Close by, George Washington and Uncle Sam listen in rapt attention.

Finally one realizes — if one could possibly have remained in the dark this long — that this is not your typical race and not your typical race crowd. It is, as the announcer is proclaiming, the seventh edition of this most venerable of Washington, D.C., gatherings, in which the high and mighty of our nation's capital will once again "prove that the

United States government 'runs.' " In a few minutes, nearly a hundred U.S. senators, representatives, federal judges, department heads and media representatives will run three miles along with hundreds of their staff, in an attempt to (once again in the words of organizers who are ever eager to phrase things in government-ese) "settle the question of who is fittest — the Executive Branch, the Legislative Branch, the Judicial Branch or the media that cover them."

If nothing else were accomplished in the seven years of the Nike Capital Challenge, it would at least deserve mention for its unrelenting, amusing use of government language. From the entry form, in which changes in team competition rules are listed as "amendments," to the press releases, one of which describes the addition of the judicial team category as the "casting aside of judicial restraint," to the signs on the course, which this year includes the notable, "Do Supply Side Runners Believe in Oxygen Debt?," race organizers clearly relish any chance for puns on governmentese.

Participants seem just as eager. Team names range from "Taxation Without Hesitation" (Treasury Department) to "Rita's Rodriguez-Elles" (captained by Rita Rodriguez, a director of the Export-Import Bank) to "With All Deliberate Speed" (D.C. Circuit Court of Appeals) to "Legs Meeserables" (Attorney General's Office). Some are worse, or better — it's always hard to tell. Competition for best and worst team names is furious.

Puns aside, some serious running does take place here, spiced up by political rivalries and squabbles. As participants line up for the start, it's hard to forget that the guy on your left may have recently slashed your budget or the guy on your right may have just blasted you in the press. One wants to be careful not to trip or elbow someone in whose office one may soon find oneself begging a favor.

"It's interesting to be out there," notes one media rep, "running and sweating with people who, if you met them on the street, wouldn't give you the time of day."

Head whistle-blower James Miller, Director of the Office of Management and Budget — or the Office of Mercy and Benevolence according to team T-shirts — has agonized in deciding whether to participate in the race or attend a Republican Leadership Council meeting at the White House. After blowing the starting whistle, he heads for the meeting. Other unnamed participants have made the opposite decision.

In fact, where most directors may blame injuries or illnesses for the loss of celebrity runners, Nike Capital Challenge director Jeff Darman points to meetings and briefings as the main culprits. This year, for example, the hearings for Supreme Court nominee Robert Bork and the visit of Soviet Foreign Minister Eduard Shevardnadze drew entrants away. A crisis could be even more critical.

"A bomb goes off in the Gulf," jokes Darman, "and there go my media teams."

With so much political power concentrated in the race, it is comforting to know that, after a mile, the only power that counts is the stuff inside that drives the runners along in a steady progression around the tip of Hains Point. There the course passes the sculpture, "The Awakening," which suggests the emergence of political power or, perhaps, a very large runner trying to get out of bed for a morning run. Rounding the turn, the runners soon reach the finish line, led by OMB staffer John Wessels, who is first to break the tape. Red tape, of course.

In this race, though, first finisher is overshadowed by more important categories — first senator (Max Baucus of Montana), first representatives (Mel Levine of California and Claudine Schneider of Rhode Island), first senate team (Baucus Caucus), first house team (Weber's Wunners, led by Rep. Vin Weber of Minnesota), and on and on.

There is more interest in these division competitions than in any other aspect of the race except, perhaps, the best and worst team name categories, which this year go to McDonald's Golden Arches (Kim McDonald of the *Chronicle of Higher Education*) and Slattery's Speedy Wheaties (Rep. Jim Slattery of Kansas). In a close contest for "Best Spirit," in which contestants were urged to "curry favor with the judges," a team from the Department of Energy (Energy In Action) edges out Baucus Caucus.

While officials dressed in colonial garb scramble to compile results for the seemingly infinite number of categories, and before Darman begins answering a stream of calls from media around the country wanting to know how *their* Congressman ran, finishers stand around as finishers always do, comparing results, aches and pains in front of signs directing "First Aid" one way, "Contra Aid" the other. It has been a once-a-year ordeal for most, and they've enjoyed themselves immensely.

"Each of us has different reasons for entering," notes Claudine Schneider, the fastest woman in the House for the past four years. "I come back to see if I can keep getting older and better at the same time." This year's race represented a 2-minute improvement for the legislator, who figures it may be time to start looking for a coach.

Whatever their motives, participants have proven a point.

"The goal of the race," says Darman, "along with having fun and raising money for Special Olympics, is to show that some of the busiest people in the country can still find time to stay fit."

According to one reliable source, there may be an even better reason why the race director keeps at this unique event year after year.

"On one day of the year," muses Darman, "the power in Washington lies with me. The high and mighty are all standing there in their shorts waiting for me to tell them it's time to move."

October 1987

LE GRIZZ

It is, I think, the point of life to explore the boundaries.

LIKE MOST STORIES, this one could begin almost anywhere. At conception. At birth. On the day I first began running. At the moment I discovered that, more than almost anything, I loved running through the woods, feeling an integral, primitive, living part of the planet.

Perhaps the best point to begin, though, is at the moment I paid my $30 entry fee. Thirty dollars, after all, is not just three sawbucks. It is, rather, a commitment — in this case a commitment to run 50 miles. And so I sat, a detached observer far above my checkbook, watching myself sign on the dotted line. Apparently I was actually going to do this thing.

For five years I had heard of Le Grizz, a 50-mile race in Montana. Out of love for this event, friends from Spokane had driven long distances, camped in freezing weather, avoided dangerous (although unseen) predators, and run, walked and ultimately dragged themselves to a distant finish line. Then, trek completed, they had soaked in hot tubs and consumed beer and pizza until the pain subsided, leaving only the memories of an extraordinary adventure to relate to friends back home. Most, it seemed, remained delirious for days, professing to having enjoyed themselves.

I found this interesting. I had always been fascinated with ultras, had once, while on an overseas exchange during my sophomore year in college, even considered running 70 miles from the English town where I lived to the ancient monument of Stonehenge. The point? Some sort of neo-Druidic experience, I suppose, an athletic-religious-cosmic adventure. My friends thought I was nuts, and talked me out of it.

Years later I ran my first marathon, and learned that it was not easy to run mile after mile after mile after mile. Eventually, the balance in the struggle between body and mind, in which the determined mind promised to prevail, would tilt in favor of the body which, bereft of glycogen and dignity, would simply refuse to function. Decimated, the body would always win. Or was that lose?

Strange things could happen in a race of only 26 miles. What lay in the void beyond?

"Fifty miles is a whole new world compared to the marathon," noted the Le Grizz entry form. "It is a world of new knowledge of oneself, of self-actualization, and of brotherhood."

One suspects that this line was penned in the delirium of postrace hot-tubbing. Still, its lure was considerable. It may be difficult to pin down the peculiar attraction of exploring the extremes of human athletic possibilities, whether one is talking about climbing Mt. Everest, swimming the English Channel, or doing one's personal equivalent of the absurd. It is, I think, the point of life to explore the boundaries.

For years, 50 miles sat on the burner in the back of my mind, simmering. Eventually, I succumbed.

THE NIGHT BEFORE

On the evening before my first 50-miler, the moon that rose over the mountains behind the Spotted Bear Ranger Station was a *real* moon. Not a fat, lazy, mellow-yellow harvest moon or one of those fuzzy, sociable kind of orbs that smiles over urban landscapes. Rather it was a piercing, ice-cold, nasty, I'm-the-eye-of-the-universe sort of moon that scattered the stars, scared wildlife, quieted the rocks and glared at all of us assembled at the campground below. We were, the moon let us know, unlikely to get much sympathy from Mother Nature for what we were about to do.

The temperature was falling like a stone through ice water. Before dawn, it would hit 15 degrees. October at 3,500 feet in the Rockies is a gamble with loaded dice.

"There is always the outside chance, this being Montana," noted the Le Grizz entry form, "of foul, horrible weather."

Actually we were lucky. The forecast showed no signs of the snow, sleet, wind or rain that visited Le Grizz in 1984. "Runners alternated between feelings of depression and stupidity as the start time approached," noted the report of that year's event. Five people who had completed a 100-mile run that same year failed to finish.

This year it was simply cold. Naked cold. Dazzling moon cold. You could see clearly a half mile to the other side of the river. It was cold there, too.

Those who run ultras, though, thrive on extremes. It is not enough, you see, to simply run 50 or 100 miles from point A to point B. Along with that, one gains status by withstanding extremes of temperature, navigating narrow trails and scaling thousands of feet of elevation in regions where the air is too thin to permit normal aerobic activity.

In terms of ultra extremes, Le Grizz is fairly moderate. The road is rocky and uneven much of the way, but it is a real road, not a trail. There are hills, certainly, but no mountain passes to scramble up and down. The elevation is 3,500 feet, high enough for one to notice an altitude effect but not enough to whimper and wheeze about. And although the temperature that weekend would threaten to freeze eyebrows to forehead, at least it would not threaten dehydration.

Still, to enter Le Grizz I had been asked to sign the following: "I understand that participating in the Le Grizz 50-Mile Ultramarathon may subject me to injuries and illnesses, including but not limited to hypothermia, frostbite, heat stroke, heat exhaustion, physical exhaustion, animal attack, falling trees, road failure and vehicle accident."

Yes, I understand. I signed. And I paid my thirty bucks.

I wasn't alone. More than forty similarly disposed adults had signed up for Le Grizz, up from twenty-five the year before. Most of us were gathered along with family and friends within a 5-foot radius of the campfire at the Spotted Bear Campground, trying to carbo-load before the pasta froze. Five feet was the approximate range at which fire overcame cold, at least on the side of one's body turned toward the blaze.

Experienced ultrarunners in the crowd seemed strangely calm. Huddled around the fire that evening, they spoke of past 50- and 100-mile runs with less obvious passion than one would expect of runners completing their first 10K. Life-threatening situations were treated as part of the sport, major bodily failures as amusing anecdotes.

Among the group were Rick Spady and Jim Pomroy, two Montana runners who between them had won all five Le Grizz runs. Spady, the faster of the two with the Le Grizz record of 5:50:56, was in charge of firewood, a job that appeared to be a reflection of his nature rather than a specific obligation of the course record holder. From time to time, Spady would kick a spent log, sending sparks flying and settling the fire, then he'd add more wood to revive the blaze. Meanwhile, Pomroy tried to explain that running 100 miles is not really all that tough, once you adjust your attitude to enjoy the social aspects of the event.

"There's a lot more going on than with a 50," he offered.

I've stood around a fair number of campfires in my life, and they all seem blessed with the same purpose: to evoke memories, inspire philosophy and shake loose a few tall tales. Staring across the fire, one sees friends and strangers lost in thought. Their eyes reflect the glow of embers from the fire, suggesting the kindling of the mind. It is the look of human beings at peace, and it is the look one imagines in the eyes of ax murderers just before the massacre. It is a look of ambiguous calm, and it was on the faces of the ultrarunners that evening.

As the night chill clamped down, most folks headed for the relative warmth of their campers, tents and sleeping bags, leaving only a few seasoned ultrarunners around the fire to tell tales of Leadville, Western States and past Le Grizz struggles. They looked like woodsmen, hunters, or perhaps creatures that came sneaking out of the woods in the middle of the night.

But they were simply runners of long races, about to begin another. In the midst of long pauses in the conversation, their eyes gave indication of the calmness one needs to stare in the face of the long, hard road ahead. And above them, the eye of the moon blasted its icy light across the wilderness, promising nothing but the indifference of Nature to human dreams.

MORNING

It was a rough night in the forest. In theory, I had the best accommodations within 50 miles of the starting line. The camper I had rented came complete with kitchen, toilet and sleeping areas for myself, my wife Bridgid, and our two daughters, Kaitlin, age 4, and Catherine, age 2. More important, it had a heater.

In spite of all this luxury, I thrashed around inside the thing all night, trying to find a spot where I could stretch out and sleep. The floor was long enough, but the heater blasted hot air through a vent there, disrupting my sleep and threatening to burn my sleeping bag. The back of the camper was quieter, but space was limited. I shifted back and forth between the two spots all night, trading kinks in the legs for dreams of setting myself on fire, and managing only a couple of hours of sleep. Sleep deprivation became one more hardship to suffer in the spirit of ultrarunning.

The Le Grizz entry form says this about the legend of Hungry Horse: "Two husky freight horses, Tex and Jerry, working in the rugged wilderness of Flathead River's South Fork area, wandered away from their sleigh during the severe winter of 1900-01. After struggling for a month in belly-deep snow, they were found almost starved and so weak that considerable care and feeding were required before they were strong enough to be led back to civilization."

This legend is reported without comment. Like most of the hard truths about this event — the rocky road, the weather, the devastated muscles, the animals lurking in the bushes — one need not elaborate. Awaking on the morning of the run, my thoughts turned to food. I ate cereal, cookies and whatever else seemed to speak the language of carbohydrates. Though not full, my stomach was engaged, hopefully giving my body a chance at survival.

Outside the camper, runners and friends scurried back and forth, puffing clouds of warm breath in the air while searching for food of their own. Many were dressed in custom-made yellow and black tights, the uniform of the day for those of us from Spokane. In the midst of apprehension, the gaudy tights helped lighten the load. Pulling on my own, I left the warmth of the camper and went hunting for the race director, Pat Caffrey. He was busy handing out race numbers at one end of the parking area.

Caffrey is the force behind Le Grizz. He is the race director, the starter, the man in charge of awards, one of the sport's tallest figures and, most important, the guy who writes such funny things about Le Grizz on the entry form that the reader forgets what a gruesome thing a 50-mile run can be.

"Contrary to Yuppie Myth," wrote Caffrey about the atrocious weather that plagued Le Grizz runners in 1985, "people become wild animals, not environmentalists, when confronted with such a wilderness experience."

It was easy to understand that sentiment. After picking up my number from him and hustling to the line a few minutes before the 8 o'clock starting time, as ready as I was going to be for this thing, I shivered relentlessly as Caffrey delivered instructions, jokes and, at 15 degrees, information on how to buy leftover Le Grizz T-shirts.

"Brrrrr. Grrrrrr," I muttered on the starting line. Others around me agreed.

"Today's temperature is a Le Grizz record," Caffrey noted, grinning. Our lips were too numb to comment. Finally, raising the starting weapon, a 12-gauge shotgun wound with electrician's tape, the man behind Le Grizz fired a single blast that echoed in the depths of the wilderness.

Numb, we were off.

ZERO TO TEN MILES

The start of most road races is a flurry of arms, legs, elbows and adrenaline. The start of Le Grizz was more like the opening of Macy's doors on the day after Thanksgiving. People were hurrying, but within recognized bounds of propriety. There was time, plenty of time, to complete the task.

It had been so complicated just getting going that morning — finding food, going to the bathroom, making sure cars would start (several needed considerable coaxing), deciding on the right combination of clothing, etc. — that I began to relate to Le Grizz as it should be. Not as a race, but as survival.

I *will* overcome all this. I *will* get to the finish.

Other than finishing, I couldn't decide on an actual race goal. To win? To break 6 hours? I had nothing to base expectations on, so I settled on simply running the distance at a comfortable pace and scaling whatever obstacles lay in the road ahead.

In any race, a runner must evaluate training, past successes, failures and present bodily feedback in determining a goal. The proximity of other runners may inspire a response. Should I run with him? In an ultra, the personal evaluation is more critical, the relationship to other competitors, irrelevant. Or at least so I found it. One must focus on one's own ability to travel the distance, not on someone else's.

After a mile or so, I was running with Spady and another runner, Jim Ryan, who was part of a two-man relay. Twenty years of trained competitive responses were suddenly meaningless. In a shorter race, one goes with the leader or gives up the victory. In an ultra, one stays with one's own pace or gives up hope of finishing. I decided to run with Spady only as long as it felt like my own pace.

As the numbness in my quads, hands and face began to subside, I found myself discussing ultra training. Spady argued the value of the weekly long run over extremely high mileage. That system had kept him generally healthy and a top contender in races of 50 and 100 miles.

"If people wouldn't worry so much about the total mileage," said the course record holder, "but would get out there and just keep going for 6 hours, they'd do a lot better."

Six hours. *Just* keep going for 6 hours. My own longest runs had been 30 miles each, less than 4 hours. On one, I covered my usual 20-mile run, finished back at my house, ate a handful of cookies, drank a glass of electrolyte fluid, and headed out for another 10 miles. Those 30 miles had seemed endless.

Long training runs, the kind that help ultrarunners, require a different perspective. Years ago I tried adding 30-mile runs to my marathon training. One evening in 1977, I left home in the dark on an out-and-back course, 15 miles each way. After half an hour I was running on a major highway, blinded by headlights and contemplating death. After an hour I turned onto a country road and things got quiet, with only the breeze in the trees and the pad of my footsteps disturbing the silence. It was more like a dream than any training I was used to. Suddenly an owl chimed, "Whooooooo ... " from a telephone pole.

I'm sorry, but this wasn't training, this was weird. It was my last 30-mile training run for a decade.

Other than that, my longest runs had been journeys from Spokane to the top of Mt. Spokane — organized races of 34 miles that climbed 4,000 feet. Those had been difficult, as accumulated fatigue, dehydration and muscular tightness became problems at the same time oxygen was getting scarce and the road was reaching its steepest incline. A few soft drinks after reaching the summit, though, I felt recovered. No problem.

"Yeah, but things get *really weird* after 35 miles," noted Von Klohe, a Spokane friend and ultrarunner who advised me on Le Grizz training. Ultrarunners are always saying things like that. Then they chuckle.

As Spady and I ran along discussing ultra training and racing, the splits he reported from past Le Grizz runs made me nervous. The man was talking 6:10 and 6:20 mile pace, much faster than my own plans. Hearing that, I was anxious for a reason to let him go. That opportunity came at about seven miles in the form of my support crew — my family. As we headed up a slight incline, I spotted them ahead.

Le Grizz weekend represented a watershed for the Kardongs. It was our first night of camping together, at least if an evening in a heated home on wheels can be called camping. Things had gone well so far, but Bridgid and I were both apprehensive about how well our two girls would tolerate six hours of riding in a camper while Dad slowly whittled himself to a nub. To get them in the spirit of things, I had put Kaitlin in charge of cookies for dad.

Seeing my crew alongside the road at seven miles, I drifted off Spady's pace, slowed, and stopped for aid. Kaitlin handed me a bag of unopened cookies. Bridgid was in the camper, changing Catherine's diaper.

A well-trained support crew is essential for ultrarunning success, providing quick access to fluids, food and emotional support. As I ripped open the package of cookies, I realized I had forgotten to give my crew any information about what it was they were supposed to do.

Up ahead, Spady and Ryan were disappearing around the turn.

TEN MILES — 1:06:48

I'm not sure exactly how fast I expected to go through the various mile points, but 1:06:48 at 10 miles, with one aid stop and a pee break, seemed about right. I was running steadily, comfortably. Spady and the relay runner, Jim Ryan, were nowhere in sight.

The main problem I had faced on the road so far, other than an undertrained support crew, was clouds of dust from support crew vehicles. It had been a dry summer and fall in the Rockies. As vehicles leap-frogged from aid station to aid station, billowing clouds of dust choked the air, smothering those of us on foot. The only option was to stay to the side of the road and breathe sparingly when a vehicle passed.

Spady had speculated earlier that the dusty conditions would last until about 15 miles, at which point the bulk of the traffic would be behind us, and the air would clear. That proved to be only slightly off the mark. After 10 miles, dust and traffic began to fade, replaced by the full beauty of the countryside through which Le Grizz travels.

Hungry Horse Reservoir is on the western side of the Continental Divide in northwestern Montana, just south of Glacier Park. Waters from here flow in convoluted fashion through Montana, Idaho, Canada and Washington, eventually joining the Columbia River. The Le Grizz course follows a road along the southwest side of Hungry Horse Reservoir, affording participants who are still in control of their faculties an exquisite view across to the Great Bear Wilderness area.

The sight itself is worth the drive — though perhaps not a 50-mile run — especially in the fall. In this part of the country, most of the conifers just hunch their shoulders and settle in for the winter with no major transformation. The tamarack, though, a species of larch, changes from green to gold, then drops its needles like any deciduous tree. At the same time, aspen, birch, cottonwood and alder are busy turning color among the evergreens, and on Le Grizz weekend, hues from green to chartreuse to deep yellow are splashed across the hills. The aspen in particular stand out among the forest giants, brilliant gold, shimmering with the slightest breeze as if charged with electricity.

On this day, too, the moon had joined the scenery, preceding us most of the way. Hanging there just above the trees, it had grown less and less harsh in deference to the ascendance of the sun and the blueness of the sky. It had, I imagined, given up glaring at us, grumbled, and simply shrugged in grudging acceptance of the lunacy of human beings.

Now that the dust had settled, running through this scenery became distinctly pleasurable. I passed ten miles without much effort. Fifty miles began to seem possible, reasonable, even easy. The view was gorgeous, my legs felt strong, and the temperature had warmed to a comfortable level. I was really enjoying myself.

The attraction of Le Grizz, the combination of scenery and challenge, became clear. It was the opportunity to run without effort through natural splendor. It was the calm of the forest and the joy of self-propulsion. It was the combination of two loves, running and wilderness, that induced euphoria. I smiled. This was wonderful. And then, at 12 miles, I hit the first big uphill.

It was no monster, just a steady, continuous upgrade of perhaps a half mile. When it was gone, though, I was no longer euphoric. I was no longer convinced of my ability to travel another 40 miles. My quads had complained on the way up, the first signal of problems lying ahead. With five hours of running left, the joy of the forest began to give way to the reality of the long road through it.

As euphoria disappeared, though, misery didn't immediately take its place. That would come later. Instead, the next few miles became a task, a goal within a goal: I must get to the 20-mile mark.

Mentally, running 50 miles is the process of putting miles behind you. Ten miles represented one chunk, 20 miles another. It's a little like filling a garbage bag with aluminum cans. Crush the can, throw it in the bag. Crush another, throw it in the bag. Crush it, bag it, crush it, bag it, crush it, bag it. It is not an elegant process, and at times it seems both endless and meaningless. Eventually, though, the bag is full.

That may not sound like fun, but it isn't agony either. There were some rather pleasant times between 10 and 20 miles, as I alternated running in sub-freezing temperatures in the shade and warmer spots where sunlight was able to squeeze through the trees onto the roadway. Gloves went off in the sun, back on in the shade. All in all, the rhythm of those miles was enjoyable.

At one point a man in a pickup truck pulled up beside me, rolled down his window, and asked, "How far you goin'?"

"Fifty miles."

The response was a big toothless grin and a shout of "Good luck!" Then off he drove.

In the wilderness, where folks spend countless hours hunting deer, gathering firewood, climbing mountains, angling for fish and otherwise passing huge amounts of time entertaining themselves, a man in black-spotted, yellow tights running 50 miles was only slightly odd. In the forest, solitary human weirdness is expected, even appreciated.

At 13 miles my support crew appeared again, better prepared this time. I took a swig of defizzed Pepsi, asked them to meet me in another three miles or so, and trotted off.

I was feeling fine, though at 15 miles it occurred to me that on most days this would have been one of my longer training runs. I noticed fatigue beginning to creep into my quads, and I worried that this was too early to be having problems. I had hoped to avoid any noticeable aches and pains until much later.

At 17 miles, my support crew showed up again. Kaitlin handed me a half glass of Pepsi, while Bridgid announced that I was ahead of Spady.

"I don't think so," I answered. "He went ahead at the first stop, and I haven't passed him."

"The only guy I've seen is that other runner," she said, referring to Ryan. "I'm sure you're ahead of everyone else."

"I don't think so."

I downed the pop and headed off again. Whether I was in the lead or not seemed irrelevant. The key was to relax, conserve energy, try to go with the flow.

I hadn't even reached halfway yet, but already the tightness was growing, from my stomach to my knees.

TWENTY MILES — 2:12:58

Twenty miles. A long Sunday morning training run, the kind that drains my legs for at least a couple of days. This time, though, 20 miles was only the beginning. Thirty more lay ahead.

My time, 2:12:58, encouraged me. My pace had held up nicely for the second 10. Later I would figure my overall rate at this stage as 6:39 per mile, but for now, inept as I am at midrace arithmetic, I simply realized that I was running the same basic speed I had run during the first 10, well under 7-minute pace.

Earlier, just getting to 20 miles had seemed crucial. Now, having reached that mark, the goal became 30: I've got to get to 30. Relax, forget about the miles, just get to 30.

Right before the checkpoint I had passed Ryan, and I began to suspect that Bridgid was right. I was in first place now. Spady's fate was a mystery, but whatever had happened to him, his crew was nowhere in sight. Apparently I was in the lead.

Was there wisdom in that? As a neophyte ultrarunner I was on thin ice. Was I running too fast? Was I feeling fatigue too early in the game? Had Spady figured that, left to my own devices, I would dig my own grave, and did he therefore trick me into taking the lead? That seemed unlikely.

Whatever the answer, I consciously slowed down. Seeing my support crew a short while later, I stopped for more fluid and a molasses cookie, hoping to delay the inevitable crash into the wall at the end of the trail of dwindling energy reserves.

As every marathoner knows, there is a point near 20 miles when the body sends notice that it has had enough. Running becomes geometrically more difficult, fatigue encompasses the body, collapse is imminent, depression sets in. All this happens very suddenly. Marathoners call this "the wall."

The wall seems to be primarily the result of the body's inability to store sufficient energy in the muscles to carry it as far as the mind claims it wants to go. As stored sugars in the muscles, glycogen, run low, the body secures more and more energy by metabolizing stored fats. That process feels different, physiologically and psychologically. It is much, much harder.

Training for ultrarunning is a matter of teaching the body to metabolize fat for energy, something that is accomplished through long training runs, which explains Spady's advice that aspiring ultrarunners "just keep going for six hours" once a week. Strategy for ultrarunning also depends on learning how to eat during the run. Consuming calories early can help delay the wall.

That isn't as easy as it sounds. To eat is to fill the stomach, which then asks the body to devote resources to the digestive process. That's not reasonable when the legs are fully employed. Somebody loses, almost always the stomach. I've never been able to run after eating without developing stomach cramps of one sort or another. Thus, in shorter races I run hungry to avoid stomach distress. In an ultra, though, that's risky, and most runners opt for stomach discomfort rather than collapse. In my own case, I was hoping that the combination of sugary pop and the occasional cookie, both easily digestible, would represent a reasonable compromise.

Any attempt to keep the body adequately supplied with energy during an ultra, though, can only be partially successful, and I knew I would eventually be running on empty. Even as early as 20 miles, I was beginning to feel slightly dizzy, moderately disoriented.

In an ultramarathon, one discovers that, as the Zen masters have always insisted, body and mind are inseparable. The mind does not sit in the skull, riding happily along as it pilots the body from point to point, detached from the organism's needs. As the body staggers, so does the mind. They are friends — connected. If you don't believe me, try a 50-miler.

Earlier, my running body had helped produce euphoria. Now the body was doing a bang-up job of foisting paranoia on the mind. There were, I was convinced, predators watching me run.

The Le Grizz entry form, a.k.a. Pat Caffrey, says the following about midrace wildlife: "The road is lightly traveled in October (before hunting season) and goes through wild mountainous country where grizzly bear still roam. Other mammals, such as deer, elk, moose, black bear, mountain lion, bobcat and coyote are common."

In this year's final instructions, Caffrey had added the following: "The Montana Department of Fish, Wildlife and Parks has been trapping our grizzly bears from the west side of the reservoir. Six have been removed recently. If this continues, you may be running 'Le Traps!' "

Ultrarunners may be able to laugh at adversity, but when you get right down to it, grizzly bears are not funny. Like sharks, they eat people, and generally without benefit of music.

"Don't worry," a ranger at Glacier Park once told me, "grizzlies will only attack if you surprise them, invade their territory or come between them and their cubs." Three things, I explained to him, that a runner could do without realizing it.

Grizzlies are both unpredictable and quick on their feet. A grizzly bear can run up to 30 miles an hour, meaning it could give Carl Lewis a head start and still feast on his carcass at 80 meters.

So there I was, running out in front of the ultra parade, a mostly solitary figure traveling through the wilderness enjoying the scenery, when it suddenly dawned on me that I was hearing crackling noises in the bushes.

I've spent enough time in the woods to know that even a tiny animal, a chipmunk for example, can make a lot of noise. A bear, then, ought to sound like a rockslide as it snaps branches, crushes dry leaves and generally bullies its way through the forest. This is what my rational mind, insisting on its ability to make an objective judgment about the cracking of twigs, wanted to say. But, I tell you, the mind is connected, in this case to a body short of fuel.

The bear could be standing very still, the mind mused, waiting to run me down. He's probably watching me right now. My black-spotted tights, which accent the giraffe-ness of my legs, are probably invoking some sort of predatory response *at this very moment.*

In past Le Grizz runs, one of the Spokane runners had spotted a pile of fresh bear dung in the road. Right about this point in the race, my weakening mind noted. Another Spokane runner had responded to the crackling and crashing in the underbrush by stopping to throw rocks, a sure sign of glycogen depletion.

I told myself that, should I suddenly encounter a big Yogi, I would respond appropriately, which meant ... well, anyway, I would *not* throw rocks. Meanwhile, as I continued toward the halfway mark, I tried to relax and imagine that the sounds I was hearing were made by chipmunks, birds and other creatures that used to delight Snow White, and not by the sort of animal that can remove a runner's head with a single swipe of its paw.

MARATHON — 2:56:14

In the 1976 Olympics, I ran the marathon in 2:11:16. Thus, a time 45 minutes slower than that should not have pleased me, but it did; 2:56:14

seemed much better than I might have expected.

There is no such thing as an "easy" marathon. Twenty-six miles of easy running still produces muscles that are sore, tight and fatigued and a mind that is tired, scattered and testy. Body and mind have had it. This, the duo agree, would be a good time to stop.

In the very first Le Grizz Ultramarathon in 1982, runners crossed this point, indicated by "26.2 miles" written in red paint in the road, and immediately observed an arrow pointing down the road with the inscription: THE UNKNOWN. One imagines Pat Caffrey on the evening before the run, grinning devilishly as he painted this.

Passing the marathon point this time, I had several thoughts.

One, I was more *than half* way. There were fewer miles to go now than I had already covered. The feeling was similar to what I've experienced during a track workout after completing six out of ten quarter-mile repeats. An odd sort of relief blossomed. The garbage bag was *more* than half full.

Two, I needed to *get* to 30. In an ultra, the satisfaction of reaching a mile point is short-lived. I wanted to be at the next major milestone immediately.

Three, I needed a potty stop. My stomach had been bothering me for the past 10 miles, and I thought a trip to the bathroom would help. Seeing my support crew ahead, I pulled over and headed for relief.

There is a Disney cartoon in which Goofy puts on a pair of stretch pants without taking off his snow skis. That's how I felt trying to do my business in the tiny camper toilet. I figured afterward that it had taken at least three minutes, most of which involved logistics rather than function. Another 30 seconds or so was also spent convincing Kaitlin and Catherine that they didn't need to visit me during this particular activity.

Back on the road I felt much better. The fresh runner from the relay team had passed me during my break, and I wouldn't see him again until the finish. Part of me was worried that Spady had also caught up during my prolonged pit stop. Mostly, though, I was concerned about monitoring vital signs rather than staying ahead of anyone.

During the next few miles, a collage of thoughts, experiences and observations from earlier in the run reappeared: euphoria, despair, impatience, fear of encountering a grizzly, determination to finish, and admiration of the scenery, which now included the brilliant, robin's egg blue waters of Hungry Horse Reservoir. It was difficult, though, to focus on any one of these for long.

My support crew was stopping every two miles now instead of every three, in deference to my flagging spirits. Just short of 29 miles, I came up a rise huffing and puffing, then stopped in front of the camper. Squeezing one nostril at a time, I blew my nose on the ground, something I wouldn't do in a crowded elevator but which seemed fairly acceptable in the midst of a 50-mile run in the middle of the forest.

When I looked up, I noticed Kaitlin staring at me in disgust and bewilderment. In her experience with parents, this was a new phenomenon. Bridgid noticed her reaction, too.

"Is that the way you blow *your* nose, Kaitlin?" asked Bridgid.

Kaitlin made no response other than to continue staring in disgust at her once-proud father.

THIRTY MILES — 3:25:20

With 20 miles — the length of my long Sunday morning training runs — still remaining, I found little solace in reaching the 30 milestone. There were too many miles left.

My time, 3:25:20, evoked no particular response. Was it good or bad? I couldn't even figure whether I had slowed down since the 20-mile mark, though in fact I had.

More important than my elapsed time was the information I had forgotten to share with Bridgid. I had meant to warn her about the drastic deterioration of my personality that I expected to occur soon. When blood sugar is low, one begins to realize how dependent the organism is on maintaining a proper chemical balance. The "personality," a supposedly fixed set of human traits and attributes, proves to be about as permanent as Mt. St. Helens. Ordinarily reasonable, pleasant folks become nasty, whining, hopeless idiots. The runner becomes acutely disagreeable as his or her digestive system cannibalizes the body for fuel. It's best to steer clear of such folks.

My support crew, though, had agreed to stay with me, and had thus relinquished the perfectly reasonable possibility of turning me over to the grizzlies when I began to get rude. At present, we were all entering a danger zone of intrafamily relationships. When the camper appeared again, I vowed to issue a warning.

"Do you need anything?" Bridgid asked nicely.

"No, but I'm going to start getting nasty pretty soon," I answered obliquely.

Bridgid has seen me depleted before. She knew exactly what I meant.

For the next few miles the road seemed to climb steadily, until it was fairly high above the reservoir. It was hard going, and I labored. At 33 miles I stopped for fluids, nearly threw up from the ensuing nausea, and was walking to regain my equilibrium when Bridgid pulled up beside in the camper.

"I think you slowed down a bit," she said innocently, forgetting about the depletion. I stared ahead morosely and kept walking. Fortunately, I was not in possession of a weapon.

Things were getting worse now. My quads had been beaten to exhaustion, and my stomach grew more and more uneasy with each step. I passed 35 miles in 4:01:11, which meant — miraculously, I was actually able to figure this out — I had 2 hours to complete 15 miles to break 6 hours. That goal seemed questionable, though, and I decided to concentrate instead on just finishing.

Suddenly some kind of large bird, a pheasant perhaps, took flight from the bushes. He may have been frightened, but I was terrified. My heartbeat soared.

I began to feel the way I had at the Ultimate Runner — a pentathlon of running events I had participated in two years earlier — when I reached the final miles of the marathon. I would travel one mile at a time, rewarding myself with a short walking break and drink at each mile marker. I asked my support crew to leap-frog one mile at a time with me.

I was surprised at this point that, though obviously suffering from depletion, I hadn't developed a craving for sweets. That would come soon. For now, though, I just concentrated on reaching the 40-mile mark, while the thought of a nice, long soak in the hot tub later that evening buoyed my spirits.

FORTY MILES — 4:38:17

I was entering a world not of sight or sound but of mind. And the signpost up ahead reads: "LE GRIZZ — 40 MILES."

"Ultramarathons are for the patient and calculating runner," says the Le Grizz entry form. "You are expected to monitor your own well-being. You are in charge of your body, your mind, your run."

Well, maybe. At 40 miles, though, it sure as hell didn't feel like it.

My mind kept returning to Von Klohe's remark, "Things get *really weird* after 35 miles." That observation seemed closer to the mark.

The next five miles would be the hardest of the day. Along with the general beating my legs had taken, my stomach continued to rebel, and my mind drifted from thought to thought like an explorer without a compass. At one moment I would be convinced of my ability to win my first 50-miler in less than 6 hours. The next moment I would be struggling against the urge to walk the rest of the way to the finish, whatever the outcome.

A good part of my concern during these miles was in having Bridgid stop the camper *exactly* at the mile mark, not 50 or 100 meters down the road. For Bridgid, though, driving along searching for the white mile marks in the road proved to be incompatible with the job of supervising two camper-bound pre-schoolers. Mile after mile, she missed it. Mile after mile, I repeated my whining request that she be exactly at the mile point next time.

"I don't know why it's so important to me," I told her at 43 miles, "but please stop right on the next mark."

This is the kind of behavior that seems so foolish later on, when one has a Snickers bar in one hand and a beer in the other. Unfortunately, at this point in an ultramarathon, it is the sort of behavior that seems divinely ordained. It was crucial that Bridgid stop where I directed.

As I came up to the 44-mile mark, I became incensed. She was not there! After all my begging, she still wasn't on the mark! I cursed, and may have even picked up the pace a bit in anticipation of seeing the camper around the next turn. She wasn't there either. One more turn. Still not there. Suddenly I realized the awful truth: She had missed stopping at 44 miles altogether. I would have to run all the way to 45 miles!

God, what a cruel, cruel world it was, in which a man had to run *two miles* without a support crew. I screamed something into the forest. Something about Bridgid. To this day, only the trees and wildlife know what it was.

I wanted to cry, to stop, to lie down and never get up again. Somehow, though, I kept going, step after painful step. Finally, an eon or so later, I reached 45 miles.

"I can't believe you missed the last mile point," I whimpered.

"I'm sorry," Bridgid replied. She seemed sincere.

My time at 45 miles was 5:18:40. I drank another half glass of defizzed Pepsi and walked down the road. Ten seconds later I threw up.

It wasn't a pleasant experience, but neither was it anything to get upset about. Just one of those things that happens when you run longer or harder than you should.

Kaitlin and Catherine watched in horror, though, while Bridgid tried to assure them that everything was all right. A few seconds later, I started running again.

Running was the only thing, after all, that would finally bring peace. At 45 miles, I was a battered, exhausted, drained and nauseous wreck.

"It never always gets worse," Dan Brannen, long-time ultrarunning aficionado, had said. He advised me not to forget those words during those miles of Le Grizz when the downward spiral of bad to worse to even-worse-than-that seemed unbroken, infinite.

"Eventually," said Brannen, "something will get better."

And it was that advice, that odd nub of wisdom, which rang truer than anything at 45 miles. It never always gets worse. We're talking about life, now, not just ultrarunning. Or at least life in the downward spiral. "Survive," we tell ourselves and others in the throes of despair. "Endure. It will get better."

Perhaps the attraction of ultrarunning lies in the simple distillation of this: the ability to envision a distant goal, another time and place when things will be better, and to survive the worst until then. It is both the thread of survival instinct that unites us to other creatures and the clarity of imagination and willpower that catapults us above them. I *will* make it, says the determined mind, and convinces the body. It never always gets worse.

Suddenly, as if on cue, I felt better. Whether it was the simple fact of having emptied my stomach, or the realization that I was approaching the finish of this ordeal, or the final inspired gasp of determination, I rallied. I felt better. Five miles to go.

At 46 miles, I came around a turn and saw Hungry Horse Dam ahead. From there, I knew, it was only a couple of miles to the end. I felt what seemed to be a shot of adrenaline, a surge of courage, speed through my system. I was on the homestretch!

I sensed again that I might win this thing, might even break 6 hours. Those particular aspirations had been buried beneath a stack of miles for the last couple of hours. Even now, the truly relevant goal was to keep going at any pace without walking.

At 47 miles, I headed across the top of the dam. The concrete roadway felt unbelievably hard, jolting my muscles and joints.

The final miles were more or less a blur of hills, sore quads, elevated spirits, low blood sugar and human conviction. The last two seemed especially tough, as I skipped the final aid station in the hope of breaking 6 hours.

"Dad looks pretty good again, doesn't he?" Bridgid said to Catherine, who was now riding happily in the front seat with Kaitlin.

"Yeah," she answered cheerfully in 2-year-oldese, "he no throw up now."

"In a 50-miler," says the Le Grizz entry form, "one competes against one's own limits, not someone else's limits. To finish is to win."

After 5 hours, 58 minutes and 37 seconds of running, walking, pit stops, vomiting, despair and determination, it was over. I had won. I finished.

FINISH LINE

Exactly two steps after crossing the Le Grizz finish line, I stopped. As it turned out, I wouldn't run another step for five days (I would have enough trouble just walking). I had committed serious, though temporary, abuse on my legs.

Bridgid escorted me to the camper, where I found I was unable to climb three steps to get inside. My quads had simply, absolutely refused to assist the lifting process anymore. Eventually Bridgid was able to push me inside, where I crawled into a seat, pulled on warm-ups and wool clothes, and began eating.

I was very, very chilled, but an hour later, after huddling inside a blanket and nourishing my blood sugar back to a reasonable level, I began to feel alive again.

Spady dropped by, looking much, much better than I felt. He had struggled with stomach problems all day but had still finished second in 6:19:57.

"I've got some real bad news for you," he said, grinning somewhere beneath his fu manchu. "In about three days, you're going to think you had fun here today."

He left, but a few minutes later he came back and asked Bridgid, "Well, how was it out there? Did he get really nasty, like for parking 50 feet away from where you were supposed to be?" Apparently, this was normal behavior for an ultrarunner.

Spady advised that I walk around a little bit, and now that strength was returning I followed his advice. Individuals and groups were finishing on a regular basis now, and I went to offer my congratulations. Our Spokane group had enjoyed good fortunes. Other finishers, too, found the Le Grizz conditions favorable for fast running that day.

In chatting with the various finishers, I discovered that one of the relay team members had seen a bear just past the marathon point. Only a black bear, though. However, another runner had sighted a grizzly at 18 miles. So was it depletion-induced paranoia or a sixth sense that told me something was drooling in the bushes as my tights flashed by? At any rate, it was the first (and second) actual bear sighting in the seven-year history of Le Grizz.

While finishers were eager to share adventures, they were even more eager to begin eating things — candy, pop, jo-jos, fried chicken — that everyone realized were unarguably unhealthy. Organizers of Le Grizz, though, understand that someone who has just completed a 50-mile run is in no mood for healthy vittles. Dues had been paid, tens of thousands of calories used up. It was time to chow down.

A few of the early finishers also enjoyed a surprisingly strong brew of beer, which more or less ignored any bodily screening systems and raced to the head. Under the steel-eyed glare of the moon the night before, the keg had frozen, and the water and alcohol had separated.

Noted Caffrey in a postrace message: "The half keg that did manage to get served was up around 8 percent alcohol, in case some of you were blaming your susceptibility to the beer on the day's activities. This special brew has since been christened 'Grizzly Beer.' "

Though long gone, the moon enjoyed the last word.

When beer, chicken and assorted junk food were consumed, when participants were finished watching a moose graze along the shore of the lake near the finish area, and as the sun began to dip toward the horizon, Caffrey finally called us to hobble and huddle together for the awards ceremony.

In an event as personally challenging as a 50-miler, organizers seem to feel that, since they told you, "To finish is to win," the least they can do is prove they mean it. Everyone gets a trophy.

The trophy for first is biggest, but it possesses no added significance. An overwhelming sense of communion permeates the ceremony — a recognition that everyone, regardless of speed, has achieved the same ambiguous victory, whose reality is etched in battered muscles and tired, sweaty lines on faces.

Pain, fatigue and sweat, of course, will eventually disappear, leaving only memories and a few tangible mementos like the trophy. And with bronze and wood symbolizing a full day of painful struggle through the wilderness, it's no wonder that officials in 1983 were mortified to discover that the running figure on the trophy for that year's overall winner, Rick Spady, was broken off at the knees.

"Though it was explained that the runner had broken off in shipment," wrote Caffrey later in characteristic good humor, "the other winners demanded similar trophies and threatened to break the runners off their trophies as soon as their strength returned."

In the end, then, I received my award — the only trophy I've chosen to display. It has a base of shellacked Montana juniper and a figure of a grizzly bear standing on its hind legs, looking fearsome. That bear has, I imagine, just spotted a skinny human being in yellow and black tights running through its domain.

Later that evening I enjoyed postrace rituals of hot-tubbing, feasting and adventure-swapping with the Spokane crew, then went to bed early. The next morning seemed a little like the melancholic final day of college, with comrades heading off in different directions, leaving shared adventures for individual lives in the civilized world. Nearly everyone took a different route home.

During the next week, I hobbled through the building where I work in downtown Spokane, hoping someone would question my gimp. ("Oh, that? Nothing serious, really, just tired legs from a 50-mile run. That's right, fifty.") Gradually, my muscles began to rebuild. In a strange way, though, I relished the residual pain, evidence of my journey through the world beyond the marathon.

And after that?

The Le Grizz entry form says this about what to expect following the event: "You might feel burned out for four days as a result of energy depletion. Then comes some euphoria."

Spady had said it differently. "In about three days, you're going to think you had fun here today."

He was wrong. It took almost a week.

TRIALS AND TRIBULATIONS

It seemed then, standing in line, oldest to youngest, as if the fire of Olympic excellence had passed through this group like a wave, blessing each of us briefly.

THE WIND IS BLOWING SO HARD that one of the favorites lies down on the starting line, a chilly thinclad snuggling with Mother Earth for warmth and security. In the distance another mother, Liberty, stands watch over the scene. The huddled masses are about to begin.

I have been placed in the center of the starting line, a conspicuous anomaly in the midst of true Olympic contenders. Somehow, the idea of running this marathon has always promised to be more subtle than this, an honor accorded to past Olympians, an invitation to visit backstage. But a place on the front line?

Yet here I am, with the Donakowskis and Petersens and Gompers of the world.

Behind us my wife Bridgid watches. She and I were unknown to each other twelve years ago, when I finished a surprising third in the 1976 Trials and an even more surprising fourth in the Montreal Olympics. We met shortly after that, and though she has watched me run many races since, this is her first breath of the air of Olympic aspirations. She has been unable to shake the notion that perhaps, as teachers and movies insist, anything is possible here in America.

"Isn't there some part of you that believes you might make the team?"

she has asked more than once over the past few months.

"Bridgid," I respond, "where is your reality principle?"

At 39, I am merely hoping to run steadily, pass a few stragglers and finish this marathon harboring the satisfaction cherished by any runner — the personal fulfillment of running as well as I can. That will be enough.

The gun fires and we're off, a pack bound by dreams and determination. I'm there with the best runners in the country, reliving an experience from my past. It is thrilling to once again be in the U.S. Olympic Trials.

And yet, truthfully, I am not really in them. I happen to be here, in the pack, enjoying a brief sense of déjà vu. But, I feel instinctively, I am the wrong player for this scene.

Many nights I've been able to wake myself from strange imaginings by realizing that I'm dreaming. At some level I recognize it, and the dream unravels. I wake.

That's how this feels.

After the heady charge through the first half-mile, I ease up, relax into a pace I believe I can run for 26 miles. The pack of contenders surges ahead, and I'm left in the dust. Behind me, a void.

For a while I try to recapture the feeling of 1976, when I put my body on autopilot in the early miles, letting capriciousness take the edge off intensity until the real racing began. I wave or shout to people I recognize, and I tell myself that I will begin working at 10 miles.

But nothing is automatic about the marathon anymore, and when I hit the first uphill at four miles, it hurts. By the top I'm gasping for air. Thankfully, I'm running with an Alaskan runner named Kris Mueller, whom I met a few weeks earlier. He seems determined to survive this experience in good humor. His attitude helps.

Over the next dozen miles I try to draw strength from the crowds. The worst neighborhoods seem to produce the best spectators, at least in animation and volume. They yell long, elaborate remarks I can only partially comprehend. Something about $50,000. Something about keeping the spirit. A chant that includes two obscene words and a lot of laughter. Young kids want to slap hands, and I oblige.

I pass halfway in 1:13:40, not far off my goal, but it has not been easy. I am fighting blasts of wind, hills, turns, swirling eddies of litter. I am all alone, too, running across the Hudson from that wonderful, intoxicating, sobering Manhattan skyline. I know I still have a long way to go.

Dreamscape again. I am running solo, and for a while I can see no one ahead or behind. It is as if I am the only runner in this race.

At about 18 miles, fatigue and nausea overwhelm. To keep from throwing up, I begin walking.

An old man approaches, face withered, eyes clouded. On another day, he might have asked for spare change. Today, though, he has a more sublime question.

"Is this the Olympics?" he asks.

I force myself to be civil. "The Olympic Trials," I say.

He pauses, watching me pass. "Yeah, but it's still the Olympics, right?"

I don't answer. The notion has a special significance to the man, but I'm too disgusted with my own condition to appreciate his perspective. My system has shut down, and I know the final miles of this marathon will be acutely painful. I'm not looking forward to it. More than that, one thought seems incredible: I once ran 2:11:16. How was it possible?

My mind flashes to a banquet a few nights earlier, when I stood in line with past Olympic marathoners — Billy Mills, George Young, Jack Bacheler and others — to be honored with applause. It seemed then, standing in line, oldest to youngest, as if the fire of Olympic excellence had passed through this group like a wave, blessing each of us briefly. In 1976, it had passed through me.

Now, though, all that is history, and I must simply get to the finish. It is a long trudge home.

Much, much later, I struggle down the final half-mile back in Liberty State Park. As I approach the line I hear two things. One, the announcement of the top three finishers — Conover, Eyestone, Pfitzinger. For whatever reason, the flame has passed to them. Two, I hear my name on the loudspeaker.

"Finishing now is Don Kardong, member of the 1976 Olympic team."

In the distance is the skyline of lower Manhattan, suspended in time, surrealistic. The eternal city, chilling and dispassionate.

Somewhere in the crowd, Bridgid is waiting with warm clothes and comfort.

June 1988

WAKE ME UP WHEN IT'S OVER

Mark Twain once said that everyone is ignorant,
only about different things. Same idea in the MVP.
Everybody's a klutz, only in different sports.

IS THIS A DREAM or what?

I'm in the middle of a cross county race, leading the pack. As in most running dreams, the route I'm following is bizarre. I jump between trees, trot gingerly along curbing, and run up and down hills following a white line that has apparently been laid down by a disgruntled, disoriented and/or inebriated prankster.

There are people present here who don't fit the context. An Olympic 800-meter gold medalist. A pole vaulter. A famous oilman. They're running behind me, of course, because this is my dream, right?

I pass under a railroad trestle, where a very young-looking official signals me to take a sharp left turn. Charging up a hill, I reach the top and spot an arrow that seems to direct me onto the trestle. I start across.

After a few steps I realize that, aside from the tracks and the ties connecting them, there will soon be nothing between me and a long fall into a muddy river. I stop briefly and yell at the official below.

"Across here?" I shout in disbelief, begging a negative response.

"Yes!" he answers, and the dream takes a nasty turn. I am soon halfway across the bridge, stutter-stepping between ties far above a sluggish, yellow-green and malevolent river. I hear yelling in the distance, a disjointed but anxious voice in the wind. Perhaps soon I'll stumble and fall and begin tumbling down, down, down toward doom. And then, of course, I'll wake up ...

No chance, Don. Better keep your balance and stay on your feet. This, pal, is no dream. This is real life.

Well, sort of. Actually this is the Jim Hershberger MVP (Most *Versatile* Performer), a ten-event test of athletic versatility — agility, coordination, endurance, skill, speed, stamina, strength and, as it turned out for some of us who went off course in the final event, composure in the jaws of death. The Hershberger MVP: a day-long agenda of sporting challenges — golf, racquetball, basketball, cycling, pitch-pass-kick, blockade-and-calisthenics, swimming, kayaking, jet skiing and cross country running — with $67,000 in prize money on the line.

On a hot day in Wichita, Kansas, fourteen professional, Olympic and just plain talented athletes (and myself) have assembled to compete in ten widely different events and thereby answer a most fundamental question of athletic macho-compulsiveness. Who can do it all?

The MVP competition, touted as "The World's Most Complete Test of Athletic Versatility," grew out of one man's frustration. Jim Hershberger is a Kansas oilman, philanthropist and aspiring politician, a 5-foot-9-inch human dynamo with a more-or-less permanent burr in his saddle. If this guy rests, it is with one eye open and one foot in the stirrup.

Along with being a Kansas celebrity for his business, charitable and political energies, Hershberger is also a sports fanatic of near-perfect constitution. In his 56 years on the planet, he has won awards in fourteen different sports, national recognition in five, and been featured on the front of the Wheaties box. He has participated in, well, everything. Sports on courts, in water, on playing fields, in stuffy rooms, on mats and in wide open spaces. Sports with bats, balls, gloves, clubs, racquets, sticks, bullets, boards, boats, well-oiled machines and bare hands. I mean *everything*.

"Well, I've never boxed," he admits after prodding, "except in street fights. My wrestling coach said never hit a man unless he's looking up at you."

In 1981, to celebrate his lifelong fascination with things athletic, Hershberger enjoyed his 50th birthday by cramming half a century of personal sports participation — and injuries — into 14 1/2 hours of multisport mania when he organized the first "Hershberger Games," a kind of precursor of the MVP.

Over the course of that day, Hershberger competed against Big Eight Conference champions and other athletic wizards in eighteen sports, including tennis (broken wrist), badminton, swimming, rifle shooting, 220-yard run, cycling (two broken fingers on his right hand and a bone that broke through the skin), wrestling (broken nose), volleyball, handball ("That's a lot of fun with a bone out."), racquetball, ping pong, basketball, waterskiing, jet skiing, softball, golf ("I was par for the first six holes, holding on with two fingers, then I got cocky."), and a 10K (pulled hamstring).

"Mind you," says Hershberger, "there wasn't one minute of rest." No kidding.

Fiftieth birthday aside, this is not the sort of man you'd expect to watch a bunch of highly paid, pampered professional athletes vie for top-dog honors in a TV multisport competition called "The Superstars" without leaping to his feet and shouting, "Those imposters!" Hershberger's pride was piqued, and he yearned to show the youngsters how it's supposed to be done.

"Not on your life!" was the reaction of organizers.

"A little scrawny kid beating those Superstars?" asks Hershberger rhetorically. "They didn't want that."

So, unable to get an invitation to the event that supposedly celebrates the best all-around athlete, Hershberger decided to start his own.

In 1984, the Jim Hershberger MVP was born.

GOLF

I remember this game. Numbered clubs, dimpled balls, wide expanses of soft green turf that are excellent for running speed sessions. Overweight heart-attack candidates wearing pastel pants and driving small electric automobiles. "Get the hell off the fairway!" they shouted when I ran by. Yes, I remember.

In junior high and high school, I idolized Arnold Palmer. The sight of that man striding confidently, regally, over hill and dale brought tears to my eyes. He *owned* life. I wanted to be him.

Unfortunately, high school was also the last time I played this game with any regularity. So when I look in my golf bag (the one held together with duct tape) after arriving at the course for the first event of the Jim Hershberger MVP, I am not surprised at what I find — clubs whose leather grips are unwinding, broken tees and balls of indeterminate and antediluvian origin: a Wilson K-28, a "Floater" (a trick ball, I think) and a few generics imprinted with names of insurance and drug companies (my father was a doctor and donor of golf balls to his children).

For the next nine holes, I am forced to use this equipment to try to break 55, a score at which we MVP-ers get smacked with negative points. In general, MVP competitors receive 40 points for first, 35 for second, 30 for third and so on down the line in order of finish for each of the ten events, provided no one slips below the prearranged standard of athletic incompetence. Sink below the standard and you get no points. Sink even lower than that (You klutz!) and you get minus 10. In golf, the bottom line below the bottom line is 55.

My partner in this futile exercise is Cliff Livingston, a 6-foot-8-inch professional basketball player for the Atlanta Hawks. At the orientation session the previous evening, Levingston had reacted with exasperation to the news that this year's MVP golf competition would be contested on a more difficult course.

"Some of us had trouble with last year's course," moaned Levingston with mostly good nature.

"Some of us can't dunk a basketball," responded Hershberger.

To give you an indication of how well this round of golf goes for Levingston and myself, on about the third hole he winds up and swings powerfully, decisively but, sorry to say, unsuccessfully. He barely nicks the ball, which jumps one inch off the tee. I, in turn, scuff my shot about 50 yards down the fairway, thereby winning the contest for the longest drive. By about the seventh hole, my caddie is advising me to use my 8 iron, which is the only club he's seen me hit with anything resembling skill, no matter what the shot. Putts too. Using the 8, I actually hit a nice approach shot, one that sails high and and lands safely on the other side of a water hazard.

For a brief moment I realize what this game is supposed to be like. Arnold Palmer. This moment aside, though, today's golf has been more frustrating and infuriating than sublime. Come to think of it, that's the way this game has always been for me.

Cliff steps to the tee, hits a powerful flat shot right at the water. Instead of splash and sink, though, his ball skips once and lands safely on the other side.

"I guess that's what this game is all about," I tell him as we walk down the fairway. "Chippin' and skippin'."

"Chippin' and skippin' ... " Cliff muses.

A few minutes later the golf competition is over. Neither of us has made the cut.

RACQUETBALL

In golf, I had reason to believe that I might, by some stroke of divine goodness, recapture at least a portion of my long-dormant, though never abundant, ability. In racquetball, I have no glimmer of hope. I've played twice in my life, and can't even remember exactly where to stand.

In MVP racquetball, competitors play four games. First player to get 7 points in each game wins. My personal goal is to score a point during this event or, if that proves impossible, to at least figure out the subtleties of the game, like which walls you can hit against.

My first game is against Bill Johnson, the 1984 Olympic downhill skiing gold medalist, who disposes of me 7-0. Brutal competitor. I return no shots.

My second game is against Bob LaPoint, five-time winner of the world slalom waterskiing championship, who dumps me 7-0. I score a moral victory by returning two shots. I'm rollin' now.

My third game is against Brad Chatfield, a former high school letterman in five sports, who is competing as an amateur today.

"Don't worry about me," he says as we warm up. "I haven't won a game of racquetball in the whole fours years I've been in the MVP."

In a way, I enjoy playing against Chatfield, because when he scores a point he says things like, "Whoops, my racquet slipped," instead of just sweating, grimacing and digging in for another swat at my ego.

On the other hand, I hate playing against a guy who hasn't won a game in four years and who I know is about to win his first. Somewhere in the ensuing confusion I score a point, thus achieving my goal. In the end, Chatfield triumphs 7-1.

My final game is against Lon Kruger, the Kansas State University head basketball coach and the top golfer of the day. A gracious man, Kruger doesn't ask whether I've ever actually played racquetball before. He accepts his 7-zip victory with aplomb.

As humiliating as this experience has been, I've learned something valuable: Racquetball is not one of those sports you should attempt to play without knowing how.

BASKETBALL

A startling thought occurs to me before the basketball shooting event: Wouldn't it have been a good idea to have found out ahead of time which events were going to be contested in the MVP and then practiced them? (Sometimes these brilliant thoughts just come to me.)

Too late for that. I played my last serious basketball about the same time as my last serious golf, and now I've got three minutes to prove I can reconstruct the dynamics and resuscitate the touch that, even in my prime, eluded me.

I dribble up and down the court, trying not to rush shots from the three designated spots on each side. I shoot a few airballs and have to repeat shots. My goal here is lofty — to try to look sort of like a real basketball player at some point in the competition. I fail, managing only 10 points before time runs out.

Later I watch Lynette Woodard, the first woman ever to play with the Harlem Globetrotters (and the first woman ever to be talked into competing in the MVP), take her turn. She scores 40, which will be good for seventh place. Cliff Livingston, the other pro basketballer, scores 47, good for fourth. In four years, no professional basketball player has won the MVP basketball event, which most likely proves something about something — or maybe not.

In 1986, the last year the MVP was held, Dave Wottle won the basketball event. He also won the overall MVP title that same year. I still remember standing in a shopping mall in Germany during the 1972 Olympics, watching television as Wottle scooted past the field in the final millimeters of the 800, and letting out a primeval "Whoop!" to the surprise of the German shoppers around me. Who would have thought the guy could shoot hoop, too?

Indeed he can, moving quickly up and down, back and forth to gather an impressive 54 points. Unfortunately for Wottle, Lon Kruger is a shade beyond impressive, scoring 60 points to finish just ahead of Wottle in the basketball battle. Kruger earns 40 points in the overall MVP contest — his third perfect 40 of the morning.

I have also been perfect all morning, scoring minus 10, minus 10 and minus 10.

BIKE AND CARRY

Mark Twain once said that everyone is ignorant, only about different things. Same idea in the MVP. Everybody's a klutz, only in different sports.

Actually some of us were proving to be klutzes in more sports than others, but even I felt like my moment of redemption should come soon. With cycling, I thought it might have arrived.

What is cycling, after all, but a test of endurance? Surely a runner's heart must be worth gold here.

The MVP cycling competition includes half-mile stretches of biking interspersed with a few meters of carrying the bike around turns. Total distance is approximately six miles, and the equipment is roughly the kind of one-gear bicycle my friends and I used to bring to a screeching, spin-out stop by reversing the pedals as close as possible to the nearest girl we pretended not to like in fifth grade.

MVP mythology indicates that this is the event that really lets contestants know what they've gotten into.

"It really takes a toll," Wottle had noted the previous evening. "It saps your energy and takes your leg strength away, and you still have six events left."

Bring on the anguish, I think. This is what we runners relish!

Once again, I have forgotten to practice. But then riding a bike is like riding a bike, right? You never forget. I pedal steadily, overtake with authority and move up with confidence, passing three competitors over the final half-mile. When it's over, I have earned 30 points for a fourth place finish.

After four events, I have pulled out of debt. My overall point score stands at zero.

PITCH-PASS-KICK

One thing you learn as an athlete is to quell doubt. As I wait to take my turn at target practice with baseballs, footballs and soccer balls, I try to convince myself that confidence and relaxation will result in accuracy. Hey, I tell myself with as much conviction as I can muster, I used to throw and kick with the best of them.

When my turn rolls around, I commence grabbing and throwing baseballs at a target three feet in diameter and ten yards away. Amazingly, I hit three straight strikes.

It's just like riding a bike! exclaims that part of my mind that controls confidence. Bring on the footballs!

Many, many throws later (many throws later than would have been predicted by chance) I score my third hit. By the time I finish kicking soccer balls and running to the finish line I have earned another minus 10 points. In the process, though, I have learned another valuable lesson: The only thing that's just like riding a bike is riding a bike.

BLOCKADE AND CALISTHENICS

Blockade and calisthenics is an obstacle course with calisthenics along the way. The idea, says our instruction sheet, is "to get from start to finish in as short a time as possible," a fairly straightforward notion.

After seeing the course, though, my personal goal becomes avoiding injury while using muscles I haven't been aware existed until now.

There is, you see, one part of this event that involves kneeling, holding onto the axle of a small wheel with both hands, rolling the wheel back and forth on the ground in front of your face, and smashing your chest repeatedly against the ground. In another part, competitors lift two 15-pound weights out to the side while shouting "Awwk!" and "Ooooff!" as they rip the muscles in their chests (well, *my* chest anyway). And in another, they do ten abdominal crunches, an exercise I've been specifically avoiding since I first heard about it.

For me, the only part that feels natural is the running between stations. By some stroke of luck, though, I finish ahead of two people, get 17 points and move out of the negative category for good.

KAYAKING

The exact makeup of the MVP changes from year to year, and kayaking is a new addition to the lineup. Contestants here must maneuver their fiberglass craft between buoys and avoid overturning. There are two major reasons to keep your kayak upright: 1) Once you fall out of a kayak, it's embarrassing trying to get back in, and 2) It's a good idea to avoid direct contact with the Arkansas River for as much of one's life as possible. Like most rivers that flow through major cities, this one is a combination of flotsam and jetsam, sludge, unmentioned chemical waste and life forms that are angry about their niches in the biological hierarchy.

So, I tell myself, learn how to stay afloat. My turn comes near the end, so I have the benefit of hearing kayaking instructions several times and observing the results of not implementing them. Several athletes, like my golf partner Cliff Levingston, have body structures that defy the laws of kayak physics. He ends up in the middle of the river, splashing around in good-natured frustration while attempting to re-enter his kayak.

"How in the world are you supposed to keep from turning over in that thing?" he wonders afterward.

In contrast, Jim Hershberger skims swiftly across the water and around the buoys, a performance that will win him first-place points.

So, I tell myself, try to look like Hershberger — quick, balanced and, most important, dry.

"Have you ever been in one of these before?" asks the instructor as I lower myself into position.

"No," I answer, "am I facing the right direction?" This is greeted by laughs from observers who, I suspect, have been wondering the same thing.

I'm racing in a heat with Bob Seagren, who looks wonderfully at home in his craft. He goes out like a shot out of a cannon and then, overturning at the first buoy, sinks like lead. If he'd stayed afloat, he'd have been dangerous.

I'm the tortoise in this story, slow and steady, galumphing my way through an unspectacular run that nets me 22 points for eighth place. Ironically, this has been one of my better events.

SWIMMING

Due to the presence of assorted debris and, I imagine, mean-spirited and poison-spiked mutant flounders on the bottom of the Arkansas River, we are required to wear shoes in the water. Seagren shows up with what appear to be black rubber frog-feet, looking unfairly well-suited for this event.

Not that any change in equipment would matter. Seagren looks and swims like Aquaman, cutting a mean wake for about a 100 meters to the spot where he must climb up a plank out of the water and sprint to the top of a small hill.

"A hill in Wichita?" wondered downhill skier Bill Johnson the night before. Then, convinced there would be one, adding in feigned awe, "And from there you can see all of Kansas."

When Seagren reaches the top, his swimming "rival," Lon Kruger, is still thrashing around out in the river like an apoplectic catfish. In the MVP, even an exceptional athlete like Kruger must occasionally face the black hole where athletic competency ends. It is a long time before Kruger gets to enjoy the view from the hilltop.

The luck of the draw pits me against Wottle for the title of fastest ex-Olympic Runner/Swimmer/Hill Climber. Neither of us considers our swimming ability worth talking about. I once excelled at "Marco Polo," but that's about it.

It turns out to be a close race. I reach my plank a tad before him, scramble out of the water a couple of feet in the lead, and then (shades of Munich!) the dirt-bag outsprints me up the homestretch. Amazingly, we end up the fourth- and fifth-fastest swimmers of the day.

JET SKIING

Jim Hershberger is sometimes accused — very quietly when he's busy thrashing one professional athlete or another in the next room, court or arena — of stringing together his ten best sports to make the MVP.

"If that were the case," he says, "I'd have put waterskiing in."

Maybe so, but when it comes time for jet skiing, there aren't many practitioners in the crowd.

"Jet ski?" asks Steve DeOssie of the Dallas Cowboys. "I've seen one in a magazine once."

If you're like me, you have this attitude about jet skis, snowmobiles and off-road vehicles. Namely, they're proof of the decline of Western civilization. Motor-driven distaste aside, I'm committed to giving the MVP my best shot, so I try to learn about this perversion as quickly as possible.

There are two schools of thought here: 1) Ride it, don't try to waterski it, and 2) Waterski it. As it turns out, riding a jet ski involves getting dragged through the water for a while, pulling onself to a kneeling position, standing up, and then making an impressive motor-enhanced splash in the Arkansas River. After a minute or two I learn how to stay up, then I learn how to turn, then I learn that my time is up and that I have earned another minus 10 points.

I'm in good company, though. Nine out of fifteen competitors receive the same score. Among those, Lynnette Woodard deserves the highest praise. She's had the good sense to refuse to get on the damn thing in the first place.

CROSS COUNTRY

Given the nature of the nine prior events, being asked to cross a railroad trestle in the middle of a cross country run doesn't seem so unreasonable, does it? And at this point I am not about to refuse anything that might jeopardize my one possible victory of the day.

Dreamlike? Yes. Dangerous? Possibly. But give up my lead because I hear the voice of reason (one of the officials actually) calling me back when I am already halfway across? No way. Full steam ahead.

Surviving the bridge, I head back up the river and connect to the intended course, then move out ahead of the field. For me it is a wonderful moment in which, after a full day of athletic frustrations, my aspirations finally unite with my abilities. I arrive first at the finish.

Wottle finishes next, then Seagren, then soccer star Kim Roentved, who is one of only four competitors in the field who hasn't scored at least one minus 10 all day, a fact that will help him finish second overall in the MVP competition.

And the winner?

Right behind Roentved, finishing fifth in the run, comes the man who has managed to survive all ten events today better than anyone. He has chipped, swatted, shot, pedaled, thrown, paddled, stroked, roared and run with the best. He seems at times to be held together with braces, tape and baling wire, and as he finishes the cross country run, he is limping and grabbing his hamstring in pain. In finishing, he totals 276 points. He is this year's Jim Hershberger MVP Champion. He is Jim Hershberger.

A FEW MVP LESSONS

Before I carry my beleaguered body to the nearest hot tub to soothe my muscles and ease my ego, let me share a few things I learned by competing in ten events over eleven hours on a hot Kansas day. I've already mentioned a few, like the value of practicing and the foolishness of asserting that anything is like riding a bike except, just possibly, riding a bike. Here are two more:

One is the trick of the MVP itself, which is to be truly versatile, failing nothing. Of the top five finishers, only Dave Wottle had an event in which he received minus points. Of the remaining four, three scored zero in at least one event. Only one competitor, Jim Hershberger, had no negatives and no zeros. And, need I remind you, he won the thing.

In MVP-land, negative points are the kiss of death. Wottle, for example, protested faulty equipment for his inability to handle a jet ski, a protest that seemed reasonable, since he successfully covered the course after switching to a new machine. But his protest was disallowed, he received a minus 10, and the point difference dropped him from first to fourth.

Seagren, to cite another example, started his kayaking with enough zip to win the event but ended up in the drink. A victory there would have meant overall victory, too. In fact, almost any one of the top eight finishers could have won overall with an event turnaround or two. The lesson? Versatile is the MVP's middle name.

The second lesson is a personal one. Whatever my past athletic history and skills, these days I'm primed for just one sport. As a dedicated runner, I've developed a specificity that's inescapable. The day after the MVP, that lesson was written painfully in muscles that a day earlier hadn't even had names.

Extreme body types on either end of the spectrum are clearly a detriment in a test of athletic versatility. I finished thirteenth overall in the MVP, right between two very large football players, Steve DeOssie and Jim Jeffcoat.

A lot of men, I'm sure, would love to be powerfully built like either DeOssie or Jeffcoat, no matter what impact it might have on their chances in multisport competition. But I suppose we're all bound to be dissatisfield at times with whatever edifice we're inhabiting.

Prior to the start of the MVP cycling event, two diametrically different body types, mine and Jeffcoat's, rested on bicycles next to each other. One of the event volunteers good-naturedly told Jeffcoat he was going to have to pare his body down if he wanted to be a cyclist.

"I plan to," he responded, "once I'm done playing football."

"Look at me," I told him, "as a model to aspire to."

He looked, and didn't seem so sure about it anymore.

TURNING 40

As I sped with my friends along familiar trails in the woods, all the numbers we sometimes use to compare ourselves — the ones that mark the years, the ones that measure our performances, the ones I had recently recorded in the lab — started to fade into insignificance.

APPROACHING 40, I BEGAN TO SALIVATE. A new age division. A chance to gear up the old bones for a second shot at world-class status.

At 38, I began to calculate where I would have placed in the races I entered had I been a little older. At 39, I subscribed to *National Masters News*. At 39 1/2, I was on the launching pad, counting down. But as the Big Four-O approached, I began wondering just how ready I was to do battle with the best masters runners in the world.

"We should get you tested again," urged Don Winant, an exercise physiologist and occasional training partner of mine. "I'd love to see what your VO$_2$ max is these days."

"Again" referred to a study of elite distance runners conducted in 1975 at Kenneth Cooper's Aerobics Clinic in Dallas. I had been a subject in that landmark research project, which broke ground in the understanding of the cardiovascular, biochemical, biomechanical and psychological makeup of top runners. Numerically, I knew just where I stood — and ran — after that study. I wondered along with Winant just how fit this formerly elite body was fourteen years later, as it teetered on the edge of a new age division.

Thus I found myself in the Eastern Washington University (EWU) Laboratory of Applied Physiology a week before my 40th birthday, about to be dunked, weighed, pinched, pricked, prodded and probed.

Most tests of physiological capability require that you don't panic. In one test you're asked to blow out all your air, ease your nearly-40-year-old bones into a deep tub of warm water, and sit very, very still ("Relax, Don.") while researchers determine how much you weigh underwater prior to drowning. In another, wires are attached to your chest, a tube and hoses inserted in your mouth, a clip pinned on your nose and a mesh girdle wrapped around your torso. Then you're asked to run normally and naturally while researchers increase the speed and incline of the itsy-bitsy treadmill belt from which you are about to be hurled.

And talk about panic. In another test, you are officially weighed while surrounded by witnesses.

"One-hundred-sixty-seven?" I asked. "Are you positive?"

They were — 167.

In 1975, when I checked into the Cooper Clinic, I had weighed 154. In those days, I was near the peak of my racing prowess, one year away from competing in the Olympics, and the training necessary to keep me at the front of the pack also kept me on the switchblade edge of the body-fat spectrum. So of my 154 pounds, a mere 5.7 percent was in the form of fat, hardly enough to pinch. After completing underwater weighing in the EWU lab on the eve of my 40th birthday, researchers calculated my body fat to be around 14 percent.

"That's one of the big differences between you then and you now," said Damon Delistraty, the exercise physiologist who oversaw my testing. He chuckled as politely as possible. "You've changed in terms of body composition."

In other words, I was fatter.

That evening, I dug out a photo of all of us at the Cooper Clinic. It brought back memories of a thinner, swifter time of life. There I was in the back row, long-haired and confident, able to run three miles at a pace faster than 4:20 per mile. And there was Frank Shorter, midway between his 1972 gold medal and 1976 silver. And Dick Buerkle, Paul Geis and Doug Brown, all about to make the 1976 Olympic team. And Steve Prefontaine, on the upswing of a spectacular athletic career that would end tragically a few months later in a car crash.

So many top runners, so little fat.

The big cardboard box in which I found the Cooper Clinic photo that evening is the closest thing I have to a scrapbook. It's filled with dusty photos of thin-looking, fast-moving runners, most of them me. Look:

Here I am in 1966, with the other members of my high school cross country team. That's me in the middle of the second row. My basketball coach encouraged me to turn out for cross country, hoping improved fitness would compensate for lack of skill. Instead, I found a new athletic future.

Here I am again, that same year, in the Seattle Indoor Meet. I'm number 38, the pimple-faced kid. If you'd told me then I'd still be running twenty years later, I'd have laughed in your face. I was having enough trouble just getting through the next few minutes, and I certainly never thought I'd continue past high school.

But sure enough, here I am again, two years later. Stanford cross country team, 1968. We were second in the nation, nearly beating the Villanova favorites. What a race I suffered through that day in New York's Van Cortlandt Park, gasping for air every step of the way, desperately trying to hang with my teammates.

Grand days, those. Here's a shot of the team the next year, racing against the University of Southern California and San Jose State. That's me leading. On my right is Duncan Macdonald, who I raced with and against over and over again from freshman year, right into the Olympics. There are piles of photos in this box of the two of us in one race or another. Duncan is 40 now, too, and recently ran a 10K in 30:34. The bastard.

Here's a shot from the Big Meet (Stanford-Cal) my senior year. That's Arvid Kretz next to me. He was once arrested running late at night, dressed in street clothes and carrying an alto sax. He was on his way home from music practice and was trying to get in a few extra miles. ("You see, officer, I'm on the Stanford track team ... ")

It was the fun and successes of college running that kept me going after graduation. Somewhere along the line, I decided I had a shot at the Olympics.

So here I am that next year, 1972, running against Frank Shorter, George Young and other big-name runners in the San Francisco Indoor Meet. I was terrified to be in such elite company, and couldn't believe it when I finished second. But what I found really amazing was that George Young was still competing. And he was in his 30s!

That year I ran my first marathon, the morning after clocking an 8:36 two-mile in the Oakland Indoor Meet. I won in 2:18:03. Here's a shot of me afterward, meeting the great Soviet sprinter, Valerie Borzov. Things were going well at the time, but my 1972 season ended miserably. I came down with mono, stopped training, and barely managed to get back to moderate form in time for the Trials. I nearly quit running.

But I kept at it, even after accepting my first full-time job as a teacher. That's me with my sixth grade class in the spring of 1975, my first year of teaching. Five miles in the morning, on my feet all day, coaching in the afternoon, 10 miles of running in the dark. Day after day. And all of that on school lunches (corndogs, succotash, Jell-O) and fast food. Hard to believe anyone could survive on that.

I did. And here's a snapshot taken in Eugene the following spring, just before the '76 Olympic Marathon Trials. That's Tony Sandoval on my left, who I had to catch and pass 23 miles into the marathon to make the Olympic team. Four years later, Sandoval won the Trials, though the boycott thwarted his own Olympic dream.

1976 was a peak year for me, but the story goes on and on in this box, past the 1976 Olympics and into the late '70s and early '80s, when running became so popular that even the President of the United States felt compelled to participate. By then, I was too much a runner to think of stopping, and thus the photos go on year after year, shots of me and my low-body-fat compadres, eagerly trying to outdo each other in California, Florida, Georgia, Hawaii, Japan and Brazil. Mugging for the camera afterward.

It's going on twenty-five years now, a quarter century of putting one foot in front of the other, far longer than I could ever have guessed at the outset. So it seems only fitting to take a close look at this picture, too. This is me at 18 months.

What was it in that kid that later led him to run, to keep running, to keep pushing himself to run faster? Talent? Dreams? Neuroses? My own daughters are about this age now, and I wonder what's inside *them.*

Decades from now will they be digging through a box full of photos, staring at their baby pictures, wondering what led them to choose one path or another?

Back in the EWU lab, I was just getting the results of my tests from Damon Delistraty.

"You're on the lean side, certainly," he said, "but definitely not as lean as you used to be."

Well, yes, I knew this. To most people, though, I'm still unbearably thin. What else?

"Your residual lung volume has gotten bigger," said Damon. For a moment I felt proud, until he added, "That's kind of detrimental. You're not using as much of your lung capacity as you could back in 1975."

Now I felt guilty. It was as if I'd been sloughing off in the intake of air, not giving it a full effort with the old diaphragm. But, Damon assured me, this was just one more thing that happens over the years. "As you get older, your lung function tends to go downhill," he explained.

And my heart rate? In 1975, I hit 198 beats per minute. In 1988, 190. Very good for my age, so they say, but still a letdown. "Maximum heart rate tends to go down, too," explained Damon.

And the total of all this, the sum relationship of body weight, air intake, heart rate and the like? In 1975, my VO_2 max the highest amount of oxygen I could use per kilogram of weight per minute, was 77.4 liters. In 1988 — 63.

At the Cooper Clinic, we had all waited to hear this number, as if it were a sign from above about who should be beating whom. Steve Prefontaine, the best runner in the crowd, had the highest score. That made sense. Frank Shorter, though, had one of the lowest at 71, and he'd won a gold medal. So much for divine determinism.

Still, a reading of 63 was too much lower than my original number to simply brush aside. I was forced to face the fact that I had, indeed, deteriorated with age. No real news there, of course, just the cold, unflinching, inexorable stare of scientific data to confirm what I already felt.

But then came some good news. According to Damon, I appeared to be surprisingly efficient. I seemed to have become more successful in recruiting non-aerobic energy sources. I stayed on the treadmill longer than predicted, substantially longer than any of a group of "pretty decent" collegiate runners Damon had recently tested.

"I really expected to see a much higher VO_2 based on the length of time you stayed on the treadmill," said Damon. "Some of those college kids I tested had VO_2s in the mid-70s."

Suddenly, this whole discussion reminded me of Steve Prefontaine. In 1975, with his VO_2 max of 80-plus, Pre had stayed on the treadmill for 8 minutes, 30 seconds. He looked exhausted afterward, just as he had at the PAC-8 Meet in 1971 in Seattle, when I came as close to beating him in a race as I ever did.

So when my turn came to get on the Cooper Clinic treadmill, I went for broke. I gasped and struggled and went for that one last increment of time, and I stayed on the thing 8 minutes and 45 seconds, longer than anyone in our group, a quarter of a minute longer than Pre.

I beat Pre once in my life, and that was it.

Three days after my testing, my wife surprised me with a 40th birthday party. I had been expecting one for over two years, but the timing, five days before the official day, caught me off guard. Clearly, age has not cured my gullibility.

The next morning, six of us went for a long run in the state park near my home. We ran familiar trails through the woods, enjoying the scenery and occasionally surging down the path for all we were worth.

Between breaths we talked about training, world events, the weather. There was some joking about my age and speculation about my chances as a masters runner at the World Veterans Games in Eugene later that season.

I couldn't think about Eugene without getting a jolt of adrenaline, remembering many of the best races of my career. A 12:57.6 three-mile, for example, when I finished third behind Prefontaine and Shorter. The 1976 Marathon Trials, when I qualified for the Olympic team. Now, at age 40, I had a chance to go back.

As I sped with my friends along familiar trails in the woods, all the numbers we sometimes use to compare ourselves — the ones that mark the years, the ones that measure our performances, the ones I had recently recorded in the lab — started to fade into insignificance. And even the box full of images, sometimes precious for reminding me of where I've been, began to seem unimportant.

It was just this movement, this feeling, this force of effort and determination that seemed to matter. Blitzing down the trail as fast as possible, surrounded by friends. Forever.

January 1989

FREEZE YER GIZZARD

Most years, Freeze Yer Gizzard entrants are hunkered down, slunkered down and bunkered down in the gymnasium of Rainy River Community College on race morning, staring out the frosted glass windows before dashing outside at the last minute to attack ten frozen kilometers like terriers confronting a polar bear.

WE ARE INTO THE POSTRACE part of the event now. Nearly a 100 fit-looking men and women from Minnesota, Wisconsin, Michigan, Canada and elsewhere in the Great North Woods are eagerly trying to undo whatever good they might have done themselves earlier in the day.

Wearing papaya-, mango- and pineapple-colored clothes that could only have hatched in a mid-Pacific tourist trap without scruples, they lounge in lawn chairs, wearing leis they bought from the mayor, flowers that will never die, tiny thermometer pins from the Chamber of Commerce and sunglasses from purgatory. Suds flow.

A band churns through an assortment of loud, vaguely rock 'n' rollish tunes which, if you really squint your ears, hum dazedly, wave your head back and forth and engage an overactive imagination, might just possibly be said to evoke summer on the beach.

A man from Winnepeg with white hair and an athletic build, wearing rose-colored sunglasses, joins a moving eyewear fashion show (the "shade parade") and wins the "Best Shades" award. Another Winnepegger, Sandra Harting, captures the hearts of the judges with her southern-Manitoban-in-the-Islands grass skirt look, and wins the prize for "Best Beach Wear."

And finally the Biggee. Though the competition is fierce and displays of tan lines are, technically at least, a bit on the illegal side of the statute, no one is arrested. A winner is finally chosen. The man has spent most of the party lying on a beach mat on one side of the dance floor bathed in red light, simulating a tanning session. Although there is suspicion that he is being rewarded for effort rather than skin tone, he nonetheless receives the most coveted prize of all. The fans hoot, holler and clap as the midwinter king is announced; the man who, though his limbs are more or less the color of bleached snow, is considered to have the "Best Tan" in the house.

Ah, yes, tan bodies. To be honest, we don't actually see any in this room, but we remember. And we remember screaming sunshine, sand under the toenails, and chi-chis with little paper umbrellas and pink swizzle sticks. We remember summer.

By late January here in northern Minnesota, though, summer's ambience is both a fading memory and a distant hope.

"Oh, it gets cold here," the natives say with that long Minnesotan "O" that sounds like the speaker has suddenly choked, midsentence, on frozen tonsils.

It starts, this cold, somewhere up in the Arctic. A heartless mass of steely-eyed air eager to do some mischief, it moves southward in deference to jet streams, atmospheric swirling and a general sense of Canadian topography, finally turning into a stream of frigid nastiness that moves directly over a small town at the very top and middle of your map of the fifty states. Winter brunt-bearer. International Falls.

International Falls, known in Rocky and Bullwinkle cartoon fantasy as Frostbite Falls. International Falls, where real live people enjoy the distinction of inhabiting the coldest spot in the contiguous United States, or at least the site of the U.S. weather station with the coldest readings. Where temperatures as low as 46 below zero have been recorded, prompting one company to prove the worth of their batteries by starting a car stranded all winter on a frozen lake here (without building a fire under the engine block, something the locals are sometimes tempted to do).

International Falls, where townsfolk eager to turn lemons into lemonade have been gleefully celebrating life in the self-proclaimed Ice Box of the Nation since 1981 by inviting the world to the annual "Ice Box Days" festival, held on the last two weekends of January.

Welcome, then, to winter in International Falls, site also of the Freeze Yer Gizzard Blizzard Run and, this evening, the second annual Ice Box Days Beach Party. Always eager for something to do on the weekend, I have traveled here along with a couple of hundred other folks to see how the old midwinter training is going.

Did I say "winter?" You call *this* winter? This morning, instead of piling on every conceivable, wildly dissonant combination of color and fabric to stave off the chill, we runners have actually been able to — I'm embarrassed to admit this — color coordinate. Most years, Freeze Yer Gizzard entrants are hunkered down, slunkered down and bunkered down in the gymnasium of Rainy River Community College on race morning, staring out the frosted glass windows before dashing outside at the last minute to attack 10 frozen kilometers like terriers confronting a polar bear. This year, though, we have been free to warm up outside, enjoying the sunshine, above-freezing temperatures and clear streets. Mud and slush, not tundra, have been underfoot.

"Too bad it's so warm out," a runner from Minneapolis is heard to comment. "I may have to wear my shorts."

We came here armed to do battle with winter. What happened?

Near as I'm able to establish, the unseasonably mild temperatures for the 1989 Freeze Yer Gizzard Blizzard Run have something to do with a displaced jet stream — hence the unusual visitation of weather from down south. It's tempting to blame the greenhouse effect, or perhaps the White House. Really, though, it's just the weather, capricious as always, that has decided to turn warmish on a weekend that is statistically the coldest of the year.

Historically, the Freeze Yer Gizzard Blizzard Run has had both nice and nasty weather since it was begun in 1981 as a way of snubbing frozen noses at Nature. In 1981 and 1983, the temperature was well above freezing. In 1982, though, it was 25 below zero with 30-mile-per-hour winds and a chill factor that reached 78 below. That year, race director Pat McKibbidge cringed about sending people outside and nearly canceled the race.

"But I had Canadians coming out of the closet at me, ready to lynch me, because they wanted to run," says McKibbidge. "We finally cut the race in half, to 3.1 miles. As it turned out, we only had two problems, a woman with stomach cramps and a man with a slight case of frostbite."

Brutal it was, and yet that's the sort of weather that piques the interest of a certain breed of runner eager for *mis*adventure, and brings him or her to International Falls. The sort of runner who will not simply sit in a warm bungalow waiting for the sun to head north and warm the hemisphere. This is the kind of creature who will travel long distances to confront the very heart of evil, the void, the meanest spot on the map.

And so here I am, along with more than 200 similarly afflicted soul mates, enjoying not a battle with the elements but a pleasant winter interlude. The beach party itself, meant to be an anachronism, verges on the logical. So much for epic confrontations.

But let's start at the beginning. This is my first trip to International Falls. I arrive via prop-plane in the dead of night at Falls International Airport, feeling somewhat like a character in an old black-and-white movie. I make a quick inspection: wide expanse of whiteness alternating with blackness, stars sparkling in the ice crystals, snow plowed up on both sides of the runway and on top of the private planes. Very quiet. Whisper of wind.

A metal tower 30 feet high stands in front of the airport, topped with a scanning device that rotates constantly like some kind of giant blue alien eyeball. Clearly, we are teetering here on the edge of civilization. "From here," notes an International Falls tourist brochure, "the great primitive wilderness stretches without a break to the high Arctic."

It feels it.

I walk into the airport terminal, notice the travel posters for getaways to Florida and Hawaii, and go in search of a rental car.

"Hertz man is fueling aircraft," says a sign. "Will be right with you."

This is a small airport. The Hertz man rents cars, refuels the plane and also works at the local high school.

A few minutes later, I'm on my way to packet pickup. With

temperatures above freezing this evening, people are out walking the streets the way they do in resort towns in mid-August. But here there are piles of snow as high as a mammoth's eye to maneuver between. As mild as the weather has been this winter, more than enough of the white stuff has fallen to fill the streets.

At packet pickup, I meet Freeze Yer Gizzard originator Pat McKibbidge, who has moved to Duluth and turned over the reins of the event to Dick Ostroot, a long-time International Falls runner, coach and high school teacher. Race directors know the vagaries of weather, and these conditions have both past and present race director chuckling.

"Dick Ostroot's over there smiling right now," says McKibbidge, "because look at it, 40 degrees, and he knows he's not going to get pooped on by Mother Nature."

Ostroot is indeed smiling, but later admits to wishing for more typical Freeze Yer Gizzard conditions, the kind that International Falls is famous for.

"I don't want it 30 below with a wind out of the north or anything," replies Ostroot. "But the one year when we got up in the morning and it was 28 below zero and by race time had warmed up to about 17 below, with no wind, that seemed like the way it was supposed to be."

For those uninitiated in the joys of winter running, this may sound a bit severe, raising the whole sanity question.

"Some people here in town think it's strange to be out running on a winter day," says Ostroot. He pauses, then adds thoughtfully, "Of course some people, my wife included, think it's strange to go out and run on a nice day."

Back in my hometown of Spokane, people begin talking about frozen lungs when the temperature drops into the 20s. I've never heard of an actual case of frozen lungs, though, even during those odd years when Spokane temperatures drop well below zero. But, I surmise, if frozen lung actually does occur, these guys from the Ice Box of the Nation must know about it.

"I read somewhere," says Ostroot, "that there are zero documented cases of people freezing their lungs."

"You take a wild animal like a deer," adds McKibbidge, spouting a personal brand of North Woods philosophy. "A timber wolf can run a deer down. Now granted a wolf has a longer esophagus, but at the same time, that deer will run flat out and breathe in cold air until it collapses, and it doesn't ever die from a frozen lung."

Reassured with that information, I ask for other cold-weather advice. Are there no real problems for a runner in this climate during a typical winter?

"The only thing is," says Ostroot, "you have to dress right around the midsection."

I have only just met Ostroot, but I still feel I know him well enough to make the following observation: If he had not been talking with a magazine writer, he would not have used the word "midsection." He would not, for example, have crossed the 1982 Freeze Yer Gizzard Blizzard Run finish line, hustled out of the 78-below wind chill and into the nearest warm room and immediately exclaimed, "Holy smokes, I nearly froze my midsection off out there!"

Our discussion of cold weather is interrupted by the long-anticipated arrival of a busload of runners from Winnipeg, members of the Prairie Sky Road Runners, who have been making the journey to the Freeze Yer Gizzard Blizzard Run for as long as anyone can remember.

Last year, for reasons not totally clear, the Canadians came dressed in tuxedos and formals. This year the theme is international business, and many are clad in out-of-date three-piece zoot suits they scavenged from Winnipeg thrift stores. It appears as if an entire busload of Gary Fanellis has suddenly descended on International Falls.

You can tell the Winnipeggers mean business. You can see it in their eyes. You can tell by their clothing and by the way they walk. You can tell because within minutes of their arrival, every pocket in every garment of every non-Winnipegger in the motel has been visited by a card that says, "Prairie Sky Road Runners — We Mean Business!"

In no time flat, the Winnipeggers have unpacked their bags, renewed acquaintances and thrown down the gauntlet to their American counterparts, a loose congregation of running aficionados known as the Bombardiers. By weekend's end, as in past years, a 2-foot trophy with various gold-colored plastic parts falling off will have been awarded to whichever group has excelled at those most important of Ice Box Days events: running, skiing, dancing and partying. So much for serious racing.

The next morning, business begins at the starting line. Blue sky, mild weather, clear streets and Rocky and Bullwinkle are there to see us off. It seems like a good day to run fast, so I stay with two-time Freeze Yer Gizzard champion Dave Avenson until four-and-a-half miles, when he suddenly turns off his jets and lets me ease ahead for the win.

At the finish line, a few serious competitors sprint home, followed by a whole lot of folks-on-a-lark. I see grass skirts, Hawaiian shirts, bare legs and Canadian zoot-suiters carrying attaché cases, umbrellas and business cards. People stand around afterward in the sunshine like Norwegian farmers, remembering the tough winters of 1982 and 1987.

"You bet," says one, shaking his head. "That was a cold one."

By the next afternoon, both the race and beach party are history, the 1989 Ice Box Days are winding down, and I'm on my way back to the airport. I have just about convinced myself that winter here in International Falls isn't all it's cracked up to be. For my part, memories of foot racing in the Ice Box of the Nation will be mostly blue-skied and toasty.

Nature, though, has a way of making up for these little interludes of pleasantness. As I pulled into the airport parking lot, the radio was announcing that a whole lot of winter nastiness that had been brewing in Alaska all weekend was headed toward the little town in Northern Minnesota. Apparently, Old Man Winter doesn't allow runners to snub their noses at him without paying the price.

By the next weekend, life in International Falls was back to normal. Further beach parties would have to be postponed. The big thermometer downtown in the Ice Box of the Nation was reading 42 below zero.

VETERANS DAY

A slightly different training strategy, a little extra stretching, a bit more consistency, a few less distractions at work or home, and we're back on track, fit and fast. No kidding.

SO THERE I WAS, 5:45 in the morning, a lonely guy in the parking lot of the Red Lion. Dippy Dog with sports bag slung over my shoulder, scanning the clouds for signs of more rain, hitching the shuttle to Hayward Field for the World Veterans Championships.

A few minutes later, I stood shivering near the track like a stray dog, reading my name posted underneath the stands: Don Kardong — Division One of the 5,000 meters — 7 a.m.

Watching myself, I managed a wry smile. This moment had entered my fantasy months ago, but had danced in my imagination with quite different choreography and props.

For one thing, it was supposed to be warm. This was, after all, track and field, the sport of late sleep-ins and sweaty, anxious afternoons. For another, there were supposed to be thousands of those world-class Eugene fans in attendance, rabid track and field folks who will gasp in unison sensing a record javelin toss mid-air or a decisive surge in the last half-mile of a 5,000.

I was here to recapture that exotic, invigorating feeling of yore, when I would circle the oval with eyeballs bursting, locked in deadly battle among elite greyhounds. Instead, I found myself in a nearly deserted stadium on a chilly Oregon morning on which, lacking a qualifying time, I had been discarded into the slowest of six divisions.

Oh, well. At age 40 on the track, one takes what one can get.

Fortunately, by race time things had improved. I had talked my way into the fastest heat. A few fans had woken up and moseyed into the stands. And I was back in familiar territory, figuring out what to wear.

Shoes?

"Go with your flats," urged college teammate Greg Brock. "You always did well with flats."

Clothing?

"It's been so long since I raced on the track," mused 1976 Boston Marathon champion Jack Fultz, "that I don't even have a singlet."

And then off we went, around and around in the cool air. A few surges. A few shouts from the fans. A few moments of speed, clarity and *déjà vu*. All in all, a good experience.

"That was all right," I told Fultz afterward, when I had finished seventh in 15:09.82. "I used your strategy of running easy for six laps and then taking off."

"Yeah," he laughed, "but I didn't know you were going to use it against *me*." Fultz finished tenth. Both of us were way, way behind winner Wilson Waigwa's 14:26.43.

My race reminded me that it's a long way back to the past. One thing I've learned about masters running, though, is that the dream never dies. A slightly different training strategy, a little extra stretching, a bit more consistency, a few less distractions at work or home, and we're back on track, fit and fast. No kidding.

Later that week, I finished third in the cross country race. About that same time, I heard that the next World Veterans Championships would be in Finland in 1991.

I could already see myself there, jitters and all. A still, clear evening. A stadium brimming with fans. And me, looping around and around the track, ethereal, transcendent, faster than ever, in the land of the flying Finns.

RUN AND GUN

She asked, "Do you shoot at each other?" and I chuckled. Now, watching Lyle's back from behind, it seemed like a pretty good idea. Fortunately, in summer biathlon you don't actually carry your rifle with you.

WE WERE NOT QUITE A MILE INTO THE RACE, nearing the firing range. Lyle was so close behind me I could have turned and spit in his eye. Whhhicck-putooey! Bull's-eye.

Not that it would have helped much.

It irked me to see him so close, but I was trying not to worry about it. After all, I had been advised to focus on the task ahead.

"Visualize yourself entering the range and picking up the rifle," Bob Delfay, Executive Director of the National Shooting Sports Foundation, had coached a few days earlier. "Then imagine the whole process — getting into position, loading the clip, sighting in the target, squeezing the trigger. Visualize each target falling over. If you can actually see it happen in your mind as you approach the range, you know you're ready to do it."

Lyle had offered similar advice about the need to shift from focusing on competition, i.e. him, to focusing on the target.

"If your concentration isn't on the center of the targets," he counseled, "your bullets won't be either. Don't think about the race around you while shooting."

So as I neared the range, I tried to get my mind off the hot breath of the former Olympian behind me and onto the procedure ahead. Relax. Zen it. Go with the force. Control those bullets with the strength of your vision. Oommmmmmmmmm ... And then ...

"This is where we should start slowing down," came Lyle's voice from behind, shattering my concentration.

Well of course it was! Did he think I hadn't been paying attention all week? And what was this business anyway of shouting advice at your main competitor when the moment of judgment was at hand? Was this some kind of biathlon mind game? At any rate, I was becoming flustered as I neared the range, something I would never have anticipated at the outset.

It had all sounded so simple, this summer biathlon, when I first heard about it. Run 1,500 meters, shoot five shots with a .22-caliber rifle from a prone position, run 2,000 meters, shoot five shots standing, run 1,500 meters. Take your total time, add 30 seconds for each missed target, walk home with your trophy. Piece of cake, right?

Approaching those first five targets, I began to wonder.

The summer biathlon is a new phenomenon, the outgrowth of summer training camps held for top competitors in the winter sport of biathlon (the *real* biathlon, as aficionados are quick to point out, which means cross country skiing and rifle shooting, not that running-cycling pretender of the same name). A few years ago, with the general public showing up uninvited at summer training sessions organized by the U.S. Biathlon Federation, it became clear that interest in a running and shooting event extended beyond the borders of the winter biathlon fraternity.

The man generally credited with noticing this is Lyle Nelson, four-time Olympic biathlete, U.S. flag-bearer for the 1988 Winter Olympics, and one-time, come-from-behind winner of NBC's "Survival of the Fittest" competition. Yes, and the guy shouting advice at me from the not-so-distant distance.

As the elder statesman and tireless promoter of the biathlon, Nelson took it upon himself to fashion the somewhat amorphous training sessions of biathletes in the off season into a brand new sport. The result was the Summer Biathlon Series, complete with prize money and a national championship event.

The championship, held at the Antire Valley Firing Range in St. Louis, was where I now found myself, shadowed by Lyle. This was my first summer biathlon, and it was billed as the battle of Olympians, me the runner versus Lyle the shooter.

That wasn't quite fair. I'm certainly just "the runner," but Lyle deserves more than simply "the shooter." A football player while at West Point, he had somehow managed to preserve a muscular physique while immersing himself in aerobic sports that whittle most bodies into tight, well-wired but not always what the unbiased observer would call "athletic" forms. Given his skiing background, Lyle's strong upper body was no surprise. But from what dusty corner of his latent athletic talent did he uncover the ability to run 5-minute-mile pace while claiming to be out of shape? Clearly, the man could do a variety of things with great skill, including shoot straight. Talk straight was another matter.

And me? Well, as usual I was in over my head in the multisports area, specifically the firearms department. My most recent memory of shooting a gun was during a freezing, frustrating trek with my brother in a search for deer in Washington's Cascade Mountains nearly twenty years ago. When we had seen enough, i.e. nothing, and had soaked up our weight in rain, we each shot twice at a tree and shivered off to the car. The tree was already dead, so we were able to hit it.

My weak shooting background was supposed to be correctable, and Lyle, always eager to score a convert, volunteered to help.

"You're a natural shooter," he told me during my first practice session four days before the competition, after I successfully fired a shot into the dirt behind the targets. I looked up at him dubiously. "No, really," he insisted. It was sometimes hard to tell when Lyle was kidding.

And that was the dilemma I faced as I neared the range. When he shouted, "This is where we should start slowing down," was he offering legitimate advice, or was it a ruse? I was fairly sure Lyle wasn't given to tricks, but in my confusion I surged anyway and headed for a rifle.

It seems obvious that target shooting is going to be difficult if one's heart and lungs are out of control from hard running, so after picking up the rifle, I breathed deeply and walked calmly to the mat, waiting for my vital signs to return to normal. By the time I had lowered myself into prone position, I felt fairly calm, confident of being able to knock over five straight targets. After all, I had done as much in practice.

A minute later my confidence was shattered. Prone is the easiest shooting position, yet I had knocked over just one lousy target. Worse, I had already heard the announcement: "Ladies and gentlemen, Lyle Nelson has cleaned the targets."

He hadn't missed. So not only was Lyle ahead of me, having fired fast and hitting all five targets, but I had just earned 2 minutes worth of penalties. I realized, as I climbed to my feet and chased after him, that I had been worrying about Lyle the whole time I was shooting, violating rule number one of the biathlon.

"That's the easiest mistake to make," said Lyle later. "And the surest way to miss targets."

A week earlier, sitting at home with my 6-year-old daughter, I had tried very carefully to tell her what I would be doing in St. Louis. When I had finished explaining the summer biathlon, she asked, "Do you shoot at each other?" and I chuckled. Now, watching Lyle's back from behind, it seemed like a pretty good idea.

Fortunately, in summer biathlon you don't actually carry your rifle with you. That seems like one of the wisest of the event's rules, reducing the likelihood of accidents committed by frustrated and/or bozo-brained newcomers to the sport. People like myself, I mean.

Earlier in the week, for example, an incident occurred during a van ride on the St. Louis freeway. Jerry Kokesh, former president of the Road Runners Club of America and one of the summer biathlon's organizers, was driving. Lyle was in the back, and I sat in the front passenger's seat wearing sunglasses and holding a rifle. Suddenly we passed a traffic cop, and Jerry looked in the rear view mirror to see if we were about to be ticketed for speeding. We held our breaths for a moment, then Lyle's voice broke the silence.

"Go ahead, Jerry," he said. "I think we can hold him off for a while."

A funny comment. But it was the tiny shot of adrenaline I suddenly enjoyed and the twitching of my index finger that worried me. Some of us should not be around guns, especially on the freeway.

Fortunately for the rest of society, though, the summer biathlon is peopled by level-headed folks. And in designing the event and offering it to the neophyte shooting public, organizers have created a combination that is mostly cerebral and very safe.

"There has never been a biathlon accident in the United States," says Lyle. "And only perfect is good enough."

That safety record means that almost anyone can feel confident giving the event a try, and organizers are excited about the result. As I headed out after Lyle, for example, I passed Craig Virgin, one of this country's top runners, who has been finding new competitive challenges recently in the summer biathlon. This wouldn't be a good day on the range for Virgin, but a few weeks earlier he had managed to hit seven out of ten targets in the Minneapolis Summer Biathlon. Like Virgin, runners with various abilities interested in a novel competitive twist to their running seem attracted to this event.

Those interested will find little to deter them. The .22-caliber rifles have less kick than Utah beer, and biathlon organizers schedule familiarization clinics for the uninitiated, which is always a large percentage of entrants.

Nor does the beginner need to fear treading into a Rambo-esque gun culture. The National Shooting Sports Foundation, which helps orchestrate the series, is interested in promoting recreational shooting sports, but they're not a political advocacy group. And though biathletes enjoy knocking over targets, they don't sleep with their guns. Well, not exactly. They do take them along on trips, something that never fails to draw attention to the sport.

"It takes a while," Lyle told me, "before you get used to walking through a hotel lobby with a firearm."

Having a rifle in the hotel, though, allows the biathlon competitor to enjoy the fine art of dry-firing, which involves drawing dots on a piece of paper, posting the paper on the wall, and taking imaginary target practice whenever the urge hits. No bullets, no noise, no angry and/or wounded guests in adjoining rooms. Just something to do when you wake up at 3 a.m. with a full bladder.

This is a great way for a compulsive person like myself to stay busy. The standing position Lyle had shown me felt a bit awkward, and dry-firing allowed plenty of time to get used to it. Practice I did then, quietly, in the privacy of my own hotel room. By the time race day rolled around, I had practiced myself into the beginnings of a nice blister on my trigger finger.

As I completed the second running portion of the event on race day, then, and headed to the range for another battle with five stationary targets, I was hoping all that practice was going to help. I had passed Lyle on the course, but I was trying once again to focus on shooting, not on him.

Since the standing position was supposed to be the most difficult, I had spent most of my practice sessions in the standing position, where the targets, a mere 25 meters distant, seem to bounce around like agitated elves as the shooter tries to get them in his sights. It was even trickier after a run.

I had gotten good enough, though, to where I could keep four out of five shots inside the 3 1/2-inch circle that represented a dead target, so I was feeling better about my chances. But after the second practice session two days earlier, I made the mistake of looking at one of Lyle's targets. Seven of his ten shots had gone through a hole the size of a dime.

"Those aren't good shots, though," he told me. "They just went in there."

Sure Lyle. I understand.

So as I walked to the mat on race day for my final five shots, I told myself I could shoot straight, too, and I would. Get in position, get comfortable, then shoot.

A few seconds later I was leaving the range red-faced once again, having hit only one target. Lyle "the Zen master" had just knocked over his second set of five targets. The competition between runner and shooter was over. I caught and passed Lyle again, but with eight missed targets on my ledger, I was 4 minutes in debt, too much to make up.

Still, as I approached the finish line, I sprinted for all I was worth, hoping to salvage some sort of dignity with fancy footwork. In the end, as in so many other combo-events I've tried, only my running offered any comfort.

Lyle finished a few seconds later and was soon back in his role as promoter and organizer, checking systems and cheering finishers. Summer biathlon entrants start in small groups based on running ability, so for the next hour they came puffing in one after another to the finish. Some had shot well, some had run well and a few had excelled in both departments. Almost everyone, though, seemed to have enjoyed themselves.

When I checked the results later, I found I had finished second behind Lyle in the masters division. If I had hit nine targets, I still would have finished second. Only fast running and perfect shooting would have made a difference. Ironically given a week's worth of practice, I realized I could have improved substantially if I had simply run into the range at full speed each time, then loaded and fired five shots as quickly as possible into the air.

"Maybe so," said Lyle when I told him this, "but you don't have much room for improvement that way."

So it's difficult to win a summer biathlon competition on running ability alone. The thing has three parts — fast running, straight shooting and fast shooting. The three push against each other like three men in a tub. If one gets too rambunctious, the tub sinks. Balance is the key.

This new sport is a little like golf. No matter how well things go, there is always room for improvement. A little faster running next time, says the optimist, and a little faster shooting. And then, as the competitor soon finds out, accuracy goes to the dogs and bullets hit the dirt.

Like golf, too, one of the advantages of the summer biathlon is that it opens up a whole new set of excuses. A bead of sweat slipped in my eye as I fired. The targets were too dark. The rifle bolt was sticky. A mosquito was buzzing in my ear.

Fortunately in retrospect, I didn't hit all ten targets and beat Lyle. If I had, I would have been tempted to quit at the top of my game. As it is, I'm like a weak stock market. Now's the time to buy in anticipation of increases. I'll be back.

And when I return for another shot at it, I'm going to remember what I learned from Lyle. When I get to the range, I'll stop worrying about the other guy. I'll get in position, get comfortable, focus on the targets. I'll concentrate totally on the range, because the summer biathlon is a sport of the mind.

"Shooting has taught me more about sports psychology and the power of our thoughts," says Lyle, "than any other sport."

No doubt about it. I learned the very same thing, in fact, the hard way. I learned it from Lyle.

February 1990

EMPIRE STATE BUILDING

Kong, sad to say, dropped out, and a long way down. Hopefully, I wouldn't.

BILL MURRAY (gasping in the stairwell): "Where are we?"

Dan Ackroyd: "It looks like we're in the teens somewhere."

Murray: "Well, when we get to twenty, let me know. I'm gonna throw up."

Well okay, I fudged a bit on this one. Ghostbusters Murray and Ackroyd weren't actually in the Empire State Building. But they *were* struggling up a stairway, about to engage in an epic confrontation somewhere in that vast, labyrinthine scaffolding of steel, stone and glass we know from a distance as the skyline of New York City. And for the purposes of this story, that's as close as we're going to get.

My friend Hal Higdon once expressed envy that mountain climbers have such an easy answer to the question of why they pursue their sport.

Because it's there.

Sadly, we runners can point to nothing that's actually there, except the roadway and a distant finish line. And most would agree that asphalt and white chalk are lacking in drama.

Well I'm here to tell you, friends, this time it's there. *Really* there.

Right smack dab in the middle of thirty dollars' worth of island real estate. The giant-est giant in midtown Manhattan. A 1,250-foot cloud-stabber. Kong killer. Gotham personified. A tower beyond the dreams of the babblers of Babel. For thirty-nine years, the tallest structure built by inhabitants of earth, and still, at age 59, ranked number three in the world.

Ladies and gentlemen, will you please give a warm round of applause to one of the Seven, Eight, or perhaps it's actually more like Ten Wonders of the World ...

The Empire State Building!

And — did I mention this? — I'm going to run up it. More applause, please.

The Empire State Building has been dominating the world's psyche since it was completed in 1931.

"In February of 1932," writes Jonathan Goldman in *The Empire State Building Book*, "the Polish Olympic ski team tried to launch a new sport when they raced up the 1,860 steps to the top in just 21 minutes. On the 102nd floor they met the Czech ski team, which had just beaten the Poles at Lake Placid. The Czechs challenged the Poles to a staircase race. At this point the management of Empire State stepped in and squelched the event — they weren't interested in causing coronaries."

Fortunately, more enlightened modern management has decided (and I say this with the deepest appreciation) to overlook such reservations. In 1978, after decades during which climbing the Empire State Building was mostly frowned upon, general manager Robert Tinker talked the New York Road Runners Club into organizing the first official muscle-powered ascent. It was (gasp!) a shameless promotion. Thus was born the Empire State Building Run Up (ESBRU), yet another of those running-boom fantasies orchestrated by the same folks who got permission to shut down a city of 8 million people so that a few hundred marathoners could run through it. Good people, those.

That first ESBRU went off without a hitch, not counting the reporter who fizzled out on the twenty-sixth floor when reality caught up with ambition. Fourteen out of fifteen starters reached the top, led by 37-year-old Gary Muhrcke, who had already etched his name in athletic history by winning the first New York City Marathon.

The event captured the public imagination for many reasons, and word of it spread quickly. In 1979, twenty-four runners made the climb. In 1980, thirty-four. Numbers continued to grow, even though prospective entrants had to admit to having committed the rare, bizarre and meaningless (both in terms of the specific demands of a ten- or fifteen-minute vertical sprint, and also just generally) act of running an ultramarathon. In some way, you had to prove your fitness to get in.

As the event grew, finishing times dropped. That first year, Muhrcke made it to the finish line at the observatory on the eighty-sixth floor, a total of 1,575 steps, in 12:32.7, while the top woman, Marcy Schwamm, finished in 16:03.2. By 1981, Pete Squires (former Manhattan College distance star) had dropped the mark to 10:59.7, a landing where it rested for the next nine years. In 1989, Australian Suzanne Malaxos took the women's time down to 12:25.

Those climbing the building, of course, are less interested in the winner's time than their own. That's because, as you'll remember, the Empire State Building, magnificent and uncaring, is *there* for us all. Still, when that wonderful window of opportunity finally presented itself to me, I turned to the guy who had done it fastest for advice. How does one prepare for this thing? How did the record holder do it?

"I just did it," says Squires, who entered the race on a dare from New York Road Runners Club President Fred Lebow. "I didn't plan anything. I went into it blind."

Helpful advice. Nor did first-year winner Muhrcke make any training adjustments in preparation for the epic uphill battle.

"I did absolutely zero specific training for it," recalls Muhrcke.

So be it. But I'm a little older and wiser than I used to be, and there were at least two bits of information that led me to approach my own vertical odyssey with more caution than the past winners I spoke to. First, I know just enough about physiology to understand that fitness is persnickety. As well-conditioned as a runner might be, the peculiar demands of racing up a stairwell were bound to be a kinesthetic world unto themselves. To be ready to run straight up, I should train by running straight up.

And second, I'm a rotten uphill runner. I have long, thin legs, not unlike those seen on giraffes hoofing it across the savanna. Giraffes are magnificent beasts, fluid in motion on level ground, but you never see one bounding up a flight of stairs. Same with me.

In my freshman year of college, for example, I decided to supplement track training with repeats on the stadium stairs. One workout left me wounded for more than a week and amazed at the new muscles I'd discovered and abused. Clearly, I had unearthed a weakness, and over the years I became convinced that I would always have trouble with the up-and-down aspects of a runner's life.

That knowledge didn't prevent me from attempting a quick climb of the Statue of Liberty the following fall, when our team visited New York for the NCAA Cross Country Championships. A teammate and I were in a hurry to spectate, so we sprinted from the ferry to the top of the Lady's torch, then back to the ferry. I'd hate to suggest that our indiscretion cost the team a victory two days later, but it couldn't have helped.

Knowing how poorly I handle climbs, I promised myself a healthy dose of stairs in preparation for The Big Climb. Three times a week, I vowed, I would run up roughly the same number of steps as the Empire State Building. I found a couple of staircases outdoors that had more than 100 steps, and I incorporated them into my daily runs. In addition, every half hour or so throughout the day I would take the elevator to the lobby of the building where I work, ascend fifteen floors on foot (dressed in slacks, shirt, tie and street shoes), then stand at the top gasping for redemption.

"Goodness!" remarked one woman I startled in the stairwell. Most just stared or shook their heads ("It's Don again, up to something").

It was surprising how winded a few flights could make me. And if fifteen floors had that effect, what would eighty-six do? Before I had time to get too worried about that question, though, my left knee blew out. It proved to be a minor glitch, but for weeks I had trouble running uphill in any fashion, a problem made worse when I had to turn left. I called Bill Noel, race director of the ESBRU, to find out which direction the staircase in New York turns.

"Mostly right," he reported. Good news. With caution, I might finesse my way through this.

To ease the burden on my knee, I decided to try the current rage in aerobic conditioning, a stair-climbing machine. Although I was skeptical of the machine's benefits, in no time I had the rhythm. My heart rate climbed, sweat flowed. I was in mostly total comfort, looking out the window at a new snowfall.

The machine proved to be pleasant, aerobic, hypnotic. And as I slipped into a trance, imagining myself ascending the staircase of the Empire State Building, I felt a connection to past memories that I couldn't quite place. There was something back there — an incident from my early childhood, an angry adult, perhaps, someone yelling ...

"Hey! You kids get off that thing! You're bothering the shoppers."

Oh, yeah. Up the down escalator. So this was not my first experience with a stationary climb.

That day on the stair-climber, I did about 1,000 steps in 10 minutes. Four days later I was in New York, facing 1,575 steps.

Standing at the dizzying base of the Empire State Building, I was both anxious and amused. "I'm going *up* that thing!" I mused. "And soon."

It was overwhelming, a monumental icon of urban life. In the base of the structure, on a sunny weekday morning in mid-February, a 100 tiny humans were preparing for a race to the clouds.

A fair number of them were runners who specialize in mostly vertical races. The ESBRU has spawned a variety of clones around the world, and survivors of building races in Atlanta, Denver, Dallas, Detroit, Houston, Indianapolis, and Melbourne, Australia, were on hand to challenge the granddaddy of the species. Maybe it was my imagination, but they all seemed to have large, gravity-defying calves. I wondered, too, whether these runners who specialize in stairwell-running have anxious dreams about being in the middle of blue-skied, wide-open spaces, unable to find the narrow passageways and stuffy corridors.

How was I likely to fare in this crowd? I felt mostly ready. In the final weeks of preparation, my legs had finally adjusted to the additional stress of stair-climbing, and I had begun to feel adequate at uphill running. One or two friends even noticed.

"I think you're running this faster than normal," remarked Kim Jones, last year's top American marathoner and an occasional training partner of mine, as we neared the top of a long hill on a run a few weeks earlier. "All those stairs must be working."

My spirits soared.

I had also watched *King Kong* for inspiration, though I found the movie has more to do with wrestling large reptiles than ascending tall buildings. Still, it had awakened something archetypal about the Empire State Building — a black-and-white vision of the Big Ape (the Beast, the id, unchained Nature, our hairy, unwashed and uncivilized primate ancestor) challenging the tallest edifice erected by *homo sapiens*. Kong, sad to say, dropped out, and a long way down. I was hopeful I wouldn't.

As 10:30 a.m. approached, we humble humans were ushered to the lobby of the building, where normal people came and went in pursuit of normal business. For a few minutes we stood, oddballs, waiting for our moment. And then at zero hour a siren blew, and nineteen women, the first wave of runners, raced for the door.

That's right, the door, which is about 20 feet from the starting line. No sense making this thing any easier. Last one there is a rotten egg.

"You've got to get *right* there," Squires had said, "and it's just a little door."

As the 86 seconds separating the women's start from the men's ticked by, I remembered what Muhrcke had said about his strategic scramble to the door.

"I lined up behind a guy who looked like an ex-football player," he had recalled, "because I figured if he wasn't first through, he was going to be second. And I figured I would be third. It would be like a quarterback sneak."

I looked around. On my right, a short, thin runner with safety pins through his left ear. In front, a husky guy in electric-blue lycra. Hike! We were off.

And then the maddest dash ever — the race to the doorway. A confusion of arms and elbows, shoving and shouting, bad language and raw terror. A panic scene out of a disaster movie. Sale day at Macy's. Somehow I got through without injury, and the ascent began.

Muhrcke had advised me that the best strategy was to get into a rhythm as soon as possible. "It's basically coordination and rhythm that's going to get you to the top," he said.

But for the first ten floors it was flat-out panic, a sprint with no conscience, like teenagers fleeing the cops. Finally, though, the ten or so runners who had gotten through the door ahead of me slipped away above, and the ones behind dropped back a notch. From that point on, I struggled for oxygen and a routine.

I remember gasping for air. Then repeated attempts to pass stragglers, a frantic process that involved surging around a turn, grabbing handrails, and leaping two steps at a time until the next turn. Then the countdown, or countup, from floor to floor, numbers on doors in an otherwise unchanging viewscape of brown walls and 40-inch-wide steps. Interspersed were shouts from above and below, the occasional janitor or curious spectator in a doorway, and sprints down corridors on the twentieth and sixty-fifth floors, where the stairway shifted to the other side of the building.

I found it impossible to hit a rhythm, and instead focused on the constant challenge of getting by the person ahead of me. Near the top, I used the handrails a lot, and I seemed to be walking more of the time than I'd like to admit.

Finally, nearing the eighty-sixth floor, I could sense the climax. A few seconds later I broke through a doorway into daylight, hopped down a short stairway, and was hit by a slap of frigid air, especially poignant after the stuffy chase up the stairwell. Around a couple of corners on wobbly legs, and there was the finish.

When it was over, it all seemed to have gone by in a blink. Nearly a quarter-mile straight up, 13 minutes and 44 seconds, about the time it takes to run two and one half miles on level ground. While I stood on the observation deck recovering, my lungs began to burn, as if I had inhaled a shovelful of hot sand — just the way they used to feel after running a two-mile track race.

The winner, 25-year-old Scott Elliott of Colorado, had made the climb in 10:47, a new record, while Australian Suzanne Malaxos had repeated as women's champion in 12:27. Elliott, Pikes Peak Marathon Champ in 1989, kept shaking his head in disbelief about the dash to the door and the fight to pass on the steps.

"It was a pain," said the winner. "There were a couple of guys who would *not* let me go by."

Standing there on top of the Empire State Building, though, and looking out for miles in every direction, the fight and fatigue of getting to the top began to fade, and I was left with the beauty of a spectacular view. Off in the distance the Statue of Liberty, my second-highest New York City ascent completed twenty years earlier, raised her torch in congratulations. There are few things part of modern urban life I can get excited about. The Empire State Building is one of them, and having made it on foot to the top felt wonderful.

The next day was Valentine's Day, a day dedicated to the heart, though the lungs might have been a better organ to celebrate. My own were rough and rattling for days afterward. Oddly, though, considering the nature of the event, both legs and affiliated muscles and joints felt fine, and I was back to normal running in a day or two.

In the end, then, two-footed mastery of the Empire State Building proved not to be the kind of prolonged struggle that marathoners relish. But it had its own idiosyncrasies, and I now see the building with new eyes, and enjoy a kind of personal affection born of understanding and respect.

I don't get to New York often, but next time I do I'm tempted to stand outside the building, wait for the inevitable tourist to gaze up in wonder at its distant top, and then sidle up.

"Big, isn't it?" I'll say, "Well, let me tell you ... "

Or I may just hang around the lobby near that narrow doorway, waiting for someone to open it and ask the question, like Dan Ackroyd did in *Ghostbusters*: "Hey, where do these stairs go?"

And I'll answer simply, as Bill Murray did.

"They go up."

June 1990

CROSS-TRAINING CAMP

Most of this was in a language foreign to me: rakes and bars and saddles and clip-ons, all of it sounding like teen styles from the '50s. Talk of aero-bars and cadences and drop-bars and discs made me hungry. Glutes and rhomboids and psoas, I recalled as being adversaries of Luke Skywalker.

PACKING IS ALWAYS PROBLEMATIC, but this was ridiculous. I was dealing with all the usual questions. Do I have gear for rain, wind, snow and restaurants with unreasonable customer expectations — like a tie around the neck? But I was also dealing with a whole bagful of new questions. Did I pack cycling shorts, the appropriate array of athletic shoes, and a swimsuit, just in case? How about a bicycle helmet? I knew where *that* was, hanging on a nail in my garage, right where I had set it, ages ago. What else would I need?

Those of us blessed with a simple love of a simple sport — running — are amazed at the complexity of life for the rest of the aerobic world. If you doubt it, ask your average winter biathlete, who must travel with skis and boots, waxes and poles, rifles and bullets, goggles and hats, gloves and long underwear and windbreakers and lip balm and sunscreen and a laptop computer to keep track of it all.

Becoming a multi-sport geek for the next few days at the Vail Cross-Training Camp wouldn't be quite so organizationally demanding, but the addition of a couple of new sports to my repertoire was straining the limits of my packing ability. Thank goodness the camp organizers had offered to provide a bicycle, so I didn't have to pack one of those things.

And thank goodness the camp staff would be taking care of a lot of other things, too. As a non-cross-trainer, I would need all the help I could get. I had filled out the running part of my camp questionnaire with great confidence. My background? "Over 25 years as a runner," I wrote proudly. But the rest of the questionnaire left me chewing on the end of my pencil.

The cycling questions focused on training, racing, types of equipment used and goals. And the swimming section included questions about frequency of workouts, weekly yardage, competitive experience and my web-footed aspirations. I had filled in both sections with a variety of negatives: No-no-none-no-none-0-no-0-0-none.

Do I swim in open water? "Not that I know of."

Do I wear a wetsuit? "Not if I can help it."

And here was one I could answer truthfully: Specific goals in the triathlon?

"To determine if I should ever consider doing one," I wrote.

Doubts and packing problems notwithstanding, I was off to cross-training camp.

TUESDAY EVENING

Over the ages, those seeking enlightenment have always headed for the hills, where physical beauty combined with thin air produces dynamic metaphysical insights that are generally recognized as nonsense back at sea level. Nevertheless, sixteen acolytes of the triathlon and I assembled high in the Rocky Mountains one June evening for five days in search of triathletic wisdom.

"We want to make training fun, fit it into your lifestyle and make it more efficient," said Jim Davis, organizer of the camp, at our first gathering.

"We want you to leave here somewhat exhausted but not ill," added sports physiologist Ed Burke, Ph.D., putting a somewhat different spin on the camp's goals.

To keep us healthy at Vail's unfamiliar altitude of 8,000 feet, Burke drew on his experience as a former technical director of the U.S. Cycling Federation. He advised us to ease into our training, sip fluids constantly to avoid dehydration, pace ourselves during the week and not worry about experiencing more difficulty than normal with demanding activities. Like sleeping.

He also spent a few minutes describing the grinding headaches that some people experience in their first day or two at altitude. Throbbing, viselike, sinus-twisting, cranium-splitting headaches, the result of the change in air pressure.

"Okay, fine," a lady in the back finally groaned, rubbing her temples. "So how do I get rid of it?"

For some, it was a tough first night at camp.

WEDNESDAY MORNING

By the next morning headaches were gone, and we all assembled at our meeting room at the Vail Racquet Club for the first of two morning lectures.

This was a stretching session led by guru Bob Anderson, the guy who you've seen wearing a hat (for some strange reason) in virtually every stretching illustration ever printed, and who spent the better part of an hour working on — no exaggeration here — his feet.

"If there's only one thing we're able to leave you with," Jim Davis had told us the night before, "I hope it's stretching."

He wasn't kidding. If we could spend an hour on feet alone — massaging, working out bumps, lumps and pressure points, pulling toes one by one, making the longitudinal arch longer, etc., etc., etc. — imagine what we'd be into by the fourth or fifth day. No body part would go unstretched.

Knowing that the time commitment such a comprehensive stretching routine entails might discourage some campers, Anderson advised us to do our stretching in front of the television.

"I guess I'm going to have to start watching TV," noted a woman in the back of the room.

When our feet were thoroughly loose and elongated, Olympic gold-medalist Frank Shorter took the floor to share his thoughts on cross-training, which he embraced a few years ago to alleviate chronic running-induced injuries.

Shorter first tried running in a swimming pool ("one of the most boring activities ever invented by humans") but soon opted for cycling. As a result of his cross-training, Shorter has been remarkably free of injuries for over a year, not counting the dislocated shoulder and bruised hip he had suffered falling off his bike during the Portland Biathlon a few days earlier.

Shorter's talk, from the perspective of a dedicated runner who has found new intrigues on the bicycle, was especially fascinating to someone from a similar background — me. He described a training ride with cycling star Andy Hampsten, who asked Shorter what turnover rate, a cyclist's measure of rpm, Frank produced while running. Since it's not a question runners normally consider, Shorter admitted to never having thought about it. Neither had I, and I spent the next 30 minutes trying to determine my own (approximately 88).

Runners, Shorter told us, normally turnover at a faster rate than cyclists do in their most efficient cycling rhythm, which is one of the reasons a runner can lose leg speed while cross-training. Shorter also argued that too many triathletes go for another couple of hours of riding when they ought to be running, working on leg speed, which is crucial in the final phase of the triathlon.

"Cycling is alluring," Shorter insisted, "kind of a refuge for people who like to train a lot."

All of this was leading tragically and inexorably in the direction of the afternoon's scheduled activity. A question by one of the campers brought us suddenly to the inescapable conclusion of Shorter's reasoning.

"I run an 8-minute pace now," said the man, "and I want to run a 7-minute pace. What do I do?"

"Intervals," said Shorter, without sympathy.

WEDNESDAY AFTERNOON

Every running camp I've ever attended has included people of a wide range of abilities, so it wasn't surprising that cross-training camp would be the same. The Vail Camp was begun in 1986 largely as a place for a few aficionados to schmooze with elite triathletes, but each year a larger percentage of recreational athletes, fitness dabblers and absolute novices have joined the ranks.

When we reassembled in the afternoon for Shorter's talk on interval training, the differences in running background soon became apparent. Shorter encouraged people to work up to three miles of intervals, twice a week, at a speed slightly faster than race pace. Simple enough.

In trying to get the crowd to embrace this form of running, Shorter encouraged them to realize that whatever fear might be associated with interval training, excitement should also be part of the picture. Don't let fear dominate, he said. At that point, camper Jane Nicolai of Seattle piped up: "Well, I'm not afraid of it, because I don't even know what it is."

Then, after a discussion about lactate levels associated with interval training, Barry Beckerman, a scriptwriter from Los Angeles, responded, "That's great, what are lactate levels?"

These questions were answered in painful clarity later that afternoon, when Frank led us through 400-meter repeats. The setting was perfect: a grass track surrounded by breathtaking scenery. In truth, at this altitude the breath would have been taken away no matter what the scenery. This was my third run since arriving in Vail, and though I had almost gotten used to my legs feeling like cement, I had never in my life felt quite so slow while trying to run so fast.

Others were having similar problems, running way too fast in the first part of each lap, then suffering anaerobic revenge (you know, rigor mortis, the bear on the back, high lactate levels) and bailing out early.

I'm not sure if Shorter made any converts. Battling intervals at altitude was a double whammy. Frank was right about one thing, though. Cycling was sounding more and more like a refuge.

WEDNESDAY EVENING

You don't have to do everything they offer at cross-training camp, but I decided to listen to the swimming lecture anyway.

Russ Marsh, the swimming coach at the University of Colorado in

Boulder, showed a fascinating video that revealed some fascinating things about length of stroke, body rotation, flexibility, reaching deep for still water, and how to hook fascinating gadgets like paddles, floats, boards and flippers onto your body. It was all fascinating. Unfortunately, it involved getting wet.

THURSDAY MORNING

"With all the top people that are here," said Donn Rasemann, a furniture store owner from Kalamazoo, Michigan, "this is much more interesting than one of those fantasy baseball camps."

Thursday morning, then, was a chance to bask in the light of luminaries Scott Molina and Kenny Souza as they discussed elements of triathlon and biathlon (whoops, I mean duathlon) training. Most of this was in a language foreign to me: rakes and bars and saddles and clip-ons, all of it sounding like teen styles from the '50s. Talk of aero-bars and cadences and drop-bars and discs made me hungry. Glutes and rhomboids and psoas, I recalled as being adversaries of Luke Skywalker.

Okay, so I was out of my element here. I still found it interesting to hear these two bike wizards talk about how to maximize power and minimize wind resistance, and how to train effectively for sports with varying demands.

"Most people have light years to go in terms of technical improvements," said Molina, which was a whopping understatement in my case.

Later, I asked if all the gadgetry of cycling didn't discourage newcomers, especially when some cyclists seem more interested in their next purchase than their next workout.

"There *are* a lot of techno-geeks out there," said Molina, who then went on to argue against high-tech addiction. Souza's bike, he told us, cost less than $1,000, a moderate price for the top gun in the sport. Training, more than technology, was the key.

"Nothing's going to replace hard work, good sleep and consistent training," agreed Souza.

That was one thing you noticed about these guys. They knew how to work, and they knew how to rest. They were especially good resters, and I liked that. But I liked something about Souza even better, namely his answer to whether he had totally given up on swimming.

"For the time being," said the man who is known in triathlon circles as having the buoyancy of granite. "For maybe the next five years."

Later that morning, before heading out for my first ride, I spotted Bob Anderson surrounded by "his toys," an assortment of stretching and massage gadgets that have strikingly familiar shapes and contours, not unlike what you might find in the nearest adults-only shop.

One, the Jerry Cane, is a 3-foot-long hook with wooden balls attached here and there. We had seen Anderson use this device earlier to massage hard-to-reach spots on the back, something he claimed to do quite often on airplanes.

"Do you find yourself sitting alone a lot?" Jane Nicolai had asked.

Now Anderson was massaging sore muscles with a polished purple stone of vaguely phallic shape.

"Now what is *that*?" I asked, aghast.

"I know what you think it looks like," he answered, grinning. "And that may be why we sell a lot of 'em."

"Jeez, look at that thing!" exclaimed Ed Burke a minute later, and at first I thought he was talking about Anderson's stone. But he was talking about my helmet. During the weekend, people also made fun of my shoes, clothes and various other indicators of a lack of cycling expertise. Of course I was just trying to prove you didn't have to be a techno-geek to be a cross-trainer.

My ride that morning — the first in ten years or so — was an eventful reintroduction to the sport. I was given encouragement by Kenny Souza. "With a little work, I think you could give Frankie a scare." I reached a truce with my toe-clips; I learned that my running conditioning was serving me quite well in adjusting to cycling; and a friendly police officer took time from his busy day to stop me and my riding buddies on the highway to give us a lecture on rules of the road.

When we had ridden out of the mountains and into the desert, I realized I was at the tail end of the group and fading fast. If I tried to go the whole distance, I might *really* get behind. It was a decision between pride and lunch, and I opted for nutrition. A while later, I ended my 20-mile ride with a sore tailbone and tight shoulder blades, but nevertheless with renewed enthusiasm for cycling.

For a moment there, too, I thought about swimming. Happily, though, I got over it.

THURSDAY AFTERNOON

A whole array of plumb bobs, geometry, biomechanics and aerodynamics, as interpreted by Ed Burke and bicycle-frame expert David Tesch, left me with two basic ideas about cycling. One, I should try adjusting my position on the bike — front to back, up and down — until I'm situated to pedal with maximum efficiency. Two, I should avoid air, at least the kind you have to push out of the way as you zip down the road. In cycling, aerodynamics is half the battle.

For the afternoon workout, we had a choice between swimming or a trail run. Tough choice. I just love the woods — so quiet, so peaceful, so dry.

FRIDAY MORNING

I joined the group for a ride up the mountain pass, a slow but steady battle with toe-clips, pesky gears, steep inclines, diminishing air supply and an 11,000-foot summit that seemed to be receding at every turn.

One of the staffers, Dave Worrel, rode up beside me at one point and, in less than five minutes, gave seven or eight pointers that changed my life. Really. Individualized instruction, I realized between gasps, was something a good camp should spend lots of time on.

When we finally reached the top, I was tired, dehydrated and proud, but pride turned to horror when I heard the rest of the group talking about going farther. I was more than ready to head back.

"You're going to go on with us, aren't you?" asked Les Lockspeiser, a Denver cardiologist. "I mean what are you, an athlete or a writer?"

I realized later, when I had let my pride get the best of me and I was well into another 10 miles of riding, what the proper response would have been: "Which answer will get me back home faster?"

FRIDAY AFTERNOON

Today's lecture featured Ed Burke on heart-rate monitors. I had been doing some research of my own with this device and found that I could only get my heart rate up to around 120 to 125 on the bike before my muscles wimped out and my form fell apart.

After the lecture, I headed up into the hills for another trail run. My heart rate approached 190, close to max.

With 2 1/2 hours on the bike that morning and 1 hour and 22 minutes of trail running that afternoon, I had nearly four hours of tough exercise in one day. I was beginning to understand what life must be like for Molina, Souza and friends. No wonder they seemed to be napping when they weren't eating.

I was beginning to realize, too, that cross-training might be possible for a guy like me. Not counting swimming, of course.

SATURDAY MORNING

Lots of us were feeling a bit ragged, and in the lecture room, Ed Burke wasn't surprised to see only a trickle of campers filing in.

"By tomorrow we'll probably only have one person," he joked.

As tired as people might have been, Fred Kiekhaefer of Fond du Lac, Wisconsin, was alert enough to fire off a couple of quips during Burke's talk on nutrition and energy drinks. When Burke mentioned that two beers are okay after a race but that more than that will contribute to dehydration, Kiekhafer was quick to note, "That's why you can only get two beer cages on a bike frame."

And when Burke showed an advertisement for a product made of testosterone-rich, pulverized deer antlers, thus showing the bizarre lengths people will go to in pursuit of nutritional secrets, Kiekhafer jumped in again.

"Maybe they could just replace handlebars with antlers and gnaw on them during a ride," he said.

Obviously, things were getting weird in Vail, but fortunately it was almost time for me to leave. The rest of the crowd would stay another day, taking advantage of additional topics offered — massage, nutritional analysis, weight lifting, gait analysis, personalized bicycle fitting — but I had an early departure planned. Plus, the heat was on. Russ Marsh was getting more persistent, and when I had almost made my getaway, he cornered me.

"How can you do a story on cross-training without ever swimming?"

It was a good question, one I pondered all the way to the airport.

June 1990

Alaska sun run

*This is the only time in my life I've seen it sunnier
at midnight than at noon.*

The thing about Alaska: it's big — 591,004 acres, one-fifth of
the total area of the United States. If Texas politicians, jealous of losing
their top spot to the forty-ninth state back in 1959, had insisted on
dividing Alaska in half before allowing it (them) into the union, it
wouldn't have helped. Texas would have dropped to third, behind the
two Alaskas.

No dividing, then, and no fudging like the mapmakers do, putting a
shrunken, tame and disoriented Alaska in a box off the coast of Southern
California. To get the real Alaska in your field of vision, you'll need to
step way north, and way back. Farther ... farther ... waaaayyyyy back.
About a thousand miles or so should do it.

Hovering out there in space, you can finally see the whole thing. A
great hunk of frontier with its two legs striding confidently across the
top of the globe like ... like ... well, now that you mention it, like a runner
at full tilt.

The lead leg, heading east, is the Alaska Panhandle, a region of steep
mountains, thousands of islands, ancient rain forests, spectacular fjords,
and at least one glacier larger than Rhode Island. The trail leg, beginning
with the Alaska Peninsula and ending in the Aleutian Islands, is a world
of volcanoes, grasslands, Kodiak bear, whales, walrus and a couple
million seals.

Above, the gigantic bulk of Alaska is bracketed by two major mountain ranges. The Brooks Range in the north, the last gasp of the Rockies, isolates the rest of Alaska from the North Slope, site of one of the largest oil and natural gas reserves in the world. And the Alaska Range in the south, home of 20,320-foot Mt. McKinley, the largest mountain on the continent, offers residence to caribou, moose, grizzly and all manner of wild things.

Between these two mountainous brackets lies the interior of Alaska, sliced down the middle by one of the planet's longest, wildest and wooliest rivers, the Yukon. The very name makes you want to take a deep swig of whiskey and start digging. And somewhere in the midst of this vast land rests a town of about 30,000, Fairbanks.

Descend now from your lofty vantage point, like an alien approaching Earth, and take a closer look at Fairbanks. As you circle down, zeroing in on your target, you realize that the town does not dominate the landscape on which it's built. Rather, it rests there humbly, a visitor to the realm. In every direction, acres of tundra, bogs and birches stretch to the horizon. Human settlement is here with nature's permission, permission that seems revocable at any moment.

And now, with an eagle's view, you notice a gathering of human beings on the edge of town, near the gymnasium at the University of Alaska. Two large hot air balloons mark the spot. Thousands of people are jogging, stretching and otherwise preparing for some sort of celebration.

You move in closer. A costume parade is in progress. A mother and her two kids are dressed up like Super Family. A human mosquito buzzes. Runner Larry Stice is dressed up like an issue of *Runner's World* ("Carbo Reloading," reads the headline, "The Pizza vs. Beer Debate"). A man is pushing an elderly woman in a wheelchair, the chair outfitted like a covered wagon and the woman in pioneer gear. Periodically, the woman fires her cap pistol in the air.

This is June 23, 1990, the Saturday closest to the longest day of the year, and you've arrived from above just in time for the start of the eighth annual Midnight Sun Run. In Alaska, the position of the sun signifies all kinds of things to all kinds of creatures. For the humans assembled, this is a day to celebrate sunlight, pleasant weather and a gentle time of year in a land of harsh extremes.

This year, the weather has been drizzly for much of the extended day, but as 10 p.m. rolls around and runners begin lining up for the 10K run, the clouds begin to break. The sun, flirting with the horizon, pokes through.

"See, I told you," says Dan King, one of the event's organizers. "It's always sunny for the Sun Run."

And no one would have it otherwise. The Sun Run has been part of the framework of life in Fairbanks since 1983, the brainchild of former San Francisco runner Mike Styles, who wanted to create a kind of Bay to Breakers on the tundra. What better time to celebrate the Alaska experience than during the longest weekend of the year?

The inescapable joy of summer in Alaska has been around forever, and the foot race has easily merged with the feeling Alaskans have about celebrating the season. The Midnight Sun Run grew from 325 runners in 1983 to 3,219 in 1990, making it the largest 10K in the state and the second-largest Alaska run of any distance.

This scene is very familiar — costumes, celebration mixed with anticipation, lacing up racing shoes and searching for the shortest port-a-potty line. But there are some odd aspects — a long day spent fidgeting with prerace jitters, warming up in the light of evening, and the bizarre path of the sun, which seems as if it might never set.

But then everything about Alaska is a bit out of whack and proportion. Things are bigger, colder, longer and shorter than they are in the Lower 48. There are 800-mile boat races, temperatures 80 degrees below zero, salmon bigger than Edsels, 1,000-mile dogsled races, cabbages too big to lift, mountains that dominate the imagination and at least one oil spill the size of New Jersey.

The disorientation of the summer solstice, then, is just one more of those uniquely Alaskan phenomena, nothing to lose sleep over. (Well, more on that later.) For now, it's just a time to enjoy a pleasant run in the evening.

For Alaskan runners, summer is a wonderful time of year, not counting the mosquitoes. Winter, after all, is never really far from mind, and winter means brittle temperatures, snow that stretches to the horizon and darkness that cuts to the spirit. Those of us who have enough trouble dealing with winter in the Lower 48 are amazed at the ability of our northern counterparts to brave the real extremes North America has up its sleeve.

Most Alaskan runners, at least those from the interior, seem to have had some experience with running at 40 to 50 below.

"I've probably run at 55 below," says 38-year-old Bob Murphy, a former Californian who is now one of the state's top runners. "It's kind of crazy, and I don't do it much any more. It was sort of novel when I first moved up here."

"I've been out when it was 130 below with the wind chill," says Frank Bozanich, a two-year resident of the tiny native village of Anaktuvuk Pass in the mountains north of Fairbanks. "You have to keep everything covered, because it doesn't take long to get frostbitten. I've had my nose frost-bit about a dozen times. It doesn't take much after you've done it once."

Alaska is a diverse region, though, and while Fairbanks and the rest of the interior may huddle against the inexorable winter, runners in Anchorage, where half of the state's residents dwell, have a much warmer time of it.

"Most winters you can go out and run in just normal outdoor running clothes, polypropylene and that kind of stuff," claims Roy Reisinger, an eighteen-year veteran of Anchorage winters and organizer of that city's Heart Run, the largest run in the state.

A runner from the interior, in fact, may prefer the frigid sharpness of a Fairbanks winter to the rain, snow and ice of other regions. But for runners everywhere in the state, short days haunt the soul.

"I'd say the biggest problem is the darkness," says Reisinger. "If you have a job that allows you to run in the middle of the day, that helps."

For Bozanich, too, the cold seems less of a problem by itself than it does in tandem with darkness and isolation.

"It's like training in a deep freeze with the lights off," he says.

How do Alaskan runners do it? They thrive on turning hardship into adventure. The state is home to a variety of wilderness and adventure runs, and winter running is just one more experience to savor. Alaskan runners may wax poetic about moonlight on the snow, the shimmering northern lights and odd sensations they experience before, during and after a run.

"When I come in from one of those really cold runs and take my jacket off," says Bozanich, "I can sometimes break ice from the inside. It sounds like glass breaking."

Writes Bobbi Fyten, a masters runner from Fairbanks, in an article on winter running in the Fairbanks *Daily News-Miner*, "As is true with Alaska living in general, a sense of humor is the most important item you can carry with you wherever you go."

Along with a sense of humor, attention to details like layering of clothing, familiarity with the course, reflective clothing, protection of nose and past experiences with frostbite all seem to keep the winter running experience on the safe side. In a land dominated by Nature, you show respect for the season.

"It's dangerous for people who don't understand it," says 63-year-old runner Jack Townshend. "Basically, you have to build an environment."

Sometimes, too, you switch to another activity, like skiing or snowshoeing, or television. Sometimes you just bag it and wait for the coldest part of the winter to pass, dreaming of the long days of summer and, perhaps, a celebration known as the Midnight Sun Run.

In a wonderful way, the Sun Run is linked to winter, like Yin and Yang, by virtue of the group that organizes it. The Yukon Quest International Association stages a yearly sled dog race between Fairbanks and Whitehorse, Canada, an event similar to its more famous cousin, the Iditarod, although many consider the Quest, with its smaller dog teams and fewer checkpoints, to be a more difficult grind. Of course any way you slice it, 1,000 miles through a sub-Arctic winter is a fair test of fortitude.

The Sun Run, then, is the other side of the Alaska spectrum — warm, sunny, gentle, pleasant. Fairbanks is not alone among Alaskan cities in celebrating the longest day — there's a Midnight Sun Marathon and Half-Marathon in Anchorage, an "Only Fools Run at Midnight" run in Juneau and assorted other two-footed celebrations of the solstice in the state — but Fairbanksans seem to have taken this event especially to heart.

Near the finish line, where one of Alaska's swiftest runners, Rick Wilhelm, has just clocked a 31:10 victory, the focus is now on the parade of costumed citizens approaching the line. A man rides a unicycle while juggling bowling pins. Several military units run in formation. A human mosquito or two, looking not much bigger than the actual Alaskan variety, jog by. An OPEC sheik; 74-year-old "cow woman" from Florida; and three people who complete the course on cross country skis — not roller skis, mind you, but the real thing.

The focus on fun continues into the wee hours, as awards are given for costume after costume. The sun is still flirting with the horizon, and midnight feels like an autumn afternoon with its golden orange tones and cool air. This is the only time in my life I've seen it sunnier at midnight than at noon. Finally, at 12:30 a.m., the festivities end, giving me the opportunity to tell friends about being at a race where the awards ceremony wasn't over until the next day.

And then it's time for bed? Of course not! This is summer in Alaska, and it's still light out. Time for a midnight snack and a trip to the Howling Dog saloon.

I can identify two problems with summer in Alaska. First, the mosquitoes, who won't give a sweaty runner a moment's rest, and who have been known to drive Alaskans to dream fondly of January. Second, a day without darkness is an assault on the body's biorhythms. It never seems like bedtime. And so, at about 2 a.m., we arrive at the Howling Dog in Fox, Alaska, a short drive from Fairbanks.

In the strictest sense, I'm not sure if this qualifies as a postrace party, since it's open to everyone and the bar is inhabited by all manner of creatures — runners and non-runners alike. I'm reminded of the scene from *Star Wars* with a universe of odd-looking creatures bellying up to the bar. But then I suspect the inspiration for that scene came from some barroom in Alaska, one like the Howling Dog.

At 3 a.m., things are still hopping at the Dog. Hundreds of people are crammed into the building demanding libations. The band is belting out "The Rattlesnake Shake," and people out in the back lot are playing volleyball. The sun has set and risen again, but there has never been enough darkness to call it night. And without sufficient darkness, the revelers seem destined to go on forever.

In winter, Fairbanksans like to brag about working from dawn to dusk, which, when an outsider finally figures it out, turns out to be an hour or so. In summer, though, some residents seem capable of partying from sunup to sunrise, which is *really* proving your mettle.

Unfortunately, my metal is tin, and without any noticeable argument I convince Bob Murphy, my chauffeur for the evening, to take me home. Ambience is one thing, smoky air is another. We're both ready to leave.

A few minutes later, as we turn off the highway and near the house where I'm staying, I spot a moose next to the road. It's after 3 a.m., cool, and a mist hovers over the bog where the moose grazes. We pull over.

Fairbanks is the kind of place where you can be sitting at lunch only to have a moose walk into your field of vision. So the presence of one next to the road isn't exactly shocking. Still, there is something reverential about this quiet confrontation, the way we stare at each other.

"Hey, Rocky," I finally say, aping Bullwinkle, "watch me pull a rabbit out of my hat." The moose stares, unamused.

By that evening, I will be exploring Denali National Park with some of the other runners who are visiting Alaska for the Sun Run, and we will see fox, caribou, Dall sheep and grizzlies in abundance, as well as moose. And while running, we will see bones that have been chewed on by ... something. But now, nearing home, a close encounter with a moose seems especially poignant, some sort of distillation of the Alaska experience.

"Do you see them often during a run?" I ask Murphy.

"It depends on where you go," he answers. "Sometimes it happens quite a bit, especially on the trails."

"Are they stubborn, belligerent or just dense?" I ask.

"They'll stand their ground if they feel like they're threatened," he replies, "but usually they just run off into the bushes. You really have to use good judgment, because if they're with a calf they'll be very protective. I've had to backtrack and go around when they won't let me through."

Somehow that seems fair, that here in Alaska wildlife should have the final word. In Alaska, Nature rules, whether it's in the scope of the land, the severity of winter or the seemingly capricious instincts of animals.

If we retrace the route that brought us here, ascending gradually to our original vantage point in space, we should begin to appreciate the size of Alaska, but also the episodes that define life here.

As we rise, circling, from an early morning encounter with a moose to a point where the full width and breadth of Alaska comes into view, the small outpost called Fairbanks becomes only a dot on an enormous landform. The rugged and beautiful and extensive Alaskan landscape dwarfs the activities of human beings, making them only a small, sometimes delightful footnote. The extremities of land and climate seem destined to prevent much else.

And yet, once a year now, it seems otherwise in the town of Fairbanks. Then, thousands of survivors of winter crawl like bears from their dens and don their most outrageous running apparel. Then, suitably attired, they celebrate with their neighbors the freaky light in the sky, the one that never sleeps, the midnight sun.

And eventually, well after the sweat has dried and the muscles have tightened, sometime early in the morning, they may head home. And then, perhaps, finally, they will dream of the other side of running in Alaska — frigid air, frosty beards and the glow of moonlight shimmering on the snow.

September 1990

PRE

He never let them down, taking on any rival in any circumstance, sometimes seeming to be on the brink of disaster and then, just when you thought it was over, dredging and grasping a final something from a place deeper than pain, deeper than self-doubt, deeper than despair.

I SUPPOSE THIS COULD BE almost any road race. The morning is overcast but pleasant. Hundreds of runners of all ages, shapes and sizes are warming up, pinning on numbers or nervously shaking hamstrings and doing half-hearted stretches. Officials scurry back and forth making last-minute system checks.

As the starting time approaches, I finish my warm-up and sit to put on my racing flats. I had hoped to be more ready for this, to have come here with the appropriate sense of athletic mission. Perhaps, even, to win. But a virus has interrupted my training, and its vestiges still rumble vaguely in my lungs. This excuse, though, the very *fact* of excuse in this race, makes me ashamed.

As I get to my feet for the final few minutes of prerace warm-up, I realize how familiar this all feels. Jitters, sweat, self-doubt, adrenaline, impending doom. All of it connects me to my past.

And then I notice a man in the street, dressed in the red polo shirt that indicates he is an official. He is short, somewhat round in girth, with dark hair and features. A mustache gives a sense of wit to his smile.

There's something in his brown eyes, too, a certain ironic spark that I recognize, and that takes me back in years.

This is Ray Prefontaine, father of Steve Prefontaine, whose life and death inspired this event. This is the eleventh edition of the Prefontaine Memorial Run, an event named after the man many would consider the greatest American distance runner of all time. This could be any road race, but it isn't. It's Pre's run, and it's held every September in his home town of Coos Bay, Oregon. I'm here on a pilgrimage of sorts.

Touring the course yesterday, I was stunned to see signs lined up in classic Burma-shave style, teasing the following:

"Who was Pre?" "Come and See." "September 15."

Who was Pre? Who, I wonder, could wonder?

At the time of his death on May 30, 1975, Steve Prefontaine held every American outdoor track record from 2,000 meters through the 10,000. In all, he set fourteen American records and broke the 4-minute-mile barrier nine times. While at the University of Oregon in Eugene, he won three NCAA cross country championships and four outdoor track titles.

Good statistics. But there have been other great American distance runners in the past few decades: Jim Ryun, Gerry Lindgren, Billy Mills, Craig Virgin, Alberto Salazar and more. Still, Prefontaine rests in a special place in the minds, the hearts and, most important, the guts of those who witnessed his exploits.

Ask the question, "Who was Pre?" and someone will tell you a story of a race, or several races. The 1970 NCAA 3-mile in Des Moines, Iowa, when Pre, his right foot laced with stitches from an accident the day before, ran a 2-minute final half to hold off Garry Bjorklund and Dick Buerkle. Or the 1972 Olympic Trials, when Pre led most of the race, shadowed by older, wiser veterans who finally faded in the wake of the 21-year-old's punishing kick. Or the 1973 NCAA Cross Country Championships in Spokane, Washington, when Nick Rose pushed to a 50-meter lead at halfway, and observers began to sense that this time, the Pre magic was smoke. Pre proved otherwise. The crowd gasped aloud as he summoned his strength, reeled the Brit back in and captured a third

NCAA title.

Ask the question, too, and you may hear of a workout. A time he gobbled quarters, halves and 1,320s like mixed nuts. A 10-mile run when the pace spiraled out of control like an argument. A track session during which a training partner seemed to challenge Pre's dominance, and the carefully planned splits suddenly became as irrelevant as last week's weather, with a furious Pre redefining the concept of speedwork.

Ask the question, and more than anything you'll hear about an attitude, an alloyed personality forged of guts, pride, determination, cockiness and a few other basic elements that were hard to identify. Inevitably, those who ran against Prefontaine were struck by his attitude, by a style unusually blunt for a distance runner and by tactics that smelled of challenge.

"Pre was the first person I met," noted longtime rival Garry Bjorklund, "where there was so much to bite off, you couldn't chew."

Steve Prefontaine was a constant source of irritation, confrontation and inspiration to those who knew him. He had a certain look, a way of glancing back as he rounded the turn in the lead, that seemed to say, "I've got this thing in hand now, and I'm only mildly interested in seeing where the rest of you are." And then he would surge.

Like so many other runners in the early 1970s, I never beat Pre, in spite of repeated attempts. In the 1970 NCAA Cross Country Championships, I caught him at four miles. He glanced back, and that was it. In the PAC-8 three-mile the next spring, I challenged him twice for the lead. He hung on both times and finally blasted past for the win. The photo in the next day's paper showed Prefontaine grimacing at the finish, painfully wasted.

"I was hurting," he told me after the race. "If you'd gone hard for a couple of laps, you would have had me."

It was the ultimate compliment, to have made Pre hurt. But it was also a sign of my inadequacy. Why hadn't I gone harder, longer? Why couldn't I be more like him?

"His talent was his control of his fatigue and his pain," said Walt McClure, his high school coach. "His threshold was different than most of us, whether it was inborn or he developed it himself."

On this September morning before the Memorial Run, I see something in his father's eyes that reminds me of all this. And as we begin the road race journey, the suddenness and finality of Pre's death fifteen years ago, the tragedy that snuffed a special spirit, and the sadness of passing things are inescapable.

Coos Bay, Oregon. Home of Steve Prefontaine and a whole lot of people in the logging industry. Much of the Oregon Coast seems designed for city people escaping from accounting, law and business for a weekend of sand between the toes. Coos Bay, though, has an edge of sweaty legitimacy, born of cutting and hauling large trees to market. In the Coos Bay of the 1990s, downtown is spruced up to lure the tourist dollar, but the railroad runs right down the waterfront, mountains of wood chips are piled up for export, and the work ethic hangs in the air like drizzle. Signs in the back of pickups announce: "This Family Supported by Timber."

Steve Prefontaine seemed a perfect reflection of Coos Bay, tough and independent. He liked to describe his teenage years as, more or less, a decision between running the hills and flashing a switchblade. Athletics won out, but one always felt he might revert at any time and join the darker elements of Coos Bay.

Those who knew Steve Prefontaine well insisted his hard shell covered a warm interior. There were times one got glimpses of a different Pre — friendly, community-minded, struggling with self-doubt. Mostly, though, he just seemed tough, irascible and terribly anxious to get on with whatever life had in store.

The Prefontaine Memorial Run follows one of his favorite training routes, and as I head up the first hill on this course, I recognize it as vintage Pre. A straight shot from the town to the hills, a gnarly test of fortitude. Ray Prefontaine remembers his son running repeats here. Others in town recall seeing their native son run up a lot of hills. But, selective memory being what it is, never down.

Pre was said to react with disdain when he first noticed cross country runners in Coos Bay, but once he tried the sport, he found himself in a fast-flowing stream. At age 16, he told his mother he would go to the Olympics one day. Senior year, he broke the U.S. high school record for two miles by nearly 7 seconds, running 8:41.5.

Pre's following four years at the University of Oregon established a legacy. The already powerful track program prospered, with Steve Prefontaine its most famous member. He trained hard, raced savagely, continued to break new ground. And when he stepped in front of the Eugene crowd, *his people* — magic.

Sport is entertainment. These days, that means color-coordination and the prancing of prima donnas who carefully orchestrate their competitive spats. With Pre, the entertainment was pure, knife-edged, transcendent. "Here I am," he announced without words, warming up on the track. "Wait'll you see what I do this time." Chills raced down the spines of his fans, and "Go Pre!" exploded from within.

He never let them down, taking on any rival in any circumstance, sometimes seeming to be on the brink of disaster and then, just when you thought it was over, dredging and grasping a final something from a place deeper than pain, deeper than self-doubt, deeper than despair. He would rally, and he would win.

Steve Prefontaine was so at home on the track, so cosmically centered there, that the Prefontaine Memorial Run is something of an anomaly. Pre never competed in a road race, never realized his sport would become the passion of the masses, never heard the term "Running Boom." He did, though, train on the course over which I am now struggling, one of the hillier, testier routes in the asphalt pantheon.

As I round the final turn and pass the house where Pre grew up and where his parents still live, I see Marshfield High School, perched on the hillside like a Tibetan monastery. A minute later I'm on the school's track, finishing 10 kilometers in 34:15, well behind winner Don Clary.

It's a pleasant place, this track, on a pleasant morning. The sun has broken through, a gentle breeze whiffles through the trees, and the finishers of the eleventh Prefontaine Memorial Run are enjoying it all in the aftermath. Looking around, I can imagine the young Prefontaine training here, alone, on one of those bone-numbing Oregon winter afternoons, with dark clouds crashing across the sky, rain pelting the face, and the runner holding onto his dreams. Five more quarters to go.

Later I visit the Art Museum in Coos Bay where a room is dedicated to Steve Prefontaine. Ray Prefontaine is there, watching the film of his son in the 1972 Olympic 5,000, when the 21-year-old went for broke, challenging older, stronger runners. But he stumbled a few meters from the finish and was nipped for third, losing the bronze medal to Ian Stewart of Great Britain. It was a hard Olympic experience for Pre; first the murder of Israeli athletes, then doubts about the meaning of the Games and the attempt to hold onto a dream that turned Kafkaesque. It left him disappointed, disillusioned and emotionally spent.

When he recovered, Pre came back strong, attacking the track with renewed vigor. In the next two seasons he set and reset American records at two miles, three miles, six miles, 2,000 meters, 5,000 meters and the 10,000. Occasionally he lost a race, but even beaten he never seemed vanquished. Oddly, he sometimes described himself at the time as just "going through the motions." Some motions. For all of us competing at the time, Pre was still the standard.

In the wake of the Munich Olympics, too, Pre seemed more accessible, more at ease, more at peace with life. His ferocity on the track seemed undiminished, but his relationships with other runners seemed to grow.

It was during this time, in June of 1974, that I chased him for eight laps of a three-mile race in front of his Eugene crowd, before he and Frank Shorter surged away in the final mile. A picture of this race hangs in the museum in Coos Bay, a black-and-white photo with a much younger me tagging along in the background. That was another epic battle for Pre, a race where the challenger, Shorter, took the lead with 200 meters to go, and that look came over Steve Prefontaine, determination overcoming inertia, pride conquering apathy, anger overpowering pain. On the homestretch, he muscled and squeezed his way ahead of Shorter by six-tenths of a second and set a new American record of 12:51.4. The crowd, *his people*, stomped the wooden stands and screamed so loudly I felt disoriented and almost stopped before the finish.

I could *not* beat this guy, but I had slipstreamed in his emotional wake to a personal record of 12:57.6, probably the best performance of my life. It gave me confidence and opened doors. The following spring, largely as a result of this race, I was invited on a two-week trip to the Peoples Republic of China as part of a U.S. Track and Field Team. When I returned, still flush from the adventure of my life, Dick Buerkle, one of the few Americans who ever beat Pre, approached me in the airport.

"Did you hear the news?" he asked, ashen-faced. "Prefontaine died. In a car crash."

The day after the Prefontaine Memorial Run, I am back in Eugene, taking a run for old time's sake. I jog along the trail dedicated to Steve Prefontaine, "Pre's Trail," and trot along streets filled with memories. I stop at Stevenson Track at Hayward Field, site of so many of his spectacular races.

This is the track where Pre raced his last race, on the evening of his death. It was a 5,000 in which he beat Frank Shorter in 13:23.8 — not Pre's best effort, but he had a lot on his mind. He had been fighting the Amateur Athletic Union (AAU) over whether he and other runners would be allowed to race when and where they wanted. And he was frustrated by the general lack of support for American track athletes.

"I'm just like any other American," he told a reporter from the *Oregon Journal*. "If I don't pay my electric bill, they turn off my lights. After college, our athletes are turned out to pasture. We have no Olympic program in this country. It's as simple as that. No sports medicine, no camps, no nothing. I'm not talking about subsidizing us. I'm just talking about a national plan. I want to see some interest from somebody. In the past, we've sat back and let our natural talent do it. Well, the rest of the world has caught up."

So Pre was feeling a bit frustrated and scattered at the time of his final race, not quite at the top of his form. Still, he finished just 1.9 seconds off his American record. It was his twenty-fifth straight win in Eugene in distances over a mile.

It was on this same track that friends and fans held a memorial service for Pre a few days after his death. The speeches ended early so thousands of fans could sit in silent appreciation while a clock ticked off the seconds of an imaginary race. And as the clock wound down to what would have been his last lap, they couldn't contain themselves.

"Go Pre!" they shouted, and cheered, and cried.

As I leave Hayward Field and jog up into the hills where Pre spent the last minutes of his life, I can't help but reflect on his impact on lives like my own. His was an attitude that was tough to duplicate, and it affected us all.

"The characteristic that separated Pre from the rest of the world was his pride," said Coach McClure. "To be the best was his only goal. Man imposes his own limitations. Limitation was not in Steve's frame of reference."

I'm feeling my own limitations at the moment, race-weary legs that don't recover as well as they used to. They struggle against gravity to carry me up into the hills above Hayward field, then down a narrow roadway overarched with trees, like a cool, moist cathedral. This was a road Pre also ran many times, but which turned on him just after midnight on the evening after his last race.

The circumstances of his death remain unclear. He had been drinking at a party that evening, but that never seemed an adequate explanation for why, at 39 minutes past midnight, his MG convertible suddenly veered off course on a road he knew so well. The car flipped over, crushing him to death.

We'll never know exactly what caused the accident, but we do know this: Steve Prefontaine lived 24 years, during which time he became one of the most remarkable and memorable distance runners the human race has ever known. And when he ran in front of *his people*...

I stop running, walk to the side of the road, and find the cold dark granite that marks the spot. After fifteen years, I still feel melancholic reading the simple inscription in 2-inch, hand-painted white letters:

"Pre 5/30/75 RIP"

April 1991

JOHNNY KELLEY

He is one Cool-Hand-Luke-of-a-Rocky-Balboa-of-an octogenarian, refusing to give up.

WE ARE NEARING THE TOP of Heartbreak Hill, the section of the Boston Marathon course named for the poor fellow who, in so many races in the 1930s and '40s, approached this point as the leader of the race, only to head down toward Cleveland Circle a few minutes later in arrears.

Johnny Kelley. And I'm right next to him.

I look at Kelley. He is not quite walking, because his arms are up and swinging. But he is not exactly running, either. This, rather, is some sort of timeless, indefinable motion, an expression of human will overcoming entropy. We've been at this for more than 4 hours and 20 minutes, most recently at a clip of 15 minutes per mile, with rain falling steadily for a solid hour. Chilled and wobbly, though, Mr. Marathon will not quit.

"Spectators, move to the side of the road," orders a policeman over a loudspeaker a few yards behind us, as he has for the past hour. "Traffic will be coming through."

Earlier, this section of the course was packed with Patriot's Day celebrants who watched first Ibrahim Hussein, later Wanda Panfil, then another 10,000 runners race, run and hobble by. By the time Kelley reaches Heartbreak, the crowd has thinned to three basic groups: 1) race volunteers, 2) people who wouldn't *think* of leaving the course until Johnny Kelley passes, even if it means risking pneumonia, and 3) drunks.

A group of about fifty of the latter has just run 100 yards with Kelley, chanting, "John-NEE, John-NEE, John-NEE" in an act of encouragement that borders on harassment.

Through all of this, the 83-year-old, 130-pound, blue-eyed, white-haired elder statesman of the Boston Marathon plugs along, flanked by two Massachusetts State Troopers and basically ignoring the maelstrom that surrounds him. Dressed in long-sleeved cotton shirt, John Hancock singlet and blue shorts over lavender tights, Kelley is not quite color-coordinated. Function overrides fashion for the veteran, who wears his wife's stocking cap and a painter's cap on his head, a white scarf around his neck and gloves on his hands, all in a determined bid to keep the wet wolves of a rainy April day at bay.

"You're looking good, John!" shouts a man from under his umbrella. "You're looking unbelievable."

And then Kelley passes, and I hear the man say quietly to his friend, "Oh, he looks bad."

And who wouldn't look bad? He's wet, weary, more than an hour from the finish and struggling up the same monster that used to frustrate his aspirations a half-century earlier. At 83, who would argue if he were to simply call it off?

Instead, the opposite happens. Cresting the top of Heartbreak, Kelley's stride changes slightly, a subtle yet distinct metamorphosis. He is running again.

Working on his sixtieth Boston Marathon, fifty-six of which he has finished, Kelley's determination still burns. Johnny Kelley is, by God, going to get through this thing. He is one Cool-Hand-Luke-of-a-Rocky-Balboa-of-an-octogenarian, refusing to give up.

For a second, Kelley's gaze lifts off the spot on the road 5 feet in front of him where he keeps it focused, and he looks toward downtown Boston. After all these years, the finish line still beckons.

Sixty Bostons! Johnny Kelley first toed the starting line in Hopkinton in 1928, but he failed to finish. He tried again in 1932, but DNF'd again. Finally, in 1933, he completed the distance in 3:03:56, beginning a streak that would carry him to the finish line every year except two, 1956 and 1968, for the next fifty-eight years, including two victories, 1935 and 1945, and seven second place finishes.

Will anyone ever equal Kelley's longevity? To do so, a runner would have to start young, stay healthy, maintain interest, avoid injuries and outrun the Grim Reaper for nearly a century.

How has Kelley managed this? Sitting in the invited runners area a few hours earlier, I am mystified by the question. I am nursing a calf pull, and I can't avoid the notion that the 83-year-old on the other side of the room, a man twice my age, is in better condition to finish 26 miles than I am. And Kelley seems as baffled by his good fortune in avoiding injuries as most of us are in why we can't.

In fact, Kelley's biggest problem this day has been dealing with the onslaught of media attention. There's no question he enjoys the limelight, but enough has been enough.

"I'm just trying to keep an even keel and keep my head above water," he says a few minutes before noon. "It's going to be a relief to get into the race."

On the starting line, a special spot has been painted for Kelley, a circle 3 feet in diameter with a shamrock and "60" in the center. Nearby, circles of past years — 59, 58, 57, 56 — surround it in ever-diminishing clarity, like memories of yesterdays' performances. Kelley, however, after an introduction to the throng, settles in on the opposite side of the road with his two police escorts just behind. I tuck in behind them, along with Colin Corkery, a 33-year-old runner who has agreed to shadow Kelley for a local TV station.

At high noon we're off. The elite runners whoosh by on our right, and Johnny Kelley begins his mile-by-mile trek to the finish line on Boylston.

MILE 1

We are in the midst of a quest to keep faster runners from knocking Kelley over. State Troopers John Murphy and William Coulter manage the task of directing human traffic around him with great skill and diplomacy. When people squeeze by, they seem irritated at first, but then, noticing him, often shout, "Awwwright Johnny!" We pass the mile mark in 10:10. Kelley will hold a pace of 10 to 12 minutes per mile for more than half the race.

MILE 2

"There's Johnny Kelley!" shouts a spectator.
   "Where?"
   "Right *there*."
   "Where?"
   "Right there."
   "Good luck, Mr. Kelley!"

MILE 3

We pass the first aid station, and a chaotic scramble for fluids ensues. The troopers have their hands full trying to keep their charge from being trampled like a paper cup. About this time, a discarded garbage bag gets caught in Kelley's feet, and he nearly tumbles.

   A minute later, a woman leans from the side of the road to within inches of his face and shouts, "Attaboy, Johnny Kelley. Sweetheart!"

MILE 4

A man bending down to his young son says, "That's the man. That's the 83-year-old man, Johnny Kelley."

MILE 5

The second water stop seems a little safer now that fewer runners are angling to get by. Kelley takes water, spits it out and throws some over his head. We pass five miles in 51:49.

MILE 6

In the town of Framingham, a runner dressed as Groucho Marx goes by, turns, flicks a cigar and says, "Hey, Johnny, tell 'em Groucho sent you."

Kelley doesn't respond to this or any similar act or comment. His gaze remains fixed on a spot 5 feet ahead. For a guy who is known to ham it up at the least provocation with renditions of "Young At Heart" and "Danny Boy," he takes today's task very seriously, ignoring runners and spectators alike. He must hear his name 10,000 times before the finish.

"Atta boy, Johnny!"

Just before the Framingham train station, a man passes pushing a canoe on wheels, with two kids in front. I hear him explaining about the old man in lavender tights.

MILE 7

Spectators run along the side of the road, then set up to take still pictures and video of the man of the hour.

"How ta go, Johnny!"

MILE 8

We head up a hill, and I sense he's slowing down. For the first time, I wonder if he's going to make it.

MILE 9

Passing a reservoir, it suddenly gets quiet. Colin Corkery, who is running with a mobile phone, reports that Hussein and Panfil are leading the race. Kelley continues to chug along.

MILE 10

Spectators along the reservoir call out, "We love you, Johnny!" and "You're an inspiration to us all, Johnny!"

Two runners pass, and I hear one say, "That's Johnny Kelley."

"Yeah," the other responds. "I understand he has an escort with him so idiots like us can't go up and say hello."

MILE 11

A woman yells, "Way to go, John Hancock." There aren't many on this course who would confuse the sponsor singlet with the man who wears it.

MILE 12

"He's a marvelous person," enthuses a middle-aged woman at an impromptu aid station. "I can't believe he's running — 83 years old! I'm thrilled that he took our water."

We pass 12 miles a few seconds after Ibrahim Hussein wins his second Boston Marathon.

MILE 13

"I feel good!" shouts a man behind us, James-Brown-style. "I knew that I would."

His enthusiasm is wonderful, but nothing to match that of the women of Wellesley College up ahead, who whoop and scream like Arsenio Hall's studio audience upon learning that Tom Cruise is backstage. If this doesn't send Kelley into some kind of ecstatic time warp, nothing will.

MILE 14

We pass halfway in 2:25:49, and Kelley seems oblivious to the thunderous applause that greets him in the town of Wellesley. A runner jogs in front, pestering him with questions, until Kelley finally has to shout, "Get outta here!"

"Isn't he precious?" says one elderly woman. "He's just precious."

Precious and fragile and tired. And just over halfway.

MILE 15

"Kell-EE! Kell-EE! Kell-EE!" chants a group of about fifty revelers near the end of Wellesley.

MILE 16

The first sag wagons, yellow school buses with marathon dropouts on board, pass. We feel sprinkles of rain.

A man who must be at least 60 years old sees Kelley go by, picks up his metal crutches, bangs them together and shouts, "Go, Johnny!"

MILE 17

Going uphill out of Newton Lower Falls and passing over Route 28, Kelley's arms drop a little. He looks tired, and I wonder if this is normal.

A man standing near an on-ramp leans out and asks if he needs anything. This is Dan Kelley, Johnny's nephew, who tells me that Johnny's grandfather came to the United States on the S.S. Marathon. He also admits that his uncle seems to be having a hard time.

"I've never seen him look this bad before," he says, speculating that the cold is getting to him. Shortly afterward, it starts to rain.

MILE 18

"C'mon, hang in there!" yells a spectator. Is it my imagination, or are his fans starting to look worried? By the time we turn onto Commonwealth Avenue, the rain is pouring down. Over two hours to go!

MILE 19

"Oooh, he doesn't look too happy," I hear from underneath an umbrella.

MILE 20

The crowds are thin now, though people occasionally rush from their houses when they realize Kelley is passing.

Finally, Kelley reaches the top of his old nemesis, Heartbreak. His stride changes slightly, his determination redoubles, and he begins the shuffle through miles 22, 23, 24 and 25, among ever-increasing cheers.

"Don't let those troopers slow you down, Johnny!" shouts a spectator near Boston College.

"Way to go, Johnny!" yells a motorist.

"You're an institution!" shouts a heavy-set man who jogs in front of Kelley for a 100 yards before being waved to the side. "You're better than the Celtics!"

"We love you, Johnny! You're an inspiration to us all!"

With just over a mile to go, a truck passes in the opposite direction and appears to hit three 8-foot metal pipes, which come careening toward Kelley. For a moment, it looks like he might end his sixtieth Boston a mile from the finish, bowled over like a duckpin. But with his escorts' help, he scoots away safely.

"You've got it now!" shouts a man from the third story of a nearby brownstone. "Less than a mile to go!"

Kelley's nose is turning purple, and there are bags under his eyes, but he is finally allowing a smile to light his face. He knows he's going to make it. Passing the Eliot Lounge, bartender Tommy Leonard greets Kelley with a red nose of his own.

After turning onto Hereford Street and then Boylston for the final straightaway, Kelley grabs the hands of his police escorts, Coulter and Murphy, thanks them, and then turns into the Johnny Kelley I've always seen in race photos. Smiling, waving and giving a thumbs up, he travels the final quarter-mile to the finish, while sirens whoop-whoop-whoop, people shout encouragement from buildings along the way, and spectators jump up and down on the sidewalks next to him, taking time from picture-taking to give one more, "All right, Johnny!"

As the clock reaches 5:42:54, Johnny Kelley the Elder, the man who represents the heart and soul of the Boston Marathon, who twice in his life has crossed this line before anyone else, finishes again. He collapses into wife Laura's arms, and they tumble to the ground. A minute later the man who has completed his fifty-seventh Boston Marathon is pushed away in a wheelchair. After nearly six hours on his feet, he deserves a ride.

I don't know if Johnny Kelley will attempt another Boston. When I asked him before the race, he just said, "I hope so."

Someday, of course, he'll be done running from Hopkinton to Boston, and the chants of "John-NEE! John-NEE! John-NEE!" at the back of the Boston pack will be history, replaced by something else. But it's hard to imagine another runner replacing Johnny Kelley, surviving enough Patriots' Days to challenge his record.

Decades from now, someone may have a shot at it, and spectators will line the course as they do every year at Boston to watch. There will be buds on the branches in Wellesley and daffodils and azalea bushes in bloom. And some man standing alongside the road, cheering this phenomenon, may remember a day in April, 1991, when he stood as a child and watched an 83-year-old man set the standard.

And he will remember his father, turning to him and saying, "See that man there? He's 83 years old."

And he will remember asking, "What's his name, Dad?"

And the name will come drifting back in memory, timeless.

Johnny Kelley.

DIPSEA

"I realize and acknowledge," you tell some future judge as you sign the liability waiver, "that this event is a footrace over a rugged, narrow, unpaved, mountainous, rocky, steep and twisting course, which is not designed for running or for crowds."

VISUALIZATION IS AN IMPORTANT PART of prerace preparation, and I was at it with a mission.

I imagined those stairs, the Suicide drop-off into Scotch broom, and the bridge across Muir Creek. I pictured the trail through Muir Woods, up Cardiac Hill, past Lone Tree and the turnoff to Swoop Hollow. And I saw Insult, the path to the highway, the ocean down below and those false dots leading into the bushes, to nowhere, like a thought unfinished ...

What a way to go to sleep. This was the night before the eighty-first annual Dipsea, the second oldest running event in the United States, and I was in good company in my preslumber preoccupation with the particulars of the trail. Nearly 1,500 other runners were almost certainly enjoying a similar evening, mulling over visual clues and race strategy. And in so doing, they were connecting with a tradition that goes back to the turn of the century.

Imagine the San Francisco Bay Area in the early 1900s. Young, bold, brimming with immigrants and bravado. Marin County, just north of the city, must have seemed like one edge of the wilderness then, close enough to explore but wild enough to urge taming.

During a hiking expedition over Marin's popular Lone Tree Trail near Stinson Beach in 1904, members of San Francisco's Olympic Club discovered the Dipsea Inn, a lodge of uncertain nomenclature built in anticipation of future development in the area. The group immediately set to work draining the establishment of its refreshments, and before they had finished, an idea had quite naturally fermented its way into the group's consciousness. It became absolutely imperative to find out which member of this group — Charlie Boas or Al Coney — could travel faster from Mill Valley to the Dipsea Inn, one rugged 8-mile trek across the flank of Mt. Tamalpais.

A race was arranged, boisterous bets were laid, and Boas won. Later, when the group had sobered up enough to evaluate the day, they realized they were onto something.

The hiking enthusiasts dubbed themselves the "Dipsea Indians." They elected a Grand Chief, Scribe, Medicine Man, and so on, and they began to organize the first open race along what would eventually be called the Dipsea Trail.

On November 19, 1905, eighty-four willing souls braved wet weather and self-doubt in the first cross country race sponsored by the Dipsea Indians. They came from clubs and schools from throughout the Bay Area, traveling by ferry to Sausalito, by train to Mill Valley, and finally, of course, by fleet foot to Stinson Beach. Seventeen-year-old John Hassard of Oakland arrived first. Forty-seven-year-old Isaac Day finished near the back of the pack, wearing a corduroy suit and hobnailed boots. The Dipsea was off and running.

The race caught the imagination of northern Californians, no doubt stirred by newspaper accounts of exhausted runners chasing each other up steep hillsides, careening down treacherous gullies and collapsing in the sand. By 1908, sportswriter W.O. "Bill" McGeehan would capture the spirit of the race and of the age in verse:

> *There's a patter of feet on the Lone Pine Ridge,*
> *And the whir of the frightened quail;*
> *Now the white forms flash in the shimmering green,*
> *And they're off on the Dipsea Trail.*

And on they pattered, year after year, clear to the end of the century. There have been two lapses when the Dipsea was not held, one during the Depression years of 1932 to '33, the other during World War II, 1942 to '45. Otherwise, the race has been engaging the imaginations of aficionados ever since Boas and Coney first settled their wager.

Its success spawned the creation of San Francisco's Cross City Race in 1913, which grew to become the world's largest road race, Bay to Breakers. The Dipsea has inspired the written word and visual interpretation, too, including the film *On the Edge.*

But most important, the Dipsea connects the present generation of runners to a rich athletic history, just as the Boston Marathon does. While the world has changed, the Dipsea has remained mostly constant, a tradition that springs from three elements: a treacherous course, a beguiling handicapping system and a mystique that borders playfully on the occult.

Consider, first, the course.

"I realize and acknowledge," you tell some future judge as you sign the liability waiver, "that this event is a footrace over a rugged, narrow, unpaved, mountainous, rocky, steep and twisting course, which is not designed for running or for crowds."

Nobody — trust me on this one — would design this course in today's world. But there it is, a remnant of a less litigious past. And remember, you signed the waiver.

Even the word "course" should be taken with a grain of salt. Though the first Dipsea race was reported to be well-marked with confetti, over the years the basic premise of the race has been athletic anarchy. As long as you start at A and get to B, you're welcome to explore C, L, or even Z in between.

Dipsea has struggled to retain this "open course" distinction, and though it has suffered under late twentieth century realities, the principle still holds. Much of Dipsea lore has to do with heroic attempts to find new, ever more bizarre and convoluted shortcuts to Stinson Beach. Really off-the-wall shortcuts often get nixed for future races, but in the meantime the inventive mind is celebrated.

Second, there is this bit about handicaps. From the beginning, the Dipsea Indians tried to make their event interesting by leveling the playing field. Or perhaps making it less level for some than others. In any case, handicaps were assigned based on information available about each runner's ability. That system was used until 1965, when the process was adjusted so that handicaps were developed according to previous age-group performances in the race.

Handicaps equal head starts. As a result, the spice of the Dipsea is the question of how fast the fastest will be willing to push the edge of reason to catch up to the slowest. Not forgetting, by the way, that rugged, narrow, unpaved, mountainous, rocky, steep and twisting course.

Third, there is this certain mystique about the Dipsea — a fusion of history and myth that erupts into poetry at the least provocation.

Every spring, for example, members of the Tamalpa Runners of Marin County officially "open" the Dipsea trail. In keeping with the primal sanctity of Mt. Tamalpais, the opening ceremony includes poetry readings by various running "gods and goddesses" of the region, many of them past winners of the Dipsea.

"Tamalpais. Sleeping maiden. Queen of the Hills surrounding the bay," began the ode of Maryetta Boitano in 1979. Her poem, written six years after she won the race at age 10, is a fitting evocation of the ancient spirit of the mountain and the native myths surrounding it. The Dipsea Indians would have beamed.

And Eve Pell, who went on to win the race three months later, offered her own poem in 1989, which began (and ended):

> *Can you run it? Can you win it?*
> *Will you finish? Will you fall?*
> *It's the Dipsea down to Stinson*
> *And it fascinates us all.*

By the time I line up in downtown Mill Valley, I have been thoroughly immersed in Dipsea verse, lore and strategy. I've read the history of the event, *The Dipsea Race*, by Mark Reese. I've been coached by Jim Furman of the Tamalpa Runners on the ins and outs of the course. And I have spent the previous evening submerged in mental imagery. Now, I will confront the thing myself.

With a slim 3-minute handicap as a 42-year-old male, I'm starting in the twenty-second group of the invited section. I'll have to pass hundreds of runners to get toward the front.

Fairness aside, handicapping is a reasonable way of spreading runners out over a narrow course. Due to high demand, the Dipsea Race Committee, which now manages the event, has had to set up a strictly regulated entry system that includes some first-come-first-served, some auctioned entries, some invitations and a lottery. Each year, hundreds of runners have to be turned away. It is *not* easy to get into this race.

"Three separate people this year requested entry based on their having terminal illnesses," reported Jim Furman in the 1990 *Tamalpa Gazette.*

Even spread out as we are, it's a mad scramble over the initial half-mile to the first set of steps. There are three flights, 671 steps in all, and only enough width for two runners. Instant gridlock.

Heading up the steps, I find myself alternately trying to squeeze by and being squeezed by. At one point, as I try to negotiate past the runner ahead, the guy behind grabs me and lifts me to the side.

"Move to the right if you're walking!" someone shouts, even though everybody seems to be walking.

I decide to follow a tall masters runner named John Cobourn, a bearded graduate of Brown University who is wearing a red hat. I figure that, being a Dipsea veteran runner and about my ability, he will be a good guide. That works. For a while.

About a half-mile after the top of the steps is the crest of the first hill, a place called Windy Gap. The original route cut straight across here, but we have to turn right and follow the highway for a few hundred yards. The "open course" has suffered repeatedly in recent years due to new homes, traffic problems and the concerns of park rangers.

The change is unfortunate, since so many Dipsea legends have to do with clever shortcuts. It was here at Windy Gap in 1937 that Norm Bright veered onto his own path, following wooden pointers he had nailed in the trees, and charged on to a new Dipsea record. Thirty-three years later, Bright was up to his old tricks again, using a strategically placed Coke can to mark the shortcut at Windy Gap and racing on to another victory.

Just before the two-mile point, I chase the runners ahead down the first big downhill, called Suicide. Suddenly, "open course" is a real concept again. A variety of paths, none desirable, unfold in front of me, while my "guide," Cobourn, has disappeared into the bushes ahead.

I remember Furman's advice to go left at the first turn, but in my anxiousness to avoid falling, I end up taking the wrong path through the Scotch broom. Grabbing onto the bushes in my desperate descent, I manage to implant slivers that I will be removing from my hands for weeks afterward.

I'm pleased to reach the bottom of this hill and rejoin the main stream of runners with only slivers to whine about. I've known at least one runner who fell here and became so disoriented that he wandered through the woods lost for almost two hours. And another Dipsea runner, Ray Locke, remains here *for eternity*. After several years as a participant, Locke completed his final Dipsea in 1924 at age 66. Obviously enthralled with the course, he asked that, upon his death, his ashes be scattered along this section of the course. In 1932, his son carried out his wishes.

At the bottom of Suicide I cross a road, traverse Muir Creek by way of a wooden bridge, and start up Dynamite Hill. The trail here is a narrow path of switchbacks, and it's packed with runners.

I consider taking a shortcut through the bushes, but I've heard enough about poison oak to think twice about it. And I recall seeing a victim at the starting line, a pleasant man with a fist-sized open sore on his leg, oozing orange pus.

"Is that orange stuff ointment?" I asked.

"No," he answered. "It just weeps like that sometimes."

I elect to stay on the trail.

After reaching the top of Dynamite, we travel through various weather systems for the next two miles, from fog to sunshine to a section of forest where it seems to be raining. This is sometimes called the Rainforest, and it's a misty, wonderfully mysterious sort of place. It's the kind of area that inspired 10-year-old, 1973 winner Maryetta Boitano to comment, "I thought a bear might come and eat me up, and I heard of incidents of sighted mountain lions and rattlers. So I guess being afraid of the Dipsea made me really excel to my fullest."

It is also a slippery, rocky place, and I take my first spill, hitting my shoulder. No problem, just part of the game. If you don't collect a few mud-spattered, blood-encrusted wounds along the trail, you haven't really tried.

"People who care about their bodies are at a real disadvantage in this race," I remember a friend of mine remarking.

After recovering from my fall, I make it past the 4-mile mark to the top of Cardiac with no further problems, unless you consider screaming quads, wheezing, and runners screeching by to be problems.

I try to ignore them and enjoy the view from the top — the deep greens of the forest, the golden meadows, the ocean below and the fog rolling over the top of Tamalpais like a vaporous spell. By now, though, I'm a bit nauseous from the climb and essentially oblivious to beauty.

A minute later, though, I'm at full speed, first in Swoop Hollow, then plummeting down the sheer, rocky incline of Steep Ravine, where overhanging tree limbs and slick wooden steps put me on the edge of insanity. A guy passes me, somehow going twice the edgy speed of insanity.

As we find out later, the first person to come through here was 9-year-old Megan McGowan. She held her lead all the way to the finish, beating favorites like 54-year-old Eve Pell, 25-year-old Mike McManus, who will set the fastest time ever on the new, restricted course, and five-time Dipsea winner Sal Vasquez, 51, who has injured his calf on Suicide.

McGowan has been over the course repeatedly with her father in the weeks leading up to the race, so she knows how to thread the needle in the ravine. Still, is this a good place for a 9-year-old girl to be running?

I don't know. Who should or shouldn't run here? Back in 1922, Dipsea officials bowed to pressure from Bay Area churches and physicians and suspended the extremely popular Women's Dipsea Hikes, which had been going on since 1918.

Apparently, the physicians thought that women's bodies were unsuited to stressful hikes. The concerns of churches seemed to be about the hiking costumes popular at the time. Maybe church leaders were anticipating the fall of Frank Grundish in Steep Ravine in 1948. Grundish took a spill nasty enough that he lost his running shorts, although he did reach the finish line. Clad only in shoes, jersey and supporter.

In 1950, despite Amateur Athletic Union (AAU) rules prohibiting mixed-sex racing, women entered the regular Dipsea for the first time. By the 1968 race, 5-year-old Maryetta Boitano would be the first "woman" to finish, and the next year women were allowed to enter officially.

At any rate, women, children and everyone in between now seem to handle Steep Ravine reasonably well. Once through it, the gully turns into an uphill that, after all the preceding struggle, has earned the name "Insult." At the top of this hill, I head out to the highway and can see Stinson Beach below.

I pass the false white dots, which appeared inexplicably before the race a few years ago and which lead down a gully to a dead-end in the bushes. Was this an act of misdirected humor, ill spirit or a desperate attempt to mislead the competition? And who was the perpetrator? No one seems to know.

I move on, follow the next set of dots into the bushes and take my second fall of the day, down a slippery embankment. I manage to roll out of the way of the runner behind me, avoiding trampling. By this point, I have just about realized that there are too many pitfalls on this course to get obsessed with fast times. I will simply cruise in, I tell myself. I will simply survive. And then I hear it.

" ... 35, 36, 37 ... " shouts an official as I pass. I'm thirty-seventh. Thirty-five finishers will get one of those wonderful, sequentially numbered black Dipsea shirts. Those things are *precious*. And here I am, right on the shirt/no-shirt border.

So I pick up the pace down another sharp path, pass one runner who takes a wrong turn into an open field, and pass two more after we jump the stile at the end of the meadow a half-mile from the finish. By the time I reach the finish, I have snuck up a few more notches to earn thirty-first place and a coveted Dipsea shirt.

Soon, hundreds of people are finishing and heading to the showers to rinse off dirt, blood and the possible kiss of poison oak. It's an exuberant crowd that shares war stories, beer and hot dogs the rest of the day.

Winner Megan McGowan walks by, enthusing, as a youngster should, "I won! I won!"

Later, at the awards ceremony, Eve Pell will say, "When I woke up this morning, I thought the motto of the day would be, 'Age before beauty.' Later, I realized it would be, 'Youth must be served.' " Five-time winner Sal Vasquez, in turn, will lift McGowan in his arms, he himself unruffled by his injured calf and lower-than-usual fifth place finish.

But the most inspiring runner of the day is 84-year-old Jack Kirk, the white-haired "Dipsea Demon," the Johnny Kelley of these parts. Kirk finishes his fifty-sixth consecutive Dipsea, wearing a long-sleeved gray dress-shirt with a yellow T-shirt over it, khaki leisure pants and canvas deck shoes. He shuffles to the finish, looking like Spencer Tracy in a hurry.

It was sixty-one years ago, 1930, when Kirk first answered the Dipsea call. In 1951 and 1967, he won the race. In 1931 and 1940, he ran the fastest time. He has been to Stinson Beach hundreds of times since 1930, but never, he claims, by car.

One day, Jack Kirk will be another Dipsea legend. Today, he uses a 22-minute handicap to finish in 2 hours, 11 minutes and 28 seconds.

Kirk is almost as old as the Dipsea itself. He's old enough to remember Bill McGeehan's words when they were nearly fresh on the page in 1908, words that gave poetic voice to the event that would inflame the passions and disturb the late-night slumber of runners for the rest of the twentieth century:

> *Oh, the eyes that are bloodshot, the lips that are white,*
> *And the stiff limbs that falter and fail;*
> *For it's no place for weaklings — the grueling course*
> *Of the men of the Dipsea Trail.*

The original Dipsea was the province of men, and today's race belongs to a 9-year-old girl. But somehow it all still works, here in the final decade of the century. Enormous changes have transformed the world, but none of these seem to have dampened the enthusiasm of those seeking to test themselves on this anachronism of a race course.

I look at my hands and see the slivers. I brush some mud off my knees. And I begin imagining places along the trail where I could have picked up a place or two.

August 1991

Wooooo, pig!

Perhaps, my oxygen-deprived brain reasons, I really am from Arkansas. Otherwise, what were those eighteen hours on the bus all about?

IF THERE WAS ONE MOMENT when I felt truly in sync with the journey, it was when our bus eased around a turn and I could finally see that mountain, looming haughtily in the distance, a granite thug on the Colorado landscape.

Or maybe it was earlier on the trip, when Stephen Tucker, a doctor by profession but a two-footed traveler by avocation, took off his shoes and socks right there in the middle of the bus, gathered all of us around as if he were about to impart the wisdom of the ages, and began wrapping silver duct tape — insurance against black toenails — around his naked toes, while the Oklahoma landscape raced past us at better than a mile a minute.

No, come to think of it, it was right at the beginning, as we boarded the buses in Little Rock. Somewhat overwhelmed at joining this group of 100-plus Arkansans, people I had never met before but who would be my traveling companions for the next five days, I was thinking about how best to break the ice when Arthur Kerns — lawyer, runner and my airport chauffeur — propped me up in front of all of those Arkansas Pikes Peak pilgrims and welcomed me in a fashion that can only be appreciated by those who know the revered traditions of Arkansas society.

"Wooooooo, pig!" they chimed in unison, as I stood there with what appeared to be a compact red pig nesting on my head — the traditional Arkansas Razorback "Hawg Hat." "Soooiiieeeeeeee!"

Thus initiated, I boarded the bus and headed for Colorado.

There are some fairly improbable things in our world, but somehow the notion of three busloads of flatlanders driving eighteen hours so they can attempt to run to the roof of the Rockies deserves a mention.

Technically, of course, Arkansans didn't invent the Pikes Peak run. The first race was held on August 10, 1956, a challenge between three smokers and eight non-smokers, none of them Arkansans. The fastest non-smoker made the round trip in 5:39:58. Only one smoker reached the summit, then promptly quit (the race, not the habit). Apparently, 26 miles was too far to walk for a Camel.

Though the issue of emphysema was largely settled in the first race, the question of who could climb from the 6,200-foot starting line in Manitou Springs to the 14,110-foot summit and back continued to capture the imagination. Over the years, the lure of the challenge spread. By 1991, the thirty-sixth annual Pikes Peak Marathon had 750 people filling all available spaces, with another 1,750 tackling the one-way Ascent, held a day earlier.

Most of those entrants come from Colorado, which seems reasonable, since they're already living there a mile in the sky. But the second-most Pikes-Peak-intoxicated state is not Utah or Arizona or anything else in the neighborhood, but rather (Soooiiieeee!) Arkansas.

According to records of the mostly official Pikes Peak Marathon Society, the first Hawg to make the top of the mountain was Max Hooper, an ultramarathon runner from Little Rock who completed the round trip in 1976. A smattering of Arkansans, apparently inspired by Hooper's success, made the trek in the next few years.

But what really started the buses rolling was the 1983 entry of one Ken Ropp. An unassuming businessman from Little Rock, Ropp was inspired enough by his own run to the top to become somewhat of a Rocky Mountain aerobic evangelist. For Ropp, Pikes Peak became a way to bring Arkansas runners together and introduce them to a unique challenge amid some spectacular geography.

"You can't find a better setting than the mountains," says Ropp. "They're so beautiful. And the magnitude of the run is such that it's really an accomplishment just to compete in it."

Ropp began a beguiling recruitment around Little Rock, managing to convince unlikely candidates that they could, indeed should, try to make the Pikes Peak journey. In 1984, three Arkansans followed Ropp's advice and earned a spot in "the Society." In 1985, six. The Pikes Peak Marathon Society was growing by leaps and bounds. In 1986, the number grew to twenty-one, inspiring the Society to rename Pikes Peak "Mount Arkansas," though Coloradans seemed not to notice.

Whatever its name, though, more and more Arkansans were developing a hankering to get up it. By the time I was invited to come along in August 1991, the pilgrimage to Pikes Peak required three buses to carry runners, spouses and friends, with even more Hawgs traveling by air and auto. In all, 141 were signed up to run.

In case the unlikelihood of this may not have sunk in, try imagining a town in which citizens have just enjoyed a pleasant spring of dogwood and azaleas, but where life is hurtling toward its customary ill-tempered, sultry summer mood. Most people head indoors, turn on their air conditioners and wait for football season. Not these Hawgs. They choose to defy the seasonal downturn and begin training for the August assault on Pikes Peak.

"I look back over last year's training log," wrote Charlotte Davis in the 1991 Society training book, "and I realize the hardest part of the Pikes Peak Marathon is the preparation — training in the sweltering Arkansas summer heat, getting up at 4 a.m. on Saturday or Sunday to run with the group. Of course, all that hard work pays off. It makes what seems impossible, possible."

Consistent training is the key. Knowing this, more than a 100 runners sometimes show up at Society meetings to train for the impossible — or at least the improbable and illogical — and to hear veterans dispense high-altitude athletic secrets. Little Rock is only 286 feet above sea level, and the highest point in the state is just under 3,000 feet. Scared breathless, novices listen for hints on how to outsmart Pikes Peak, whose summit offers 40 percent less oxygen than home. Mostly, they run uphill a lot and practice drinking fluids.

By the time they've completed the process, runners will be deluged with training guides and information, T-shirts, shorts, posters, gloves, pins, hats, bumper stickers, certificates and a mostly personalized letter of encouragement from Arkansas Governor Bill Clinton.

And then one day they find themselves on a bus galloping across Oklahoma, watching some guy wrap his toes with duct tape.

"He's giving us a 15-minute demonstration," announces Arthur Kerns, "so he can write this whole trip off. And then he's going to send us all bills."

It's a long journey, during which even a man's toes can seem interesting.

When enough time and scenery have passed, the big sky darkens, and our proud little caravan pulls into a rest stop. We convert the seats in our three rigs into sleepers, or at least to horizontal quasi-beds. For the next eight hours, we pilgrims will travel surrounded by dozens of our equally horizontal, tightly packed new best friends. Close quarters certainly, but I sleep soundly, secure in hawg heaven.

Many hours and several states later, we pull into the Silver Saddle Motel in Manitou Springs, Colorado. It's 10 a.m. on Friday, and the Society has already annexed the motel for the weekend. Railings are bedecked with Arkansas flags and banners.

"Welcome Arkansas Pain Lovers," announces one. "The *Marquis de Sade.*"

The Marquis, occasionally known as Jim Johnson, is a 56-year-old advertising executive from Little Rock, who made his first Pikes Peak journey in 1979. He is also the founder of the Marquis de Sade Running Club, an organization with no dues, no meetings, and not much else that might normally be expected of a club, although they do have a lot of bumper stickers, paraphernalia and strange ideas about amusement. Like running Pikes Peak.

This year, the Marquis is sporting long locks on the perimeter of his balding skull, a promise made to his 17-year-old son Alex. "Run the Pikes Peak Marathon and I won't cut my hair," he told the kid. What teenager could resist that? Now, Johnson must dodge endless comparisons of himself with Ben Franklin.

The Silver Saddle, with real beds and a large hot tub, is base camp for the Arkansas assault, as well as a crucial part of Society lore. The story is told, for example, that in 1985 runner Larry Cook returned to the motel after successfully completing the round trip, then asked his fellow Arkansans to go to their rooms and retrieve their Gideons. Eventually, the story goes, Cook put his hand on a stack of seventeen bibles and swore never to run the Peak again.

Cook, who is on this trip, claims the story is apocryphal, although he admits the sentiment is accurate.

"I don't know why I'm here," he says, not quite moaning. "It's terrible. It's horrible. It's the toughest thing I've ever done in my life."

So much for the pep talk.

The next morning, I walk out of my room and take a look at the mountain, pink-hued at dawn. It's a 13-mile journey by trail to the summit, but it looks much, much longer than that. On the tippy-top, up among the stars, I see a pure white light blinking, beckoning.

At the starting line a few minutes later, I listen eagerly for last minute bits of wisdom.

"Get up with the guys in front," advises Dr. Tucker, "because it's too hard to pass on the trail."

"Let me give you a real bit of advice," interjects Arthur Kerns, who has overheard Tucker. "Don't do that. Stay back and take it easy."

Before long, I'm scuttling up the narrow trail, switchbacking in a conga line of runners. Instincts developed through years of cross country running, that urge me to take advantage of tangents and openings in the crowd, are worthless. In the end I settle back and just keep climbing, antlike, following the critters ahead.

After about 40 minutes, the trail flattens out for the first time since the start, and I relish the brief respite. A few minutes later I pass an aid station at French Creek, manned largely by Arkansas volunteers.

"Go, Arkie!" someone yells, seeing my Society T-shirt. It startles me.

I'm very comfortable at this point, but it's still early, and I haven't forgotten the warning in the runner instruction booklet: "Typical medical problems encountered during this race are altitude sickness, hypothermia, hyperthermia, heat exhaustion, dehydration, cramps, foot blisters, cuts/abrasions, sprained knees and ankles and bee stings."

So far so good, here at 9,000 feet. Not even a bee sting. But like most first-timers, I'm headed for higher ground than I've ever trod before, and I'm wary, especially of dehydration and altitude sickness. My mouth is dry, but breathing seems fine at this point, so I wonder when the effects of altitude might zap me. Reams of information about altitude problems have been provided by the Society, but the most graphic is a report by the Marquis on a 1986 episode.

"I must have stood up too fast," he wrote, "because a dizzy feeling slowly spun the horizon to vertical. I rolled out across the trail looking up in the trees. It was rather nice lying there alone on my back in the middle of the trail. The clouds were nice."

Most descriptions don't sound nearly this friendly. Altitude sickness is capricious and nasty, and only a timely descent to lower elevations can alleviate it. Cautiously, I monitor for danger signals and, finding none, continue running.

After climbing steadily through the woods for more than an hour, I begin to look forward to breaking into a clearing and seeing my goal. When I finally do, it amazes me. Pikes Peak is still way, way up there.

Near Barr Camp, I hear medical personnel yell, "Halfway!" and I realize I'm starting to experience shortness of breath. In a while, I begin alternating walking and jogging. Jogging is a little faster. Walking is a lot easier. On I trudge, power-walking up the mountain.

This is a good time to remember the "Three Steps to Running the Peak," as offered by the Society: 1) Run until that gets too hard. 2) Walk until that gets too easy. 3) Repeat steps one and two until the finish line is behind you.

At about 2 hours, I pass through a few hundred meters of twisted, bleached-out ghost pines, the last, stubborn trees on the mountain. I'm at about 12,000 feet now, and above the tree line there is only a steep, rocky climb left, through what seems to be a perpetual field of boulders.

"Two and a half miles to go," says a volunteer as I pass. I do what little figuring shortness of oxygen will allow, and determine I have a chance to break 3 hours. Bad time to find a new goal.

I can manage very little running, or even jogging, anymore, just the steady fast-walk up the face of the mountain, accompanied by lots of huffing and a slight pounding in my temples.

I find myself battling a mild case of vertigo as I look out and down to the trail below. It is a spectacular, cloudless morning, something that doesn't always happen here. In fact, I almost wish for the kind of fog they've encountered in past Pikes Peak races to muffle my fear of heights.

Finally, though, I hear shouts from the top and realize I'm closing in. As I enter the final climb, a series of switchbacks called the Sixteen Golden Stairs, I try to count them, but lose track at five.

I'm running this last section of the climb with Bill Coffelt, an Arkansas ultrarunner who is using today's ascent as a tune-up for tomorrow's round trip.

"I have found that 16 to 18 miles of repeats is a good maximum," Coffelt once advised potential peakers, speaking of uphill mile repeats. For most, he might just as well have advised flying.

Periodically, people shout, "Go, Arkansas!" at both of us. Perhaps, my oxygen-deprived brain reasons, I really am from Arkansas. Otherwise, what were those eighteen hours on the bus all about?

Quads, calves and hamstrings are all tight and tired now, but I realize I'm going to avoid disaster and reach the summit. At 2:56 I cross the line. Nearby, speakers are blasting an old Beatles tune. "Fool on the Hill"?

Up here among the angels, runners have been greeted with hail, fog, rain, snow, thunder and lightning. Today, it is simply a spectacular sunny day, with a view to the ends of the earth. It is the kind of morning that inspired Katherine Lee Bates to write "America the Beautiful" after a trip to this point in 1893.

Nearby, Scott Elliott, who eats, sleeps and trains on this mountain for three weeks each year, and who won today's climb in 2:12, seems amazingly fresh. The last time I saw Elliott was a year and a half ago, when he won the Empire State Building Run Up. Today, I believe I can almost see that New York City landmark from where I stand.

I can also see way down the mountain, past the switchbacks, into the forested downslopes to Manitou Springs, and it seems to be a long, long way. I am proud of my journey, pleased to have reached the top, happy to be enjoying this spectacular view.

More than anything, though, I'm hearing the whining in my muscles, which makes me very, very happy about one other thing: I don't have to run back down.

By the next morning, those who are doing the full marathon and *will* have to run back down are lining up in Manitou Springs. I hike weary-legged with the rest of the Arkansas crew to the 4-mile point at French Creek and help set up the aid station, then shout encouragement, pass out water and refill bottles until the last of the round trippers is headed up the trail. Hours later, I hike back down to Manitou Springs and watch them finish.

There, announcer Roger Ellison stands dressed like Zebulon Pike, the army officer and explorer who discovered this mountain in 1806. The look-alike congratulates people from age 16 to 73, finishers of this year's race. The real Pike once failed to reach the top, calling the feat impossible. Now his likeness welcomes modern-day adventurers with great enthusiasm, as if the spirit of old Zeb can't quite believe what he sees.

Along with looking quad-thumped and dragged-out tired, most round trippers seem to have suffered a spill or two on the descent, displaying bunged-up knees, abrasions and raspberries. Most falls are painful but not dangerous, lessons in caution.

"I was skippin' from rock to rock like a bighorn ram," says Society member Dale Stiles later, relating the fall that bruised his hip. "And that was about when I went whomp! I ran down from there like a big cautious dog."

I have to admit that, in spite of hearing stories such as this, I am feeling just a bit envious of those who have made it both ways. Maybe another year?

Of course, in the world of adventure running, no feat stands unanswered. If you run up a mountain, someone else will run down as well. If you run both ways, someone will no doubt mention that they did the ascent the day before to get ready for the round trip. And so on.

On this weekend, Coloradans Scott Weber and Marshall Ulrich will complete four Pikes Peak round trips, catnapping next to the trail along the way. I am tempted to ask about duct tape, when I learn that Ulrich has had his toenails surgically removed. Hearing this, I steer clear.

Most finishers today, though, are not supermen without toenails.

They are simply human beings who have decided to push against the personal edges of the possible. Like many of my busmates, for example, people I share stories with on the trip back to Little Rock the next day. Like sisters Martha Rogers and Rosemary Haluzka, who rendezvoused with two more sisters in Colorado and made the summit a successful family quest. Or 50-year-old George Ann Billingsley, who startled her family a few years ago when she, a total non-runner, began training for a five-mile race. Now, she can tell her children about the view from the top of the Rockies.

Not every Arkansan makes it. In a postrace bus survey conducted by Celia Storey, a columnist for the *Arkansas Democrat*, eleven of seventy-five confess to not making the top, including Celia. More than a third of those surveyed report symptoms of altitude sickness, including "slight headache, headache, backache, slight dizziness, dizziness, nausea, vomiting, dry heaves, severe diarrhea, disorientation, lightheadedness, lethargy, hallucinations, palpitations, sleepiness, tingling fingers, ear pressure and gas."

In spite of these problems, or maybe because of them, Arkansans on the return trip will show an amazingly high rate of interest in poetry and existential philosophy.

"I will marry this rock," writes Celia Storey. "I will bear his fern- and sun-flecked children. I will never move again."

Humor helps. An anonymous Somebody pens this limerick:

> *There once was a peak named for Pike.*
> *A mountain that's not meant for tykes.*
> *I think that it's clear,*
> *The next time I'm here,*
> *I'll make the descent on my bike.*

There is, after all, eighteen hours on the road home to try to make sense of the experience. Mostly this is a personal task, an attempt to impose meaning on the scramble up a heartless mass of granite. If you make it, you feel blessed.

"Thirty years from now," writes Jim Sweatt, "who will remember what I did on Pikes Peak? I will."

And if you don't make it, you remember the attempt, pride yourself on it, and remember that you're not alone. Like Celia Storey's husband and fellow columnist Michael; he was turned back during the Ascent but drove to the top the next day to cheer on his teammates.

"Calling the hawgs for four hours at 14,110 feet," he wrote, "is almost a religious experience."

This was a team assault, and the camaraderie is palpable.

"We are pleased to report," Celia Storey will sum up, tongue-in-cheek as always, in the final newsletter of an especially animated crowd from Bus 3, "that from our little experience together, four engagements have been announced, three shaky marriages have been saved, two folks have found 'significant others,' six people reported meaningful religious epiphanies, two have become blood brothers, and eight people had out-of-body experiences. All-in-all quite a time."

Enough of a time that even as they swear never to attempt the impossible again, they are already planning for next year.

In the end, they seem to know that, like many "impossible" tasks, this one is within reach. You don't need to be a bighorn sheep to make it to the top of Pikes Peak. The buses are filled with people just about like you, and many of them have just earned a spot in the over-200-strong Arkansas Pikes Peak Marathon Society, earning these words of praise: "Said person has paid his dues for life and commands the respect of his peers forever and ever."

What does it take? The Jackalope Award, which is given to members who conquer the mountain twice, offers this view: "Nerve, persistence and pure dumb luck are all you need to make the 'impossible' come true."

Of course, I couldn't help but notice there's one other thing that seems to help. Being a Hawg.

Wooooooo, pig! Soooiiieeeeeeee!

February 1992

HO CHI MINH CITY MARATHON

As marathoners, we play with this notion of survival. In real life, in times of war and peace, it sometimes becomes the only thing a human can focus on.

I WAS NEARING 20 KILOMETERS, not quite halfway through this sweaty stewpot of a marathon. Almost from the start, I had been feeling a tightness in my right calf. I wondered if I would suffer another muscle pull, the bane of my life as a masters runner. Perhaps, I thought, I will reinjure it, limp around for weeks, and pique people's curiosity back home.

"What happened to your leg?" they would ask.

"I injured it in Vietnam," I would answer.

Somehow that struck me as funny, a bit of incongruity to lighten the marathon load. I never served in Vietnam. I did my utmost, in fact, to avoid involvement in a war that seemed totally wrong, a vicious, dead-end quagmire of American foreign policy. So to consider limping from a Vietnam injury sustained twenty years after the war seemed funny. Sort of. Maybe if there hadn't been disabled Vietnam veterans on this trip, it would have been funnier.

Running through the Thu Duc marketplace, I caught up to two young Vietnamese runners. One of them turned and asked me something, but I couldn't understand. He repeated the question, but to no avail. Thus stymied by our inability to communicate, we tacitly agreed to run side by side for a while, past cheering spectators, market stalls and three young girls dressed in what looked like scout uniforms, beating drums. They smiled, we smiled, and in spite of the heat and humidity, the long road ahead seemed kinder.

Then, climbing one of the only hills on the course, we passed more spectators, eased through the pungent smoke of a cooking fire, and I left the two Vietnamese behind. I was closing in on another runner, and I recognized him from behind. Actually, I recognized the singlet — stars and stripes. Even though I knew he would be dressed in the flag, the sight startled me.

The runner was Jim Barker, a Vietnam vet and San Francisco Bay Area veterans center counselor. Barker had traveled here to the former city of Saigon along with three wheelchair-bound vets to run in the first International Ho Chi Minh City Marathon. The wheelchair athletes, after what seemed like an endless dialogue with Vietnamese officials, had finally been refused permission to run. Barker, able-bodied, had gone ahead and entered as planned, and was now midway through a marathon that sometimes seemed a simple if torturous act of sport, at others an epic journey of spirit and emotion.

Looking on from behind, I was struck by the enormity of it, or perhaps the irony. Two decades after the Vietnam war, a conflict that ripped through Southeast Asia and split the United States more savagely than anything since the Civil War, it had come down to this simple image of peace. Barker had once gone on training runs through the central highlands of this country as an army intelligence officer, wondering if God or blind luck would protect him from Vietcong snipers.

"I always held on to this dumb faith," he said, "that I was going to look so eccentric that even the enemy would wave."

Now he was running through a swarm of Vietnamese spectators with an American flag stitched into his running clothes. Absolutely defenseless. And hurting like hell.

"I was really beginning to feel the buildup of the humidity and the heat," Barker told me later. "Internally, I was starting to focus less on being real competitive and more on trying to pace myself in a way that would ensure consistency and dignity to the finish."

Earlier that morning, before heat and fatigue had challenged will power, Barker's experience had been somewhat different. In the first miles, the very fact of being back in Vietnam, and of being greeted warmly, had been overwhelming.

"Kind of a bursting sense of exhilaration," said Barker, "and of freedom and joy. The thrill of being alive, the thrill of being out there and of being in a very positive rapport, reciprocated from the Vietnamese community."

Americans who served in Vietnam remember it mainly as a land of imminent danger — death lurking behind every bush and building. But today, Barker was enjoying a different reception.

"It was all very, very positive," said the man wearing the flag, who speaks Vietnamese fluently. "It was 'USA number 1!' and 'American, hooray, hooray!' That kind of thing."

Now, though, as Barker and I passed the halfway point and headed through Sunday morning traffic on the Korean Highway, the shouts from the crowd seemed to help less and less. The sun was beating on our backs and climbing higher in the sky. We wondered how far it would be to the next water stop. The marathon itself, not camaraderie or history or politics, was on the front burner.

"I saw at that point," said Barker, "that this was going to be a long day on the Plains of Marathon."

Everything struck me as bizarre when I woke that morning, which was not surprising, since it was 4:30, darkly humid outside, and I was about to run a marathon through the streets of Ho Chi Minh City.

I fussed around with the usual marathon questions, most of them having to do with placement of pins and vaseline. I imagined dropping out midrace and having to hail a pedicab. To be safe, I stuck a $5 bill in the key pocket of my shorts. Finally, after filling two water bottles to the brim, I headed to the lobby.

Like many other foreigners in town for the marathon, I was staying in the Saigon Floating Hotel. The hotel had been towed to Vietnam from the Great Barrier Reef a few years ago by Japanese businessmen and was moored in the Saigon River. It reminded me of a Swedish cruise ship. The bellboys dressed like swabbies in pastel green sailor outfits and berets with white pom-poms on top, and the maids always remembered to fold the toilet paper. "Welcome to Vietnam!" said the information sheet for runners at the front desk. "Check with your hotel or tour operator to register with police within 48 hours."

Bill Rodgers was doing some last-minute carbo-and-caffeine loading in the hotel cafe with his friend, Mark Callahan. Rodgers was the marathon's invited runner and prerace favorite, and Callahan had come along for the run. Ironically, it was Rodgers' conscientious objector status during the Vietnam War that, by causing his relocation to Boston for hospital work, provided fertile ground for his marathon talents. Now, the marathon had brought Rodgers to Vietnam.

Outside the hotel it was still dark, and people were just beginning to wake as I walked to the start about a half-mile away. In doorways, I could see a lighted cigarette or two and the dim glow of human faces. Here and there, the smell of rotting vegetables or a whiff of incense caught my nostrils. Upstairs in one building came the anxious cry of a hungry baby. Ho Chi Minh City is said to have 4 million inhabitants, almost all of them living at subsistence level or worse. In the midst of this, I was on my way to the start of a marathon.

The starting line was on Nguyen Hue Boulevard, in front of the old French City Hall, now the headquarters of the Peoples Committee. The Hall is an elegant yellow building with white pillars and balustrades, a remnant of colonial stateliness. Nearby, a statue of Ho Chi Minh, his arm around a young Vietnamese girl, glowed in harsh spotlights.

I checked into the runners' area, then sat down to wait for the start. Vietnamese runners in new Adidas outfits were warming up nearby, doing sharp, exaggerated motions that looked like a cross between calisthenics and tai chi. The oldest Vietnamese in the field was 33.

Aside from the bright spotlights on Uncle Ho and the occasional loudspeaker broadcast, it was a still, muggy, peaceful morning. A cricket chirped in a potted bush near where I sat, and every few minutes a motorbike would putt-putt-putt its way down a side street. Next to me, a young Vietnamese soldier sat on a chair, guarding the entrance to the Hall, an automatic rifle across his knees. He looked like a gang member.

On the officials' stand near the statue, the two men most responsible for Vietnam's first international sporting event — Bruce Aitken and Le Buu — were comparing checklists. Aitken, a fit-looking American in his mid-40s with short-cropped hair and a graying beard, is an investment counselor living in Hong Kong. While looking for opportunities in Vietnam a year and a half earlier, Aitken had offhandedly suggested to officials that the city sponsor a marathon.

" 'What's a marathon?' they said," remembers Aitken with a grin. " 'You know,' I told them, 'that long race.' "

Vietnamese officials had a keen visceral sense of what a tropical 42-kilometer footrace would be like, and were understandably dubious. Aitken showed pictures of marathons in other unlikely locations and somehow managed to win the point. The idea of hosting an international event, something to project a positive image to the world of their once-hostile, war-torn country, appealed to leaders. Maybe, they thought, it might help convince Americans to lift the economic boycott that has stifled the country. And so a marathon was born.

Local organization fell chiefly to Mr. Le Buu, a 58-year-old former Vietcong colonel who now heads the city's Sports and Gymnastics Service.

"Isn't it ironic," noted Bill Rodgers at the prerace press conference, "that the race director's name is Le Buu? Like Lebow."

Unable to leave that one alone, I asked Mr. Le Buu if he planned to direct traffic by standing and waving from the lead vehicle. He indicated he would do something like that.

"Then," I told him, "you will remind us all of the famous director of the New York City Marathon, Mr. Lebow."

Properly translated, that drew a hearty laugh from the director.

As 6 a.m. approached, more than 200 runners from a reported twenty-six countries began drifting toward the starting line. More, I suspect, would have run, but after having spent a couple of hours myself trying to figure out how to obtain a visa at the airport a few days earlier, I couldn't help but imagine there must be thousands of would-be marathoners still there, trying to maneuver their way through that Kafkaesque process.

The field included about ninety Vietnamese and fifty Americans, with thirty women and ten U.S. veterans among the ranks. It seemed to me there were a whole lot of people who, drawn by the uniqueness of the occasion, had chosen a tough venue — the steamy streets of Saigon — for their very first marathon.

On Nguyen Hue Boulevard, young Vietnamese runners squeezed to the front, toeing the starting line. Behind, mostly older, experienced foreign marathoners stood placidly, chatting. It would be a long day, no need to rush.

Nearby, street vendors were opening shop, including one or two selling shirts emblazoned with "Apocalypse Now," a nightclub in the vicinity, which was named after Francis Ford Coppola's hypnotic Vietnam war movie. A helicopter thumped overhead. I looked up and could see a planet, presumably Venus, sparkling just above a ragged edge of cloud cover in the east.

The gun fired, and we were off in the darkness.

"I was a conscientious objector during the war," Bill Rodgers had told a reporter a few days earlier, "and I'm here racing with American veterans and Vietnamese veterans. I think we all feel this marathon is a symbol — something to bring all of us together."

A symbol is one thing. The marathon is another. When Bill pulled up beside me a half-mile after the start, he began asking about our pace and seeking confirmation for his strategy, which was to run conservatively. Bill was in great shape, but his body was winter-trained, and he couldn't decide whether to race or just go the distance. The reality of humidity and jet lag was hard to ignore.

"Once I got here," he told me the day before, "I wondered about the competitive part. I've been fluctuating."

We were running a 7-minute pace, which was reasonable for me but too slow for Bill. As we ran along the Saigon River past the Floating Hotel, I urged him to go ahead. A minute later, I was alone.

It was still early, and the course was thinly populated. But as dusk brightened, market stalls along the course sprang to life. In retrospect, the course would seem like a long journey through endless market areas swarming with people. Veterans and others who knew Saigon before 1975 claim the city has changed little since then.

"I haven't been here since December 23, 1973," Andy Anderson, one of the three wheelchair racers, told the *New York Times*, "and when I went out through the streets here this week, it was like I left last Friday and came back on Monday."

To others it seemed more crowded, the bustle of makeshift storefronts more pervasive, the smooth flow of pedestrians, bicycle riders, motorcycles and the occasional Toyota through the streets more improbable. It's hard to imagine what rules guide rush-hour activity.

Traffic control for the marathon, though, was good at this point, so my concerns centered on water. I could see umbrellas marking the first water station at 5K, and I eased over, stopped, and prepared to fill my water bottles. I expected to pick up a plastic water bottle with a cap on top. What I saw instead was an open tub of water with a block of ice floating in it.

I found out later from a Hong Kong runner who was working the stations that the water was good. Distilled water had been emptied into the tub for easier distribution. But what I saw at the time presented an enigma: Was I looking at the fluid that would save me from dehydration or doom me to intestinal eruption?

I drank, and hoped for the best.

At five miles, the course followed a bridge across the Saigon River. Coming off the bridge, a group of teenage girls wearing traditional full-length white dresses stood cheering. For the next few miles, we ran through countryside. The crowds had become more sparse, individuals more noticeable: an old man wearing what seemed to be pajamas; people in peasant garb, wearing cone-shaped straw hats; young boys squatting on the cement barriers on the center line of the highway, perched like brown birds.

We were running north, with the sun dappling the road as it shone through the trees on our right. I could feel the heat rising, and I was drinking and refilling my bottles so often that the constant spill of water turned my fingertips to white raisins.

The road was paved and mostly smooth. It carried us past rice paddies, factories and finally into the village of Thu Duc, where I passed the two Vietnamese and encountered Jim Barker and the stars and stripes. For many Americans who lived through the '60s, the flag and Vietnam are entwined in the mind in a haunting dance of conflicting emotions and sentiments: love, hate, patriotism, alienation, terror, idealism, disillusionment. For Barker, the jersey represented his mission.

"My sense was going back to make peace," he said, "but more to interact with the people and re-embrace the nation and the culture in which I feel hundreds of thousands of us have emotional ownership. I didn't go just to shake hands and accept the conditions that exist with the current government."

Those conditions have been bleak, to be sure. Vietnam is one of the poorest nations on Earth, a reflection of its history, economic system and isolation. Things have improved some in the past few years. Tourism and investment, especially from Japan and Hong Kong, are on the rise. New cars, motorcycles and spruced-up buildings suggest a brighter future. Across the river from the Floating Hotel, a 15-foot-high "SONY" sign lights up the evening, announcing the return of consumer products.

As I moved ahead of Barker and began the second half of the marathon, the old and new jangled in my field of vision. Traditional marketplaces. A video store. Wagons pulled by water buffalo. Busloads of Vietnamese, leaning out to watch the runners. Old bicycles, rusty and ragged. New Honda motorbikes, with amateur video photographers shooting from the back. An old, toothless woman dressed in purple and wearing a straw hat. A young Vietnamese woman in black, with exotic eyes and dark, waist-length hair, riding on the back of a bicycle, like a character in a James Bond movie.

From the left, across a brilliant green rice paddy, a blast of direct sunlight broke through the haze, and I realized how hot it *could* be, if not for the occasional shade and protection of cloud cover. I knew I was close to the bridge, though, the passage back to the city proper and the final trek home. At 20 miles I reached the marathon's critical point, where fatigue and dehydration so often spell collapse. In the Ho Chi Minh City Marathon, the "wall" was the Cau Son Bridge.

It was at about this point that Jim Barker encountered the only negative comment he heard during the race, and it had nothing to do with the flag.

"It was from an elderly lady," remembered Barker afterward. "I heard her from the sideline say, 'Oh, he's going slowly, like a tortoise and a water buffalo.' "

Indeed, so were we all. To make matters worse, once over the bridge, we ran into a new dimension of congestion. The densely crowded streets would at times lock up entirely, bringing runners to a halt. The preferred method of crowd control during the marathon had been for motorcycles to drive along each side, red flags flapping, officials gesturing and sirens blaring. That worked as well as could be expected early on. Later, though, when crowds estimated at over a half million all seemed to congregate in the same spot, the path ahead would vanish like a trail through the jungle.

Two scenes from this point stand out in my memory. In one, I'm looking down a long street into a swirl of pedestrians, bicycles and motorbikes. Heat waves and exhaust fumes mixed in the broiling street ahead and rose in a blue haze. I was escorted by a motorcycle, its siren throbbing in my ears, but I could see no clear path ahead. Dizzy and claustrophobic, I took a deep breath, a swig of water and tried to relax.

The second scene occurred a mile or so later. I was somehow directed into an entangled conundrum of bicycles and motorbikes. They all appeared to be headed in different directions, their riders smiling at me, all of them pointing in several other directions, trying to get me back on course. It felt like a "Where's Waldo" drawing.

At about this point, Rodgers, who had been leading for most of the race, bonked in the heat and began walking, eventually managing a wobbly-legged 3:07:52 finish. I saw him on television that evening, running the last miles of the course holding a block of ice on his head.

"I was massively dehydrated," said Rodgers later. "I just couldn't get enough water."

That left an opening for Tim Soutar, a 36-year-old British lawyer from Hong Kong, to slip in for the win. When I asked Soutar later how he got through the crowds, he smiled.

"I just kind of ... " he said, making huge sweeping gestures with his arms. "It really got my adrenaline going."

For at least one American veteran in the crowd, the experience had an additional poignancy.

"I felt like I was kind of a POW," said Jim Barker, "going down an endless, eternal corridor or gauntlet, and there was no exit. The only way out was to push forward. The alternatives — one was dying, the other was emerging alive."

As marathoners, we play with this notion of survival. In real life, in times of war and peace, it sometimes becomes the only thing a human can focus on.

Perhaps, in spite of the cruel conditions that challenged runners in the first Ho Chi Minh International Marathon, Vietnam is exactly the right place to host this event. If there is any land that has been home to struggle and survival, it is this one.

All I know is that when I headed down the homestretch, past the former American embassy and through the gates of Reunification Palace, I was profoundly glad to conclude this adventure.

My watch read 3:02:46, slow by competitive standards. But I was still standing.

The day after the marathon, a small group of us went to the American War Crimes Museum, certainly one of the oddest tourist attractions in any town. Seeing all that dusty weaponry — tanks, howitzers, helicopters — might have been almost nostalgic in a strange sort of way, but the photos of massacres, victims of napalm, phosphorus and pellet bombs, and the graphic depictions of techniques used to try to break the enemy's spirits were just plain demoralizing.

Brutality may be the currency that combatants trade in the hell of war, but by the late '60s, many Americans had concluded that the Vietnam conflict was a hell with no end in sight. And weren't we supposed to be occupying the moral high ground? By 1974, America had extricated itself from Vietnam. By 1975, the Vietcong controlled the country.

On the afternoon of the Ho Chi Minh City Marathon, an old man climbed to the top of a car outside the Floating Hotel, where the media were lodged. In long white beard and traditional garb, he proudly waved the flag of the former South Vietnamese Republic. Immediately police grabbed him and the film of any photographers deft enough to have captured the moment. For some, the battle goes on.

For most, though, that phase of history is over. Even the War Crimes Museum, eager for the tourist dollar, seems less interested in documenting American imperialism and more inclined to make a few bucks selling engraved lighters left behind by GIs. The world moves on.

"I don't have any animosity," shrugged Bob Farmer, one of the wheelchair racers, who was permanently blinded in one eye by shrapnel while serving in Vietnam. "They were soldiers, we were soldiers."

No doubt, the future will witness the visit of more and more U.S. veterans. Hopefully, many will be like wheelchair racer George Gentry, who visited the site where he was crippled in a mine explosion in 1967, but whose real mission was to introduce disabled Vietnamese veterans to the joys of athletic competition.

It appears that the marathon will be a permanent part of Vietnam's future, judging from the enthusiasm of those watching the first one. After finishing, I found myself surrounded by young Vietnamese eager to see my finisher's medal and older people wanting to tell me about their friends in America, people they hadn't heard from in almost twenty years. Close by, I saw Barker surrounded as well, nearly overcome by it.

"They were curious to death to talk to a Vietnam veteran," said Barker. "I was fighting suffocation, or claustrophobia."

Among the Vietnamese, there is a palpable yearning for contact with the outside, a desire that transcends issues that may still divide us. As I sat on the steps of Reunification Palace after the marathon, watching Vietnamese girls dance to M.C. Hammer, I felt good about the gladness of heart we marathoners had experienced from the crowd that day.

In a footrace inspired by a legendary battle in ancient Greece and the messenger who announced victory to his people, modern victories are more private. One person struggles, another applauds. One person suffers, another offers help.

When the race was over and Jim Barker was reflecting on his experience, he suddenly remembered an incident late in the race.

"This lady on a motorcycle," said Barker, "like an angel delivered from on high, came out, zoomed by and handed me a 36-ounce bottle of spring water. I was coming up on a number of Vietnamese runners who were walking, and I shared that water with them."

For the veteran who once experienced more hostile reactions in this country, the gesture mattered.

"That was the kind of moment that I was really hoping for in terms of unification. I shared with them, and they accepted gratefully. It was perfect harmony."

AMAZING RACE

Why is it that on the day before Lent, New Orleans gets Mardi Gras, while Liberal and Olney get the International Pancake Race? We don't know, but people in those two towns don't seem to mind.

HERE'S A POSTCARD FROM KANSAS to catch your attention: A line of women, knees lifted in the first steps of what appears to be a sprint, and yet, what's this? These women are dressed in skirts, scarves and aprons, carrying, what's that? Frying pans?

You look at the title on the bottom of the card — "LIBERAL" — and you wonder what image of the future the reactionary right is proposing now to discredit their left-leaning adversaries. Advancing feminist troops, armed with kitchenware?

By the time you've come to stand at the finish line for this event, though, watching the fastest women in the town of Liberal, Kansas, round the second turn and lean into the homestretch, skillets flailing, police sirens blazing, spectators screaming, you know the truth. This is no vision of the future but a tongue-in-cheek homage to the past. And it would be stretching the truth only a smidgen to claim that you are witnessing a celebration of the oldest footrace in the world. Four hundred and fifteen yards long, over 500 years old, and a women's-only event at that.

Okay, now, what *is* going on here?

Well, we're not exactly sure, because 500 years takes its toll on memory, leaving a sizable gap in which legend takes root. According to the most popular myth, in 1445 a medieval housewife in Olney, England, late for the traditional "Shriving Service" on the day before Lent, rushed out of her kitchen and down the street to church, skillet in hand, pancake in pan, much to the delight of her neighbors.

In a determined attempt to prove that they had the liveliest sense of humor in Christendom, Olney's townsfolk decided to celebrate the woman's desperate dash every year from thence forward, lining up young local women for a footrace down the main street of town. With skillets, of course.

Thus it began, nearly a half-century before the voyage of Columbus, and thus it has continued, through plague and pestilence, war and peace, rain and shine. Gaps have occurred in the yearly celebration, and other towns in England have practiced a similar ritual, but in the end, Olney has always rallied with the greatest conviction around its destiny as the capital of world-class skillet racing.

Well enough, then. These are *Brits*, after all, inclined on the slightest whim to metamorphose from Her Majesty's stiff-backed subjects into characters from a Monty Python sketch. But what about Kansas?

The town of Liberal, 17,000 strong, springs amid a patchwork quilt of fields in southwest Kansas, supported by crops, cattle, oil, natural gas and whatever tourists it can convince to visit the nearby Dorothy House and Museum, where aging Munchkins are invited each year to celebrate the Oz Festival. It is an unpretentious, prosperous-looking prairie town where almost every girl seems to grow up to be Miss Something-or-Other, including the 1991 Miss USA, Kelli McCarty.

Liberal got its name because of the generosity of early trading-post owner S.S. Rogers, who was known to hand out scarce water to passersby without charging. "That's mighty liberal of you," they all seemed to respond, not knowing that remark would be considered an insult by the end of the twentieth century.

Shortly after World War II, Jaycees in Liberal were looking for a way to connect their community to the larger world. Or maybe there was a lingering Anglophilia rampant among returning GIs. At any rate, when

Jaycees President R.J. Leete noticed pictures in *Time* magazine of Olney's pancake race, the idea struck him like an iron pan on the side of the head. Liberal already had a pancake celebration. Why not add a race?

"I sent a wire to the vicar," recalls Leete, who today enjoys emeritus status at the event, "and said we'd like to do the same and be part of the tradition."

Vicar Ronald Collins of the Parish Church of St. Peter and St. Paul in Olney responded immediately. He had revived the pancake race after the war, and seemed eager to establish a link with the Kansas Yanks. In 1950, then, the two cities lined up their best women and blew the battle horn. Olney was used to this stuff by now, but in Liberal such behavior was new territory.

"You don't run down the street flipping pancakes in front of your neighbors when it's never been done before," says Virginia Leete, wife of R.J. and publicity director of the event. She managed to rise to the occasion anyway, spurred on by a "Go, Mom!" midrace, and finished second in the first pancake race ever held in Liberal. Or North America, for that matter.

When that first race was over, the towns compared times by phone and found that Olney's Florence Callow had won by almost 8 seconds. Even in those days, the media ate this kind of thing up like a short stack. "We had press coverage from all over the world," says R.J. Leete. "It caught their fancy."

By 1952, Liberal enjoyed its first winner, and since then each side has had its share of victors. Going into the 1992 race, the Brits had a 21-20 lead, leaving out 1980, when a BBC press truck in Olney interfered with the runners. And so, as the Liberal women poised to race down the main drag in March 1992, one couldn't help but hope that a Kansan was about to even the series.

"In a way, although I'm supposed to be representing Olney and shouting for the Olney girl," said Robert Gordon of the British Consulate in Chicago, on the morning of the race, "it would probably be nice if a Liberal girl won, and that would tie the event at 21 wins each."

Or at least that's what he was telling folks on this side of the Atlantic. Back in England, sportsmanship had understandable limits.

"May the best girl win," noted Olney's race manager, Edwin Horlock, in a prerace letter. "As long as she lives in Olney!"

The Brits seem to enjoy this friendly rivalry as much as the Kansans, and Robert Gordon was the perfect stateside representative. Diplomatic as required but twinkling in both eyes, Her Majesty's Consul managed just the right combination of decorum and wit for this event, representing the Crown with dignity but appearing ready to render the latest gallop from the Ministry of Silly Walks if necessary. Who could blame the citizens of Liberal for cherishing their link to a Britain capable of producing such people?

"You wouldn't get this number of people up this early in Olney for breakfast," reported Gordon on the morning of the run, as he surveyed the 6 a.m. pancake breakfast crowd. "Olney is a little different in its structure." More of a horizontal structure, that is, at this hour of the morning.

For those of us used to the grafting of carbo-loading onto running events, it's important to remember that, with the pancake race, things happened the other way around. First came the pancake-eating, then the running event. And in Liberal, the "Pancake Hub of the Universe," serious attention is given to the flapjack. The world's largest pancake was once cooked here. And a contestant once ate seventy-six cakes at a sitting. Eight women will eventually compete in the featured race, but *everyone* joins in for the carbo-loading part of the celebration. (You marathon directors out there might want to take a note or two about this.)

Breakfast loading completed, the Pancake Day Celebration staggers heavy-bellied from the high school gym to downtown Liberal, where activity and excitement build toward the 11:55 a.m. International Race. Racing begins with children's events, miniature versions of the main feature, in which tykes are equipped with tiny scarves, aprons and plastic pans. These are followed by the "Last Chance Race" for women 50-and-over, kind of the frying-pan version of masters competition. And finally, just before the women's race is the "Men's Pacer Race," which includes embarrassing clothes but no skillets. Perhaps the possible combination of competitive men and iron pans had liability underwriters nervous.

At any rate, it is the very last event everyone's been waiting for, and at 5 minutes till noon, it is finally on the front burner. Eight women line up on Kansas Avenue, including Miss Kansas, Robin Wasson, a willing but unofficial entrant. A pancake race may seem like light-hearted fun, but there *are* rules, including a residency requirement. In addition, entrants must be at least 18 years old, have "housewifely duties," and wear aprons and head scarves. If any rules seem excessive in this context, remember that even centipede racing has regulations. And when international sport is involved, things often get downright litigious.

The women flip their pancakes — another rule — on the starting line, and then they're off. The course in Liberal, like the one in Olney, has two turns, though the English bends are rounder. The sharp turns don't seem to hinder Victoria VanSickle much, as the former collegiate 400-meter runner comes out of the second one squarely in the lead.

At 5 feet, 11 inches, VanSickle is the image of stately athleticism, strong and quick, never tying up. A woman running in skirt and apron in the late twentieth century is about as anachronistic as things get in the age of lycra and thermonuclear sunglasses, but I have to believe something here is worth keeping: the frying pan. Imagine how interesting some of those nasty European elbow-throwing track races *could* be.

At any rate, VanSickle crosses the line in 61.5 seconds, flipping her pancake again to satisfy the final rule of the race. She has beaten Sue Jones of Olney by a full second, bringing home the, uh, bacon to Liberal, tying the series at 21-all. Both names will eventually end up on the sidewalk on Kansas Avenue, not far from Pancake Boulevard, where the history of modern pancake racing is etched in stone.

With the race over and Olney accepting their defeat, we are left with two questions. One: Why is it that on the day before Lent, New Orleans gets Mardi Gras, while Liberal and Olney get the International Pancake Race? We don't know, but people in those two towns don't seem to mind.

Second: Where do we go to get shriven? Shriving is the process of confessing and receiving absolution for one's sins (leading us to suggest the following religious bumper sticker: "How's my shriving? Call 1-800-555-LENT").

In Olney, shriving takes place at the parish church, the focus of community life since well before an anonymous medieval housewife accidentally established the world's oldest footrace. In Liberal, the Shriving Service is at First United Methodist Church, and may be the only worship service outside of England that concludes with an awards ceremony.

As the Liberal service reaches its climax, we are treated to a favorite hymn, "Amazing Grace," without doubt the best shriving song ever written. A hymn, incidentally, written in the late eighteenth century by John Newton, curate of a small parish church in the middle of England, in the town of Olney.

I imagine John Newton's introduction of his immortal, profound, soul-scorching song to have gone something like this: "Ladies and gentlemen, I'd like to end today's service with a hymn I've written that I hope will meet with your approval. But first, let's have a round of applause for the winner of this morning's pancake race... "

THE OLYMPIAN VS. THE LIBRARIAN

Janet, I think with cruel glee, my victory is overdue.

LIBRARIANS MAY NOT ALL LOOK ALIKE, but if someone told you to pick out the woman in the crowd mingling at the start of the fourteenth annual Bud Light Stadium Run in St. Louis — the woman who looked most likely to scold you for an overdue reference tome or to glare at you over the top of her bifocals and hiss, "Shhhhh!" — you would have picked Janet Glassman.

Or maybe that's just my perspective. I know she's not *that* kind of librarian, but this is my rival after all, so I have to imagine unsavory personality traits. This is *the enemy.*

But even if Janet were as bad as I could imagine, I know the matchup of the 63-year-old librarian and the 43-year-old former Olympian in this age-sex handicap race would have the fans in the cheering section rooting against me. I accept that. Still, when I reach the part of this story where I finally get this woman in my sights, when I'm charging down Broadway with the St. Louis Gateway Arch in the background and Janet looming larger in my field of vision, I insist on just one thing: No fair feeling sorry for her.

First of all, she doesn't need it. I know this female can handle her own sword and shield. Grandmothers can be flinty and tough, and this one ran a marathon in 3:12 at age 57. When she races, she churns along at 7 to 8 minutes a mile. Younger runners envy her tenacity.

And second, this was a fair fight, one in which I spotted my opponent a 14-minute head start. And whatever the outcome of our personal grudge match today, in the end I'll be beaten by three men older than 60 and a 12-year-old girl. When the playing field is leveled, life gets like this.

So let's view this race, with the librarian in the lead and me chasing after her, with dispassion. This is, after all, just *for fun*.

There was a time, by the way, when this sort of battle of mismatched foot racers was fairly common. In the early days of local running clubs, when a handful of runners would show up for races, handicap events were a regular feature. It was easy then to figure out how much faster Bill was than Bob, and just as easy to give Bob the corresponding head start. This was no different than what happens every day in most schoolyards.

"I'll give you a head start, Bob," says little Bill, "and still beat you to the fence."

"No you won't, you fast-twitch twerp," says little Bob. And off they go.

Early handicap races, organized by small running clubs, weren't much more sophisticated than playground antics. Bill usually beat Bob by a minute, so Bob got a minute head start. With only a few runners to figure handicaps for, it didn't take advanced brainwork to spit out a number for everyone in the field. And as in golf and bowling, an athlete of any ability armed with a handicap could compete against the most talented. Each week, *anyone* in the field might cross the finish line first.

As the number of runners boomed in the 1970s, though, and participants of unknown ability began showing up in droves, handicap races began sagging under the weight of their own ideology. Who had the time and information necessary to figure head starts for a thousand runners?

And so, like lumbering dinosaurs, handicap races hobbled toward extinction under the pressures of modern life.

Except in St. Louis.

One weekend in 1978, Tom Eckelman and some other members of the St. Louis Track Club were in the middle of what might otherwise have been one of the last handicap races in the country. About 150 people had gathered at Forest Park, seeded into different starting sections based mostly on the honor system (the Pinocchio method), and were happily trying to chase the people in front of them and stay ahead of those behind, when St. Louis Cardinals General Manager John Claiborne drove up. A runner and friend of Eckelman's, Claiborne asked what was going on. Eckelman explained.

"Maybe that's something we could do downtown," said Claiborne. "We could finish in the stadium."

And with that, a dinosaur was saved.

And it flourished. In 1979, nearly 2,000 runners showed up for the first Stadium Run 10K. The crowd was no doubt lured more by the chance to race to the second base line in Busch Stadium and enjoy a Cardinals game free-of-charge afterward than by any fascination with long-distance-running handicap systems. Still, when one of this country's best runners, Craig Virgin, had to hustle his world-class buns down the homestretch to overtake 10-year-old Chris Koon for the victory, it made for interesting theater.

Eckelman and company had given up the honor system in favor of more manageable age- and gender-based handicaps, and the scramble of the fastest in the world chasing after old men, women and children who had been given head starts had a unique appeal. Maybe it was the plight of the underdog, struggling against the young and the swift. Whatever it was, people were fascinated.

The second year, returning champion Virgin was outdueled by 11-year-old Wesley Paul. The headline in the newspaper the next day must have really piqued the curiosity of uninitiated St. Louis sports fans. It read: "Virgin beaten by 11-Year-Old."

Craig hasn't shown up since, but the run has continued to thrive, generally drawing between 2,000 and 3,000 runners a year. Winners between 1979 and 1991 have been as young as 11 and as old as 59. Eight have been male, five female. World-class runners like Virgin and Marty Cooksey have won, and so have people you've never heard of, unless you happen to be finely tuned in to the world of St. Louis age-group running.

But those people aren't my problem on this warm, sunny Labor Day weekend. My problem is Janet Glassman.

I have been told, you see, by my friends at *Runner's World*, that this librarian from Rodale Press (which publishes *RW*) is going to wax the streets with me. And even though this is just *for fun*, I'm determined not to be on the losing end of the fun. So when Janet and I meet for the first time for dinner on the night before the race, I size her up.

"I haven't run a 10K in two and a half years," she claims.

You're sandbagging, I accuse silently, and decide to push for more information.

"How fast did you run then?" I ask.

She answers, "46:49." And I calculate quickly. With her handicap, 17 minutes, this would give her a net time of under 30:00. My performances in recent years have been deteriorating faster than my ability to adjust my goals, so I'm not sure if I can match that. I feel a shot of adrenaline, knowing I may need to run way over my head to beat her. Then she adds, "But I'm a lot slower than that now."

No doubt about it — a sandbagger. Later in the dinner I become convinced of it, as she explains how little training time she had during July while her grandson was visiting.

"I know just what you mean," I counter. "I had a horrible month, too. My calf was bothering me the whole time."

Janet switches the conversation soon after, remarking about the beer I'm drinking and how alcohol causes dehydration. An obvious ploy to create self-doubt, but I stop drinking anyway.

Later on during dinner, Tom Eckelman describes how tricky it can be racing down the ramp into the stadium, suddenly having spongy astroturf underfoot. A person might stumble there.

I imagine racing into the stadium just in time to see Janet trip and fall, sliding like a baseball player headfirst into second. An ethical question here: Do I stop and help, or do I hurdle over her for the victory?

Stop and help, I finally decide. After all, there might be photographers nearby.

The next morning, I meet Janet near the start. I try to peer into the soul of my nemesis, but I am stopped by steel-blue eyes flecked with gold. I know, though, that she is feeling nervous about the possibility of leading the race.

"I've never in my life been in the lead," she had said the night before. "I don't think I'll like it. All those exhaust fumes."

Like it or not, Janet's age and sex guarantee that she'll spend some time up front. As the countdown of groups begins, Janet takes off down the street, hotly in pursuit of a woman named Dottie. After a mile, out of sight, she edges into the lead.

Meanwhile, I wait nervously for my own send-off. Each time a group takes off, I feel a small surge of adrenaline. Finally, the 3-minute head starters toe the line, a group that includes 15-year-old boys as well as 42- and 43-year-old men. Eckelman announces that, "Don Kardong, member of the 1976 Olympic team in the marathon," is in this group.

"Oh, great," groans a kid beside me. "Just what we need." I hide my identity, but a minute later I'm off with a vengeance, racing through the streets of St. Louis, chasing not after gold, silver or bronze, but rather a short, steely-eyed, 63-year-old librarian who is somewhere out there in the distance.

In any standard road race, runners sort themselves out quickly by ability. Shortly after the gun fires, everyone is running alongside someone pretty much the same speed they are.

Not in a handicap race. Here, runners are constantly running past, or being passed by, people of widely divergent abilities. As one of the passers, I highly recommend the exhilarating experience of flying through the streets, bobbing and weaving through the crowd, passing more people than would otherwise be possible in a year of racing.

In amongst this crowd, though, I miss the mile mark, and it isn't until two miles that I get a split. Since everyone has started at a different time, one's own watch is the only reliable measure of performance. Passing two miles in 10:49, I figure I have a shot at 34 minutes for 10K. Will it be enough to catch my prey? I try to imagine her up ahead, and wonder if she can sense the cross hairs I've focused on her back.

It's a warm day here in St. Louis, but the first part of the race enjoys the shade of downtown buildings. By three miles, though, I'm in direct sunlight and starting to feel the heat.

Suddenly a runner passes me. I recognize him as Bobby Williams, 39 years old and a past winner of this event. My immediate instinct is to try to stay with him, as I would in a normal footrace. Today, though, normal racing instincts are essentially worthless. Williams has started a full minute behind me, and he has already caught up. He is, I quickly figure, running *a lot* faster than I am. If for no other reason, this becomes apparent with the ease with which he moves ahead. Good-bye, Bobby.

We are heading for the turnaround point at the Anheuser-Busch brewery now, and I see the lead vehicle coming back the other direction. An older male runner, who I later figure must be eventual winner Jack Gentry, is in the lead. Close behind is my favorite librarian.

I check my watch, continue to the brewery, then head back north toward downtown St. Louis. When I pass the point where I saw Janet, I check my watch again. I'm only 3.5 minutes behind. Janet, I think with cruel glee, my victory is overdue.

At about 5.5 miles, fate comes to pass. As we head up a small incline on Chouteau Road, I charge by on Janet's right. My lofty goal, defeating this poor woman, is accomplished.

Poor woman? Let's remember our deal now. No fair feeling sorry.

I know *I'm* not. In fact, my first instinct is … that I should hold my form and push hard to the finish, so my opponent doesn't come back and outsprint me on the homestretch.

But I suppose that isn't going to happen, not after I've made up a big deficit. Suddenly I realize there are all kinds of people ahead of me who I should be trying to pass. I begin picking them off as best I can. In a final impressive burst of speed on the way to second base in Busch Stadium, I catch 67-year-old Pat Gallagher, thereby nabbing tenth place. I am proud of my sprint, even though it is not enough to reel in Melissa Sapa, age 12. In most road races, you learn at the awards ceremony how well the age-group wizards have done. In this one, you find out on the homestretch.

A number of matchups have been settled today: 64-year-old Jack Gentry has held off the challenge of 60-year-old, four-time Stadium Run winner Leon Fennell; 33-year-old Zean Gassmann, with a mere 1-minute handicap, has managed to move all the way up to third, just ahead of Bobby Williams and 65-year-old Ernie Hirschfeld; and so on. It is a bizarre and entertaining set of finish results.

Janet finishes twenty-third, and is clearly discouraged.

"My legs just weren't working the way they're supposed to," she says. That lack of training in July and a recent return to speedwork seemed to have eroded her strength, and a too-quick first mile didn't help either.

"I came through the first mile in 7:25," she says, "and I thought, 'Oh, no ... ' I've been able to run that fast before, but I'm not ready for that now."

Anyway, so it went, our personal battle. On this day, the librarian has proven vulnerable. And in the end, I have to realize that Janet wasn't sandbagging. Her training wasn't quite up to par, and she knew it. So when the 43-year-old kid went by, she wasn't shocked.

I, in turn, can't really savor this victory. What kind of bragging rights have I earned? "There was this really tough librarian," I might begin, "and my friends thought she could beat me ..."

In the end, I'll just keep quiet about this. After all, this was just *for fun*. And so, in the spirit of fun, I'll fondly remember Janet and our little duel in St. Louis.

And with fondness, too, I'll imagine her back home, doing speedwork at the track. And hill repeats. And increasing her mileage. And I can't help but wonder if I might answer the phone one of these days and hear a soft, grandmotherly voice on the other end — innocent, no hint of calculation.

"Any chance," the voice will say, "you might be interested in a rematch?"

November 1992

Grand Canyon

"Warning: Do not attempt to hike from the rim to the Colorado River and back in one day. Many people who have attempted this have suffered serious illness or death."

THIS WAS THE PROVERBIAL MOMENT OF TRUTH. A moment of time in this ancient landscape as inconsequential as one drop of water in the river below us. But, for me, the moment that mattered.

It was 3 p.m., and I had been running, jogging, walking, and otherwise traversing the rocky path beneath my feet for 8 1/2 hours. From the interminable drop off the South Rim of the Grand Canyon to the Colorado River, followed by the steady climb to the North Rim, and then the long trek back to the Colorado River, I had pattered along, determined to complete this 41.2-mile journey before sunset.

Since dawn, freezing weather had steadily warmed, and for the past two hours conditions had edged on hot. Dehydration was a worry. Blisters, too, were a concern, and I could feel their throbbing on my right heel and big toe. Mostly, though, it had been the steady thump down, and up, and down again, carving a visceral map of the Grand Canyon in my quads, that was making life difficult.

When my running partner for most of the day, Steve Utley, came skipping past me at Phantom Ranch, I felt the way an old, lumbering plant-eater must have when tyrannosaurus rex danced the two-step of death around it. I had no life in my legs to respond. I was unable to take another running step.

Now, crossing the suspension bridge, I could look down at the copper-brown rapids below me, or up at the cold, black rocks of the Grand Canyon's inner gorge, the top of a mountain range 2 billion years old. Either way, it was a scene without pity.

There at the nadir of my journey, I knew I had nearly 3 hours left. If I took longer, it would grow dark on this part of the Earth. I was tired enough to wonder what the bottom line was on exhaustion in the bowels of the Grand Canyon. Overnight at the ranger station? A helicopter airlift? Face it, though, I wasn't going to stop. There were many reasons, but one main one: Back on the South Rim, my 9-year-old daughter, Kaitlin, and her grandmother were waiting. I imagined panic if I didn't show up.

"Where's Dad? Is he all right? Why isn't Dad back yet?"

I couldn't quit. And a little more than six miles from the finish, nearly a mile straight down in this majestic hole in the ground, there was only one way out. Left foot. Right foot. Up. Up.

I had heard about runners in the Grand Canyon as long as fifteen years ago. Immediately, way back then, I felt inclined to join. There is something about the wonders of nature that elicits an instinctive human urge to wander, explore, assimilate. For many of us, that can mean only one thing — a good, long run.

The romanticism of the quest was severely strained, though, when I finally stood on the South Rim. I could see 10 miles straight across to the North Rim, the halfway point, and could follow the trail as it wound down through the yellow, orange, red and purple cliffs, buttes, castles and crags that define the landscape. It's a stunningly beautiful sight, but it was going to be a long, difficult run. The first precipitous drop took my breath away. Could there be a reasonable trail down there? Could I manage this, or would my fear of heights turn to panic, leaving me a whimpering mess, clinging to a rock somewhere down below? My fear had been softened when I finally met my fellow travelers for dinner on the night before the run.

"This hardly qualifies as a trail run," Ross Zimmerman had said, one of about twenty ultrarunners who would be making the trip. "It's more like a road."

Steve Corona had nodded in agreement. Corona, already a veteran of nine Grand Canyon round trips, was my advisor, so I paid attention to his nod. I found it comforting.

Still, these were ultrarunners, so their lack of intimidation was understandable. Used to 24-hour treks in rain, snow, burning daylight and foggy darkness, traveling on narrow trails, at high altitudes and through improbable territory, they develop a firm conviction that whatever will happen, will happen. And they will be ready for it, because they have a couple of Band-Aids, a Power Bar and a penlight in their fanny packs.

One of their ilk once did the rim-to-rim and back in 7:43. Others have managed a "double double," 82.4 miles, in one fell swoop. I love these people, with their sublime confidence, their steady yet intense eyes, their ultimate faith in themselves. They calm me.

Back in my room, though, I reread the visitor's guide. In bold print, it read: "*Warning: Do not attempt to hike from the rim to the Colorado River and back in one day. Many people who have attempted this have suffered serious illness or death.*" I took this warning seriously, knowing we would be going over three times that far.

I reviewed my fanny pack. Food bars, packets of replacement fluid, three water bottles, first-aid supplies. The pack was heavy, so I removed my flashlight. If I didn't make it back before dark, I would travel as ancient canyon travelers did. By moonlight.

DAWN

"It can snow, it can rain, it can do anything," Corona had told me weeks earlier. When I awoke, though, after an agitated, mostly sleepless night and looked outside, the ground was dry, the temperature was below freezing and the stars were crackling.

I wanted Kaitlin to see these blazing desert stars sometime during our trip, but she was still asleep. I fidgeted with my pack, dressed and walked to the lodge to catch a ride to the trailhead.

A few minutes later, four of us stood at the top of the Kaibab Trail, waiting for first light. There were no timers, no starting instructions, no crowd to cheer us on. This was a totally unstructured adventure. Some runners had already left, others would start later. When it got light enough, we went.

I hadn't seen the Kaibab Trail before, and it was probably a good thing. It may be a road to some, but to me it was a slithering serpent of a path, marked by mule-hoof holes, rocks set across the trail to inhibit erosion and a variety of natural stumbling blocks.

It was a swift descent for the first three miles down to and across the crest of Cedar Ridge. In places the scenery soared downward on both sides, and I was glad to focus on the trail to avoid flirting with vertigo.

Zimmerman and Corona had both assured me that heat, not cold, would be my canyon nemesis. Sure enough, after only a few minutes I began peeling off windpants, windbreaker and gloves, gear I wouldn't need again and that I would have to carry for the rest of the journey.

The previous evening, Zimmerman had asked if I had done any long, sustained downhills, and he stared mutely when I answered no. Now, trying to skip as dexterously as I could from spot to spot down the trail, avoiding the brakes as much as possible, I appreciated the point of his question. I had tried to simulate jarring as much as possible in my training by running repeats down steps, but it hardly seemed to be making a difference. Neither that nor my longest training runs of 18 miles were going to help much today.

Our group of four made no attempt to stay together, but instead headed down following separate agendas, stopping to adjust packs, remove clothing and take a swig or two of liquid. I was drinking Wild Bill's XXX Grand Canyon Mix, a high-energy concoction personalized for this occasion by an ultrarunner friend of mine.

It was incredible to imagine, but after an hour of steady downhill running, I still hadn't reached the bottom. I had descended through gold, orange and red sediments deposited before the birth of dinosaurs. I had reached a plateau formed half a billion years before this part of the continent began uplifting against the flow of the Colorado River, but I still hadn't bottomed out. From the Tonto Platform where I now jogged, I was enjoying the dawn of one more day, the warmth of one more sunrise, the glow of one more morning deep in the Grand Canyon. And my quads hurt like hell.

Finally, trying in vain to buffer my ever-tightening muscles, I made the final descent down one last series of switchbacks into the canyon's inner gorge and reached the Colorado River. After descending from 7,200 to 2,450 feet and completing perhaps one-tenth of my journey, I could already tell it was going to be a long day.

Steve Corona had warned me that there would be only two places on the trail that I could rely on for water. One was a spigot at Phantom Ranch, a hiking, riding and overnight area on the north side of the river. Even there the water supply was tenuous, though, due to a recent break in the pipe, so I was grateful to be able to refill my bottles.

A part of me wanted to stay at Phantom Ranch, where campers were frying bacon for breakfast while deer grazed nearby. I could dunk my feet in the creek, kick back for a few hours, have a meal, and join the run back up the canyon in a few hours.

Just a thought. A minute later I was back on the trail, winding up the dark, narrow gorge of Bright Angel Canyon, the handiwork of one of the many side streams responsible for the extensive erosion that defines the Grand Canyon. Not much direct sunlight gets in here, and the granite walls are nearly vertical. I began to feel isolated, even lonely. I wondered where the other runners were.

A few miles later I found out, as I caught up with three men, none of whom I had met before. Two of them, Irv Nielsen and Tom McFarland, were members of the Utah Symphony Choir and were singing a Mozart tune in honor of the scenery. The third, Steve Utley, seemed to be listening. I offered to sing something by Jim Morrison, and despite this they allowed me to tag along.

All three had some experience with ultras, they seemed to be in no pressing hurry, and they were eager to share stories and information. Irv, a pharmacist and the trail supervisor at the Wasatch 100, had a good understanding of local vegetation and a seemingly endless supply of really bad jokes, which got even worse at higher elevations. In short, this was the perfect group to trudge along with to the top of the North Rim.

We reached the pump house near Roaring Springs, nearly nine moderately uphill miles from the Colorado River, without a whole lot of grief. The pumphouse caretaker, Bruce Aiken, moved to this spot from Manhattan twenty years ago, raised a family here, and spends his free time painting landscapes. He seemed genuinely pleased to see us using the spigot in his front yard.

It would be nearly 2 hours, five miles, and 3,600 vertical feet later that our gang of four would reach the North Rim. We could see it most of the time, but we didn't always seem to be getting there very quickly.

"Every time I look up there," observed Irv at one point. "it's farther away."

"Well then," scolded Tom, "stop looking up there."

I remember running occasionally during this long uphill march, and lots of moments when I felt like Wily Coyote, standing on a trail carved precariously into a rock face, staring out past one long misstep to what could be a very nasty landing hundreds of feet below.

"Isn't it *beautiful?*" bellowed Utley as we skirted around one cliff. I was hugging the inside, averting my eyes. How was I going to get past this point, I wondered, coming back down? Eventually, the trail headed into the trees and my fear passed. Around 11 o'clock, we began passing runners on their way back.

One woman, who must have been 50, was beside herself with joy on her return. "Isn't this great?" she enthused, beaming.

I think most ultrarunners are like this. The only opponent on race day is the distance, and fellow runners are greeted with open hearts and honest enthusiasm. Their encouragement helped me reach the North Rim, finally, 20 minutes before noon.

As I stood munching a granola bar, I remembered something Steve Corona had said: "What people should do is come here in October, run to the North Rim one day, stay overnight, and run back to the South Rim the next day."

Good advice, I thought, going just one direction during late spring or early fall, when weather conditions in the Grand Canyon are reasonably pleasant, and catching a ride back.

"Have you ever done that?" I asked Corona about his suggested overnight rest.

He just smiled, of course, as people do who never follow their own good advice.

NOON

By noon, our group was on the way back down. Given my skittishness coming up some of the dicier sections of this trail, I was amazed at how quick and panic-free the run back to Bruce Aiken's was. The tensest moment came a few hundred yards from his house, when we faced off with a mule deer on a rocky section of the trail. He finally blinked, turned and clattered off.

Reaching Aiken's, we stopped for a rest, refill and tall glass of lemonade. I'd been running in T-shirt and shorts for most of the day, so I was amazed when a woman runner in tights and windbreaker stopped for water.

She introduced herself as Lorraine Gersitz, but I found myself over the next few miles trying to remember if she had said Eileen or Irene or Ellen, and was that Gershwitz or Dershwitz or something else? I recognized my confusion as normal deterioration of brain function in the latter stages of a long, long run.

I followed Gersitz down the next nine miles, still surprised that she was dressed so warmly while I was struggling more and more with dehydration. I was also amazed at her flowing ease down the trail, in comparison to my own fumble-footedness. After that second long downhill of the day off the North Rim, every small barrier had become a high hurdle.

The final stages of Bright Angel Canyon narrowed to the dark corridor I remembered from early that morning, but the trip seemed infinitely longer. At every turn I expected to see Phantom Ranch, but every turn produced yet another dark corridor and yet another turn. My legs were really giving out now, as was my stomach, which finally rebelled against lemonade, warm weather and the general human condition. I retched, paused for a minute, then continued.

"You all right, partner?" asked Steve Utley, who was running behind me.

I was, but I was also promising myself, with the sincerest conviction, that I would *never do this again.*

By the time Utley and I reached Phantom Ranch, I realized I was within reach of my goal. Crossing the Colorado River, I vowed to put my head down and make it back to the South Rim before dark, before my young daughter could panic.

"The climb out is the real killer," Corona had told me. "I call it the hardest 10K in the world."

It was also a nearly 3-hour return to "the present." From rocks half as old as the planet itself, upward through geological layer after layer, winding through a landscape chiseled and eroded by the elements over millions of years, I hiked as fast as I could, anxious to reach the top. Being in the Grand Canyon is a compelling reminder of how long the Earth has been here, and how short our own stay will be. It made me want to get back to the present, to family and friends, as soon as possible.

There were places on the upward journey where I could look straight across at some of the most impressive monuments in the canyon, landforms that the first white explorers here named after ancient shrines and temples, and which still inspire hushed reverence in visitors.

The Kaibab Trail had nowhere to refill my bottles, so I rationed water, rewarding myself for every 10-minute increment of time with a swallow of liquid. Ten minutes, drink. Ten minutes, drink. Steadily my bottles became lighter, and I got closer to the top. If I stopped my legs would cramp, so I kept moving. Utley promised me a cold beer on the top, and I began dreaming about it.

Coming around a bend in the trail halfway up, I startled two ravens the size of Labradors. They jumped off the cliff and floated away, soon becoming two whirling black dots in the infinite space below.

Hikers began asking us if we were the rim-to-rim runners, and I was proud that our fame had spread. We passed a sign advising, as had the visitor's guide, not to attempt to hike to the Colorado River and back in one day, and I enjoyed the irony. With only a mile or two left, a pale moon rose on the other side of the canyon. The only sound, other than our own huffing and plodding, was the breeze.

Looking out over several especially precipitous drops, Utley and I agreed that, no matter how tough this had been, tempting fate by riding down here on the back of a mule would have been worse.

On our own two feet then, finally, at 5:34 p.m., after more than 11 hours in the Grand Canyon, we reached the top. A few minutes later, the light began to dim.

DUSK

Back at the lodge, I reunited with Kaitlin and my mother-in-law, and we shared our day's adventures. They had gone horseback riding. I had gone for a long run. We were all glad to have ended the day alive and well and back together.

An informal gathering of canyon runners scheduled for that evening failed to materialize, so I wasn't even sure how many runners there had been. Twenty? I ended up comparing notes, one-by-one, when I recognized someone I had seen along the trail. Some had taken a little over 9 hours, others, like 61-year-old Hal Winton, weren't quite sure and didn't really care.

Still, without a ceremony or celebration of some kind, I was curious about how to put the day in perspective. Was this the hardest run I'd ever done? My legs felt as if someone had been beating on them with a hammer all day. My back was sore from the weight of the fanny pack. There was a fairly impressive blister on my right heel. Both feet were shriveled up like raisins.

I had no trophy to display for all this, just a couple of shoes caked with orange dust. And, of course, a whole lot of images to carry around in my head.

I began fading toward sleep. Then I heard a voice.

"Dad?" said Kaitlin, her voice tinged with concern.

"Huh? What?"

"Are you okay? Your breathing is kind of weird."

"I'm fine, Kaitlin," I answered, smiling in the dark. "Yeah, I'm fine."

September 1993

OLD-TIMERS ON THE KLONDIKE TRAIL

"The thing you have to remember," said Murphy, "is that the other masters team is just as old and decrepit as we are."

STARTLING SCENES OF HUMAN AMBITION have been acted out in Alaska and the Yukon. Early on, native people managed to carve out niches in the hostile, frozen lands through a combination of unimaginable ingenuity and determination, finding food and shelter where none seemed to exist, and enduring for ages. Later pilgrims were no less hardy, prying riches, or at least sustenance, from the land, or dying in the attempt.

The northern environment forces humans to think and dream big, and to refuse to be intimidated by inadequacy or mortality. Witness the scene on the Chilkoot Trail in the years 1897 and '98, when gold lust created a human conga line, a vertical ant-path from the sea over the top of the nearby mountain pass, an icy formidable trip to the sky, and yet the most feasible route for those trying to reach the gold fields of the Yukon.

Over and back, over and back, and over again, and back again, twenty trips each, dreamers hauling provisions enough over the Chilkoot Trail's precipitous snow fields to reach the other side, ride the Yukon River from the rapids near the town of Whitehorse to Dawson City, stake a claim and become wealthy. Or so they hoped. Some froze along the way and were buried in the spring.

And now, nearly a 100 years later, another quest through these rugged mountains, from the town of Skagway at the northernmost part of the Alaska panhandle to Whitehorse in the Yukon, the two end points of the most rugged section of the golden highway of the Klondike Gold Rush of 1897-98. Another ant-trail of sorts, fueled again by human determination. Another attempt to thwart nature's plan to keep us humans in one place.

Ah, but this time we have runners, not miners. And it is late summer, mostly snowless. It is nighttime, too, with car taillights giving a modern, neon halo to the trail of ambition. It is the Klondike Trail of '98 International Road Relay, and my team is lusting for the lead.

These days, travelers at the top of Alaska's Inside Passage no longer take the Chilkoot Trail from the town of Dyea into the Yukon, but rather disembark at Skagway and follow White Pass. Miners a century ago sometimes used this mountain pass, too, since it was more gradual than the Chilkoot. Sadly, though, they also found it had challenges of its own, in the form of steep precipices, boulder fields, broken timbers, swamps and interminable bogs, which together frustrated the miners' journeys and claimed the lives of an estimated 3,000 horses.

With the completion of the White Pass railway in 1900, the route became reasonable for those not suffering from vertigo, and though the gold rush was over, this became the preferred course for those still seeking passage into the Yukon interior. Modern convenience made its mark again in 1978, when a highway opened through the pass. And this is where I found myself one very dark night in September, running uphill as fast as my wretched legs would carry me.

But really, can a modern road relay, a two-footed tromp on dry highway, be mentioned in the same breath as the struggles of ancient gold-seekers in an untamed, sub-zero wilderness? Yes, and not just because my teammates and I would be straining to conquer the same mountain range to reach the same endpoint. In today's world, we have challenges of our own. We are, you see, masters runners. We are all over 40.

"C'mon, Nellie," those old miners would chide their pack animals. "Don't give up on me."

They spoke to their horses. We speak to our calves, or sometimes to our hamstrings and Achilles tendons. "C'mon, down there. No blow-outs today."

Our conglomeration of over-40-year-olds first met at the pier in Skagway after traveling by car, plane and boat from farther north in Alaska and farther south in Washington and Idaho. We were divided by geography, but united in our interest in sharing stories of our maladies. We were called the Carcross 10, a team named after one of the towns along the route we would travel, but our supposed ten members was actually nine (not counting Archie's tripod; more on that later), and if initial indications held up, we would be the Carcross 8, 7 or 6 before we were done. A quick inventory revealed we had knee, tendon, calf and neuroma problems among us.

Fortunately, packs of desperate mosquitoes kept our team meeting at the dock short, so the issue of who had the most impressive injury was never settled. We had soon divided up relay legs and decided who would travel with whom in which car and sleep where. Even in the modern era, there are plenty of logistical challenges for those hoping to prosper in the Far North.

The Klondike Relay begins in the evening, starting with the slower teams. We had spent the afternoon eating, strategizing and touring Skagway, a town clearly catering to visitors, but whose pioneer past still manages to emerge from the tourist trade the way the yellow cupola of the Golden North Hotel rises above the gift shops. After watching the first teams begin their 110-mile quest, we had been train-whistled onto our own journey, and now I was racing up into the dark mountain pass, carrying my team's hopes for the first 8.8 miles.

Actually, it wasn't totally dark. Behind me, two of my team members drove steadily, van headlights intending to light the roadway but more often projecting dancing, wraith-like shadows on the nearby cliffs. Now and then the van fell behind, and it was just me and the void. I remembered that the entry waiver had mentioned possible contact with wild animals. I had also been told by one relay veteran that cars stayed with the runners "to ward off the wolf pack." Of course the guy *had* smirked.

Mostly, though, I was stewing about my Achilles tendon, still sore after a tear months earlier, and my calf, not quite totally mended from past muscle pulls. The tendon ached and the calf twitched sporadically during the ascent, neither quite comfortable with the 1,500-foot elevation gain.

I was determined to make it, though. After all, my teammates — wherever they might be nesting at the moment along the dark, golden highway — needed me. More important, I didn't want to be the master who disastered. So I pressed onward and upward, slowing when the darkness engulfed or my calf clutched, and after nearly an hour I reached the exchange point. Having suffered no major blowup or breakdown, I happily handed off to our second runner, Bob Murphy, a middle school vice principal from Fairbanks.

Near as we could tell, our Carcross 10 was in second place among masters teams and fourth overall. First was the Alaska Masters, also and better known as the Smokin' Old Geezers. We had seen the Geezers on the ferry trip up from Juneau, where most of them lived. Cruising through fjord-like waterways of the Inland Passage — no roads, no buildings, only mile upon mile of green hillside and mountain tops sawing through the clouds — we kept bumping into Geezers who wanted to know which of our team was running which leg and how fast that particular person might be expected to run. We evaded clear answers and called team meetings in response.

Now, the Geezers seemed to have the best of us. The previous year, they had won the Klondike Relay outright, passing the top open team in the final leg to win the 11.5-hour race by less than a minute. Their presence ahead of us was, of course, unacceptable, and Murphy took off after them.

The graph of my leg of the relay, from Skagway into White Pass, had looked like an up-charging diagram of the federal debt. Murphy's 5.8-mile leg, though, was even worse, like the pitched roof of an A-frame.

Worried about a calf problem that had kept his training to a bare minimum, "Murph" had suggested we be on alert in case he needed to bail out before reaching the exchange zone at the summit. We watched fretfully.

The only way out of the Skagway cul-de-sac is over the mountain tops, and, highway or not, it is a climb that daunts the spirit. The prevailing wisdom among veterans of the relay was that this second leg is best run in the dark, never seen in broad daylight by those drafted to elevate themselves to the top. Be that as it may, we watched Murph climb with conviction, smooth and effortless as Canadian whiskey. As each mile passed, I began to relax. I would not have to substitute on this particular leg.

The Klondike Relay has been known to suffer rain, sleet and even snow at this time of year, or all of them at once as it did in 1992. This year, though, Murph crested White Pass in an eerie fog bank and handed off to our third runner, Ron Downey.

We had begun at this point to mix in with dozens of the ninety teams that had started before us, and it was hard to know what place we were in or, more important, where the Geezers were. We followed Downey, a financial analyst from Anchorage, as he hunted down one bouncing florescent vest after another on the snaking neon highway. On either side of the road, one imagined, were breathtaking drop-offs into oblivion.

Over the top now and heading steadily downhill, Downey flew with power and ease into British Columbia. Downey had recently returned to uninjured running form after falling off a ladder and breaking bones in both hands two years earlier.

By the time he reached the end of his 7.6-mile leg — in what would be the fastest third leg of the day — and handed off to our fourth runner, Fairbanks attorney Dan Callahan, Downey had succeeded in moving us ahead of the Geezers. Or maybe it had happened during Murph's spectacular ascent. In a relay where runners and support vehicles are constantly trading places, it was difficult to tell. Either way, we were now in the lead.

We were especially relieved when Callahan took over, since we had not seen him since earlier in the day, when he and other team members left Skagway to stake out their places along the route, catnapping patiently until we arrived.

"Let's remember rule number one of relay racing," a teammate had insisted when we parted. "Somebody be at each exchange point."

Now, with the exchange made, our team in the lead and our runner well in control, we could relax and enjoy a pleasant evening cruise in the upper northwest tip of British Columbia. I was hoping for a view of the northern lights, which I had heard had whiplashed the sky in a vivid display during other Klondike Relays.

"If it's clear you can almost always see them," Mike McKrill, a Juneau runner and veteran of several Klondikes, had reported. "A couple of years ago you could *hear* them, popping and crackling."

And so I leaned out the window, seeing stars and even a crescent moon among dark clouds, but no other light show. And then...*Callahan was leaning against our van, stretching his calf!* It was a kind of epiphany, a guy with red tights, yellow shorts, purple shirt, orange vest and silver hair, stopped to stretch in the middle of the wilderness.

Later, we would hear that his calf had been cramping on the downhills, and he was hoping to prevent a full-scale spasm. At the time, though, I could only panic, wondering if I should warm up and get ready to replace him, a legal substitution that would cost us a 5-minute penalty, while merely substituting one shaky calf for another.

We watched in anticipation as Callahan got back in motion, and we waited for a sign that the jig was up. Instead, on he went, mile after mile, running smoothly and never pausing for another stretch. We got a report from behind us, and it appeared the Geezers were not gaining on us in spite of Callahan's achey muscle.

"The thing you have to remember," said Murphy, "is that the other masters team is just as old and decrepit as we are."

Indeed. And so at the end of Callahan's 13.3-mile leg, we retained our lead, and Callahan passed off to our fifth runner, John Schulte. A Spokane training partner of mine, Schulte is also an electrician. That meant, I hoped, that he would have brought along some duct tape to fix whatever problem might beset our team next.

Schulte had been suffering from a neuroma of the foot, but as he passed vest after vest along the trail of glowing taillights during his 15.4-mile leg, the foot held up nicely. By this point we had passed most of the teams that had started ahead of us, so the competition among us, the Geezers, and a mixed team known as Take No Prisoners, began to emerge.

It was early in the morning and still dark when Schulte entered the Yukon and our sixth runner, Jeff Corkill, took over. Those of us who train in Spokane know Corkill as a ferocious 50-year-old who seems especially suited to steep, nasty hills. A minute behind him, though, was Take No Prisoners' Don Clary, an Alaska native and 1984 Olympian who would fly by Corkill after a few miles like a mountain lion running down a deer. Then, too, the Geezers' Guy Thibideau was also stalking our man over the 14.6-mile course.

As the sky brightened in the Yukon, it became all too clear that

Thibideau would make up a 2-minute deficit and bring his team even with ours. The final miles would see Thibideau and Corkill battling like a couple of grubstakers eager to settle a barroom dispute. With their feet.

The two dropped out of the mountains and headed for the town of Carcross — our team's namesake and the home of George Carmack, Skookum Jim and Tagish Charles, the three men who made the original gold strike on the Yukon's Bonanza Creek in 1896. With steep, snow-dusted peaks and yellow sparks of cottonwoods and birches among the evergreens, the scenic Yukon autumn reflected in the still lake across from the exchange point.

"There are two seasons in the Yukon," a local radio broadcaster, Ron McFadyen, had told me earlier. "Winter and next winter."

This, though, was clearly autumn, and a stunning one at that, creating a perfect backdrop for a two-footed duel. As the challenge transferred to each team's seventh runner, the Geezers had a slight edge.

Our next runner was a repeat, Ron Downey. With nine on our team and ten legs to run, it had fallen to Downey — through some stroke of careful strategy, team intuition, or perhaps the simple recognition that he was almost the only member of our team not nursing an injury — to run twice.

Downey had already run the fastest third leg of the day, and now, starting a bit tight and chilled in the near-freezing weather but steadily warming to the task, he accelerated past the seventh Geezer. It happened so suddenly and decisively that I couldn't help but make whooping sounds into the expansive Yukon wilderness.

Turning in yet another best-of-the-day relay leg, Downey passed the baton to our next runner, Archie George, giving our team a 1.5-minute lead over the Geezers. A minute ahead ran Take No Prisoners.

Our lead over the Geezers doubled during the next leg, and we passed Take No Prisoners, as Archie overcame the knee glitch that had been plaguing him for months and turned in the day's fastest time for the 12.3-mile eighth leg. The only thing that seemed to be moving faster than the Carcross 10 at this point was Archie's camera tripod, which had disappeared at the dock in Skagway, hitched a ride to several points along the route before being cornered by Archie in Carcross, and seemed destined to bolt again at any moment. Some of us wanted to either sign it up as an additional team member, or at least rename ourselves

"Where's Archie's Tripod?" in deference to his constant befuddlement over the whereabouts of the three-legged traveler.

Or at least we had discussed it earlier. Now, with the masters and overall lead, we were sniffing victory, a heady aroma like bacon at the campfire. Two legs to go, and if we could just hold together, pick up a minute or two and hold off those tenacious Geezers, we could be first to stake our claim in Whitehorse. The payoff was nigh.

Canadian writer Edward McCourt, in *The Yukon and Northwest Territories* (New York: St. Martin's Press, 1969), says that the dream of gold represented "for the middle-aged and old (and there were many on the gold trail who had reached, and in some instances far exceeded, their allotted span), the chance to begin again, to atone for defeat and failure, to blot out the past by a single smashing triumph."

And I suppose that's what — in a modern, athletic, simple-minded sort of way — we wanted. But when it was all over and we were soaking in Takhini Hot Springs outside of Whitehorse, the sting of failing in that quest took quite some time to melt away. Fool's gold, that's what it had been, our ambitions on the golden highway.

Of course most of the team members were simply glad the specific problem hadn't happened to them. Instead, it became the fate of Jeff Sink, a high school history teacher and three-sport coach from Fairbanks, to suffer the master's nightmare on behalf of all the Carcross 10. Shortly after taking over the 11.1-mile ninth stage, a pesky Achilles from an old basketball injury went south. Sink tried to hobble through it, but it wasn't to be.

The best option seemed to be to put our final runner, Ted Fortier, into the race early, take the 5-minute penalty and hope for a miracle. Perhaps Fortier, a Jesuit priest, might have some pull in that department.

As it turned out, though, the guy with the most pull, push and acceleration was the Geezer's Greg Tibbetts, who passed Fortier shortly into the final, 11.9-mile leg and soon disappeared over the horizon. The Geezers went on to a masters course record, reaching the finish line at the S.S. Klondike sternwheeler next to the Yukon River in Whitehorse in

11:14:05. We fell to third behind Take No Prisoners.

If you have to nurse injuries and egos, a natural hot spring isn't a bad place to do it. Nor was the postrace party, with good beer and timely results, stage by stage, team by team, division by division. Those who live in the Yukon obviously develop good organizational skills, most likely to avoid freezing.

I assume those returning from the Yukon 100 years ago carried, if not fortunes, at least stunning memories. We certainly did. But when you've almost, but not quite, struck pay dirt, there's this nagging little voice in the back of your head that won't shut up.

Now, having returned to the parts of the world from which our team was originally assembled, most of us can't stop hearing that voice, urging us to get back on the golden trail again. And since the voice is insistent, we can't help but wonder what the Geezers are up to at the moment. And, pondering that thought, we generally find ourselves massaging our calves and Achilles, along with our egos.

September 1993

MÉDOC MARATHON

I had almost forgotten about the mollusk challenge. Suddenly, though, as I turned right and began the final four kilometers, they twinkled on the edge of my field of vision, nagging shellfish on a table at the side of the road. Oysters!

THE LAST FEW MILES of any marathon can be brutal, and this French event was no exception. We had enjoyed early miles of high-spirited celebration, then flowed across grape-laden hillsides and past magnificent country estates. We had been greeted at every turn with music, cheering spectators and volunteers eager to keep us happy, or at least vertical. But now, with less than three miles left, too many among us were struggling against total collapse during those last, eternal strides to the finish.

This is a common feeling among marathoners in the final stages of the journey, and the French are not immune. It can be a grim test, but also one whose bleak edges can be softened. Struggle, yes, but stop to smell the rosés. Or at least the clarets.

Thus it was, at that point of the Marathon des Châteaux du Médoc et des Graves when despair had settled in among the runners like rain on the Riviera, like black mold on cheese, like an especially despondent mime on your shoulder, that organizers were ready with the one thing that could lift the sagging body and soul and inspire the spirit to seek that distant finish line.

There it was, on my right. An oyster bar.

I plucked one of the salty, cement-colored blobs off the half shell, glanced at it a moment and sucked it down. I followed with a couple of swallows of Mouton Cadet Bordeaux Blanc. Then I went to catch Julius Caesar.

This was one weird marathon.

Not that I was surprised. My Dutch friend, Michel Lukkien — coach, manager, businessman, running-travel enthusiast, oenophile — had told me of the celebratory details of this marathon for years.

"The route is beautiful," he said. "You run over rolling hills of vineyards and pass more than thirty different châteaus. Most of the runners are in costumes, there are bands all along the way and there are wine stations. The one at 24 miles serves oysters. It's crazy. You should do it."

Michel sent me a souvenir T-shirt showing a red-nosed cartoon figure running down the middle of the street carrying a bottle of wine, zigging and zagging between vineyards on either side of the road. The inscription read: "Médoc — Le Marathon Le Plus Long Du Monde." (the longest marathon in the world). Indeed, the guy on the shirt looked unlikely to reach the finish. And could I, after wine and oysters?

In search of the answer to this tantalizing question, I joined Michel's group of Dutch and Belgian runners for a mid-September trip to the Bordeaux region in southwestern France. It was nearly harvest time, but the frantic scramble to collect the precious grapes at just the right moment was still a few days away. Meanwhile, 6,000 marathoners were descending on the town of Pauillac, where the Marathon des Châteaux du Médoc et des Graves — the Châteaus of Médoc and Graves Marathon, or, simply, the Médoc Marathon — was about to begin.

A region whose economy lives and dies on the weather becomes sensitized to the subtleties of sun, rain, temperature and humidity. The way nature smiles and broods over bunches of Cabernet Sauvignon, Merlot, Sauvignon Blanc and other varieties of grapes changes the final product — wine — in ways that are esoteric but critical to artistic and financial success. Runners, who also prosper or fail based on the weather's whims, should empathize.

"Growing grapes for wine is like chess," Michel had said during our drive here.

I had suggested that any kind of crop production had always seemed to me more of a crap shoot than a chess match.

"No. Chess," Michel had answered with conviction, explaining how a clever vintner learns to react to nature's moves — deciding which grapes to grow, how to tend the fields and when to pick which bunches from which vines, always strategizing against the elements.

Of course it didn't take a genius to figure out that a major windstorm like the one that buffeted southwest France a few days before our arrival would *not* be greeted with happy vintner hearts. Nor were race organizers thrilled to be dealing with the threat of thunderstorms in the days leading up to the race.

When we arrived at race headquarters in Pauillac on Thursday, officials were faced with the prospect of desertion by caterers hired for the prerace party. The thought of lightning hitting the metal pole supporting the party tent had the caterers on edge, and the thought of having no food at the party had organizers scurrying around frantically at race headquarters.

"This is French, this panic," said Michel. "If there is *no* panic, then there's panic."

Personally, I would have expected more of a *c'est la vie* approach from the French. In any case, on Friday evening the tents at the prerace party were pummeled by rain but suffered no fried waiters, and race morning arrived overcast, a bit humid, but mostly pleasant.

A boisterous crowd packed the starting area in Pauillac. More than half of the entrants in this marathon were wearing costumes, much of the garb surprisingly elaborate considering the 26-mile journey ahead. The town's 800 children were the official judges of the costume contest, and entrants seemed eager to play to the young crowd.

There were Polynesian dancers in grass skirts; dozens of cartoon and comic-book characters, hundreds of clowns, jesters and mimes; teams dressed like rabbits and flies and circus entertainers; and an inordinate, startling number of men in drag. It may help to remember that *costum* is a French word, as is *ambians*. Or just think of a Bordeaux Bay to Breakers or Médoc Mardi Gras, and you should get the idea.

I lined up in the middle of the pack, ahead of the Chinese dragon and the fire truck, and just behind the Viking ship. This was the most joyful marathon crowd I'd ever seen. They chatted, sang, laughed, chanted and kissed, but eventually a starting pistol cracked somewhere up front, and the athletic festival began flowing forward. We were on our way.

Packed together like bunches of grapes in a press, eager to perform for the children of the village, and still hours away from those spirit-sapping final miles, the runners shouted and sang their way through town, the sounds of celebration echoing off stone walls and roaring up alleyways.

The first 15 minutes of the marathon must be especially heart-warming to its founders, who intended just this sort of raucous bon voyage for athletic *bon vivants*. The Médoc Château Marathon Association, which created and oversees this affair, is essentially a group of five friends — three doctors, a wine grower and an engineer — who started running to lose weight, had a wonderful time in the New York City Marathon, but were disappointed in the somber, competitive character of their next marathon in the city of Bordeaux.

"It was very sad," noted Hubert Rocher, an orthopedic surgeon who was this year's race director. "We said we must do something in our region with the châteaux, something for pleasure and not only for time."

The friends began working with the Commanderie du Bontemps de Médoc et des Graves, an organization whose mission is to celebrate and promote the great wines of Médoc and Graves, two of the best wine-growing areas of the Bordeaux region. Members of the Commanderie, or Brotherhood, wear burgundy-colored velvet robes and matching hats with white linen on top. The hats are designed to look like the bowls (*bontemps*) used to whip egg whites for one of the final steps in the production of great wines, part of a process dating back to the Middle Ages. Imagine a French combination of the Chamber of Commerce and the Shriners, and you get a pretty good picture of the Commanderie.

The Médoc Château Marathon Association and the Commanderie were natural allies, both groups being committed to having a good time while advancing the reputation of their Bordeaux wines. The first marathon, in 1985, was a rousing success, and word spread quickly about the costumes, the châteaus, the wine stops, and maybe even the oysters. By the second year, organizers were already having to turn people away to protect the spirit of the event.

"We said we must keep things convivial," says Rocher, "something between friends. But each year — more and more people."

Word of a good party spreads fast, and by 1993 the race included runners from seventeen European countries and a handful from the United States and Canada.

"Most important for us," says Rocher, "is not the internationalities but the reputation and the fact that the sport is good for your health — like wine, if you don't drink too much. I think sport is good also, but not too much. All is bad when you do too much."

There wasn't much moderation in the celebrating, of course, but mid-race wine-drinking *was* restrained. I had decided to stop at as many of the eighteen reported wine-tasting stations on the course as I could. The first, though, at 1K, was blocked by a human windmill enjoying a glass of red, and it would be another five miles before I could have my first sip.

In the meantime, we left the narrow streets, crowds and music of Pauillac and ventured out into the vineyards. I began moving up, passing cavemen dressed in gray-and-white wigs and leopard skins, two windmills and five millers, Mickey and Minnie Mouse, French sailors shadowing a shark, Catwoman, two killer bees, six rabbits, and a dozen guys pushing a cart with a huge, round loaf of bread on it, one of whom (the runners) looked like British distance ace Sebastian Coe playing an accordion.

At times I could see the human parade stretch in front and in back of me, flowing over the vine-woven hillsides, making a better running fence than Cristo ever envisioned.

When I finally got my first sip of wine near 10K, I was surprised. It hummed and glowed and slid happily all the way down, with nary a hint of rejection. Not an ideal mid-race replacement drink, perhaps, but not a bad way to liven up the middle of this particular marathon.

Organizers of the Médoc Marathon have traveled to major running events around the world doing "research" into what runners enjoy, but it's unlikely they've found another marathon quite like their own. In fact, they've sensed somewhat of a prejudice against a Frenchman's favorite beverage, and are quick to point out the benefits of a glass of the red stuff, in terms of iron content and, most important, outlook on life. And from what I've seen, the French have pretty much got outlook on life figured out.

Just past this wine stop, the course diverted through the grounds and almost up to the front door of Château Branaire Ducru, a dignified, rectangular, two-story brick building with red tile roof and a balcony above the front porch. A handful of the privileged gentry stood there sipping wine, waving and shouting encouragement to the runners.

"*Très bien!*" one yelled, which means, I think, "Let them eat oysters."

There were a few aristocratic heads from this region, by the way, that rolled during the French Revolution, and I had gotten a good indication at the prerace party the night before of what that social clash might have been like. We arrived at the banquet at Château Lanessan, a stunningly elegant three-story stone mansion, at about the same time as a group of about twenty runners dressed in punk attire — spiked Day-Glo hair, chains, graffiti faces and sporadic lycra on the legs — twentieth century rabble with an aerobic twist.

During a horse-jumping exhibition on the grounds, the group drank too much wine, scared the horses with firecrackers, and generally intimidated the crowd with a totally believable punk act. For the first time in my life, I felt sorry for Marie Antoinette.

That party, by the way — punks or no punks — was one more indicator of the prevailing attitude about the next day's race. Combine eating, drinking, dancing and a particularly rousing sing-along reminiscent of Otis and the band in *Animal House*, only with French accents, and you leave wondering how anyone is ever going to make it through the race the next day. I've never been to a prerace party that was more like a postrace party.

Of course celebrating does have its limits, and as I moved up through the crowd from 10- to 20K, I noticed that costumes were becoming less and less elaborate, and the sober side of marathoning was beginning to emerge. We enjoyed African drums, Spanish music and some bluesy rock and roll, but runners were pausing longer at the water aid stations, which were frequent and well-stocked.

Halfway through the course, we came upon many of the most beautiful châteaus, which are home to some of the world's most famous wines. At 21K, I passed two guys in purple singlets and chartreuse tutus in front of Château Pontet-Canet, a two-story yellow stone building with an Alpine look to it. A kilometer later, we headed up the gravel driveway of Château Mouton-Rothschild, elaborately landscaped and painstakingly tended. And finally, we passed Château Lafite-Rothschild and Château Cos d'Estournel, two of the most striking estates in the region.

Château Lafite-Rothschild is more famous, producing a world-class red wine that is one of only five top-rated wines (*premier grand cru classé*) from the Médoc-Graves region, a rating earned in an 1855 classification of Bordeaux wines that has remained virtually unchanged since that time.

Château Cos d'Estournel, on the other hand, seemed to me the most impressive estate on the course, with its arched doorways, towers with copper-colored roofs, decorative work around the rooflines and an overall Moorish attitude. Like many of the other châteaus in this area, its caramel-colored stones are not unlike the surrounding gravelly soil in hue, suggesting that the buildings have essentially sprung from the ground. Wine-colored trim around doors and windows completes the illusion that the rich soil and grapes have given birth to the ornate structures, which isn't far from the truth.

By this point, bicycles and a tourist trolley had joined the runners for the final 10 miles. I passed Wonder Woman — tall, physically imposing in blue-caped superhero garb, with sleek, muscled legs. Truly an uplifting mid-race vision, which I later discovered was deceptive. Wonder Woman used to be Wonder *Man*, I was told, or maybe just Average Guy, before his operation.

I stopped for wine several more times, passed a very Degas-looking pink clown, heard Elvis singing over loudspeakers, and noticed that the costumes were looking a bit more ragged. In the Médoc Marathon, there are plenty of real, amber-toned sandstone walls to run into, but at 32K, volunteers had instead erected a simulated one made of plywood. I passed through an opening in the 32K "wall" and headed back toward Pauillac, joining hundreds of the slouching, physically downtrodden masses on their final, weary march home.

As I ran down the hills of Saint-Estèphe through the last vineyards and reached flat land next to the Gironde Estuary, I had almost forgotten about the mollusk challenge. Suddenly, though, as I turned right and began the final four kilometers, they twinkled on the edge of my field of vision, nagging shellfish on a table at the side of the road. Oysters!

Well, a single oyster anyway, for me. Salty and passive and down the hatch. And then wine, the Bordeaux Blanc, my last of the day. Strange, wouldn't you think, to finish this marathon meal with white wine, instead of a full-bodied red?

Proud of myself for successfully wrestling the bivalve down my gullet, I finished strongly, passing Julius Caesar and a large ladybug. I hustled down the sycamore-lined final kilometer to a sub-3:30 finish with one of Michel's group, Arie Kauffman, executive director of the Dutch Track and Field Federation and a first-time marathoner.

Afterward, I found out that the fastest of our Dutch-Belgian group, Philiep Steelandt, had battled for the lead with a young French runner for 32 kilometers before slipping back to second. Neither man drank wine, ate oysters, or was dressed like anything but a top runner — at least not during the race.

For their mid-race abstinence, these two were awarded wine at a postrace ceremony presided over by the Commanderie. Both men's and women's winners received their weight in wine, a feat accomplished by seating them on one end of what was essentially a large teeter-totter, then piling case after case of Bordeaux's finest on the other end until the board balanced. To the delight of the audience, race organizers placed mostly surreptitious hands on the makeshift scale, making sure the winners actually got *more* than their weight's worth.

Finally, for good measure, the top finishers were inducted into the Commanderie, as was Michel, an honor limited to a chosen few special friends of Bordeaux wines.

After the induction, each was asked to comment on a glass of wine they were served on stage. When the second-place female, an Englishwoman, seemed flustered by the French questioning, the inquisitor tried to get beyond the intricacies of bouquet, flavor, body and vintage, and make it as simple as possible for the confused foreigner.

"C'est rouge?" he asked.

And what about all those tired clowns, Vikings and rabbits out on the course, finishing their journey as the sun broke through the haze? Did they collect their free bottle of wine at the finish, wash the makeup off their faces, enjoy the postrace festivities, then stagger home for a solid week or more of regeneration?

Not this crowd. By the next morning, nearly a thousand revelers were at it again, this time jogging an 8K "recovery" run through the vineyards surrounding Château Smith Haut Lafitte in the Graves region. The sight of a 1,000 people trotting together over hillsides and through patches of forest, carrying flags and banners and plundering local estates of their fine wines, was a vision of medieval proportions, at least until the vision began to blur.

But finally, of course, that postrace romp, too, was over, and the troops did head home. Many, no doubt, had been touched by the mood of the region and its blessed liquid bounty. Back home, they would spread the word about the spirit of the weekend, the noble châteaus and rolling hills, the carnival atmosphere, and the marathon's commitment to the finer things the Earth has up its sleeve.

They might even wax as poetic about their experiences as did that Romantic Englishman John Keats almost two centuries ago in singing the praises of the good life:

"Give me books, fruit, French wine and fine weather, and a little music out of doors, played by somebody I do not know."

To which twentieth-century athletic pilgrims to the Médoc Marathon, rethinking those final miles, would almost certainly want to add: "And don't forget the oysters."

June 1994

SPORTS MEDICINE WITH A HUMORAL COMPONENT

There seemed to be so many displays, lectures, workshops, symposia and colloquia going on concurrently that attendees were scurrying around like rats trying to keep up with things. That seemed like a fair turnabout, considering how often rats have had to scurry around to earn Ph.D.s for these people.

EARLY IN LIFE, I VOWED NEVER TO GET INVOLVED with people who used words like "hydroxypyridinoline." I don't care if it's Xolile Yawa or Mr. Myzyzptylk, I'm not listening. And don't get me started on "etiology."

When sports medicine people — physicians, physiologists, psychologists, nutritionists and associated sport and fitness wizards — get together, though, it appears that hydroxypyridinoline is as familiar as toast. And they're always studying the etiology of things, usually with the help of rodents.

I found this out when I attended the annual meeting of the American College of Sports Medicine (ACSM) in Indianapolis, which was wedged into a seemingly infinite number of rooms surrounding the Hoosier Dome. The ACSM is the largest organization in the world devoted to a scientific understanding of sports and fitness, so they need a lot of space and, if possible, a few tickets to the Pacers-Knicks game.

Knowledgeable running writers are regular attendees of this meeting, where they learn actual information and suffer various forms of brain damage from overexposure to hydroxypyridinoline. Later they write articles about what they've learned. The information is good.

I was on hand, on the other hand, on behalf of those runners who overeat, overtrain, undertrain, underachieve and suffer chronic injuries, but who are having so much fun doing it that they're not much interested in the science of it. They'd rather read about runners who have kidney explosions than actually learn how to prevent the problem. They think that an actual study at the ACSM convention called "Breast Support for the Active Woman: Relationship to 3D Kinematics of Running," and especially a chart showing "left vertical breast displacement," is really funny. These people are cretins, but they also make up a large proportion of the running population, so I was there to represent them.

This was my first ACSM convention, and I wanted to know more about this group of stunningly fit health professionals, so I conducted an exclusive interview with retiring ACSM president Russell Pate, Ph.D., just outside the Hoosier Dome snack bar, where delegates analyzed the lack of nutrients on the menu and then ordered coffee, the merits and demerits of which continue to be debated and then consumed.

"I think of ACSM and its members as being interested in the relationship between physical activity and health," said the coffee-stirring Dr. Pate, a former elite marathoner who I have trouble calling "doctor" since I used to know him as "Russ." "There are a whole lot of applications of that, but I think that's really what the organization is about."

Wanting to immerse myself in the concerns of this group, I was advised to start at the poster display, which was held in one of the big exhibition halls. Let's say you've spent a good slice of your life trying to understand the composition of sweat. Well, then, the poster display is where you'll want to eventually present your findings to your peers.

"You should never have used college students," your peers will say, shaking their heads.

"Tell me about it," you'll respond, pointing to a mass-spectrometer printout. "I still haven't figured out what some of these substances are."

The poster display is only one segment of the ACSM gathering, but for someone with a low understanding of the etiology of things, it's certainly the most entertaining. It has the feel of a science fair, but with an inordinate number of judges.

"Which Method of Assessing Abdominal Adiposity is the Most Predictive of the Insulin Resistance of Aging?" was the title of one display. If this had been a question posed by a college professor early one morning, I might have been inclined to answer, "Uh, the first? The second?"

Years ago I spent an evening at a political rally in an intensely crowded auditorium in Paris. Squeezed in the back, I couldn't see any of the speakers. One of them was Jean-Paul Sartre. My understanding of French was next to nil, so I had no idea what the speakers were saying. After three hours of this, a man spoke directly to me in French, possibly asking for a cigarette or the time of day. *"Je ne parle pas francais,"* I said proudly. He looked at me, no doubt wondering why a non-French-speaker was attending a rally for French radicals. Perhaps I was CIA. Perhaps, I thought, noticing his sidelong glances, I'd better leave.

Most of the ACSM poster display felt the same way. "Exercise Induced Motor Neuron Excitability is not Endogenous Opioid Mediated," read one. "Effects of Membrane Depolarization and Elevated Extracellular Calcium on Transverse Tubular Charge Movement," said another. And, of course, "Effects of Downhill Running on Leg Strength, Creatine Kinase, Hyroxyproline and Hydroxypyridinoline."

"Do you have any questions?" eager presenters would sometimes ask, and I would have to scuttle off, thinking, *"Je ne parle pas anglais ..."*

Imagine, then, how pleased I was to come across "Effects of Diet and Workload on Exogenous Glucose Utilization by the Isolated Working Rat Heart." I didn't understand this study, either, but I was almost giddy from the poetry of it. I immediately imagined a distraught lover, writing to the woman who has chosen her career over him:

> *"I love you!" I cry,*
> *But you cherish your briefcase and chart,*
> *And I hang my head, crushed by*
> *Your isolated working rat heart.*

I felt great after that, knowing poetry could mingle with science, and I decided to move on to other parts of the convention.

The main problem with doing this was deciding where, exactly, to go. There seemed to be so many displays, lectures, workshops, symposia and colloquia going on concurrently that attendees were scurrying around like rats trying to keep up with things.

That seemed like a fair turnabout, considering how often rats have had to scurry around to earn Ph.D.s for these people. I observed numerous studies of rat livers, rat muscles, rat brains, rat splenic non-adherent cells and, of course, rat hearts, isolated and not. I had heard that scientists are beginning to use lawyers instead of rats in experiments. Attorneys are more plentiful; researchers don't get attached to them; and, well, there are just some things a rat won't do. But I saw no lawyer studies, so apparently this is just another despicable joke that many runners, being cretins, might enjoy.

At any rate, it was very difficult knowing where to go next at the ACSM convention. "It really is a three-ring circus," said Russ-the-Doctor Pate. "But my view is that it's a good problem. I'd rather have people come to this meeting and say there's too much to do than not be able to find things to do."

Floundering around, then, I tended to walk into rooms just as very interesting topics were winding up, mostly with the conclusion that further study (i.e., grant money) was needed to *really* know what was going on. I came across snippets of information on children's running, carbohydrate replacement and heat problems, things that I'm actually interested in. As I entered one room, the lecturer was explaining, "you'd have to drink four to six 12-ounce beers a day to significantly raise HDL cholesterol." *Lots* of people wrote that down.

But most of the time I just watched in confusion as a lecturer would dance his or her red pointer-dot over charts and graphs that seemed mostly out of focus, saying, "as you're well aware" and "as everyone in this rooms certainly knows" and "of course we're all familiar with."

I was a little uneasy sitting in any of these rooms, partially from past classroom experiences when the teacher would suddenly interrupt a perfectly good daydream with words every student dreads: "So, you there in the back, what do you think?" More than that, though, I was afraid someone would show another slide of a muscle biopsy, a procedure that involves sticking a very large needle in the belly of a subject's muscle to remove a piece of fiber. I've had a muscle biopsy, and I survived the experience, but as everyone in the room was well aware *there is no need* to keep showing it!

When I felt inclined to actually learn something, I followed around people like Owen Anderson, editor of *Running Research News*, who is really good at interpreting physiological information for people like me.

We were at one discussion of the effect of cycling on running performance, when an audience member pointed to a chart and said to the lecturer, "The slope of your curve makes it look like VO_2 at zero velocity would be negative."

I looked at Owen. "They'd be dead," he explained.

With and without this kind of expert interpretation, I found that studies that seemed to present conclusive evidence of one thing or another were likely to wither under the scrutiny of one's peers. Of course the damage was done with detached politeness.

"Very nice study," a peer might say. "But do you think, perhaps, that the high torque values observed might suggest a miscalibration of your apparatus?"

"No," the researcher might respond in defense of years of work. "But do you think the density of your cranium might suggest heavy metal?"

Of course this was simply the hum of science — the careful, emotionally detached examination of variables to determine the certainty of things we already know. Or think we do.

I was not overwhelmed, for example, to learn that participants in a 24-hour run "felt worse following the run than they did before" or that children served a low fat lunch will selectively eat the high fat items. Heck, I'm a runner and a parent, so I *know* these things. But science does have a way of surprising you. If you thought full-time surfers were just spoiled rich kids bumming around in fatuous swimwear, you should know that the study "Body Fat Content and Maximal VO_2 of the Upper and Lower Body Among Surfers" has demonstrated that you're a total idiot. Surfers are actually beach rats (ha!) in *great* shape.

Those of us who don't live our lives within the confines of science do certainly tend to get a little impatient with the tedious, plodding advance of scientific understanding, with its constant whining about more study. Mostly, if a guy beats us in a race, we'll eat what he ate, stretch like he stretches, and try to date his girlfriend in the hope it'll improve our performance. We're not picky.

But it's hard not to be impressed when you hear where an organization like ACSM has gotten to over the forty years of its existence. A medical star like Dr. Ralph Paffenbarger, for example, is clearly not prone to make wild statements, as evidenced by the lecture he gave carefully reviewing studies of the relationship of physical activity to various diseases. And so, when he made a rare departure from text to give the bottom line — "For every hour of exercise, you get to live that hour over, plus one additional hour" — you listen.

Likewise when David Costill, white-haired icon and humorist of exercise physiology, began his lecture with a slide showing Roger Bannister breaking the 4-minute mile in 1954 and 41-year-old Eamonn Coughlin doing the same in 1994, you begin to sense how the forty-year life span of the ACSM has encompassed, and in many ways nurtured, fantastic improvements in human performances.

So as the weekend moved along, I found myself getting more tuned in. There were things going on here — injury prevention, running biomechanics, carbohydrate replacement — that could make a difference in the pursuit of my favorite sport. No kidding.

And at the end of the conference, when I was back perusing the poster displays and Costill walked by, joking, "I hope you're getting *all* of this," I could at least feel I was getting some of it.

"Training Alters Serine Esterase Activity of Mouse Splenic Non-adherent Cells." No, not that one. But "The Effects of Training Frequency and Volume in Novice Marathoners" was right up my alley. There was information here that might come in handy. And members of Costill's lab even presented a couple of studies in which I had been a subject. My muscles twitched with pride and remembrance of biopsy. Now, the twitch was joined by an increase of understanding. Science was advancing, step by step, here in the Hoosier Dome, and I was starting to march right along.

And then I hit this one: "The Hyperventilatory Response of Runners: Lack of a Humoral Component."

Now wait a minute, I thought. That's not true. It's just that, sometimes, we're a bit low in hydroxypyridinoline, and our mood suffers.

Or at least we think that's what's going on. If you really want to know, more study will be needed. And while you're at it, order us another twelve dozen rats.

LEADVILLE

At the top of a hill just outside town, those runners would be able to squint into the moonlit distance and see nearly the entire flank of the mountains they would be traversing. With a little imagination, you could almost make out the sharp-toothed, predatory grin of the Rockies.

OBSERVING A 100-MILE RUN, you're prepared for the struggle. You know this will be a grand sumo mismatch, where each human — steeled through months of training, myopically focused, and yet appearing small, wizened, not quite up to the task — will square off against his or her colossal opponent: a rugged, sometimes precipitous, intermittently gloomy, seemingly unending stretch of wilderness.

You're ready, then, to watch a few hundred individuals burrow deep within the dirt of their own souls to find that essential light, the spark of survival that will get them to the next mile, and the next, and the next.

What you are not ready for, though, is the race. You did not come here expecting to see a riveting battle for the lead, from before the first light of dawn until well after dark. You did not expect to find yourself standing halfway up a steep trail in the Colorado Rockies in the middle of the afternoon, wondering if this time when you see them pass, the woman will have built her lead over the Indian. Whether in fact she is on her way to beating all the legendary mountain runners of Mexico's Copper Canyon, along with most of the rest of the male and female ultrarunning world in this, one of the sport's premier events.

"I mostly just wanted to run the best race I could," says Ann Trason, long after she has completed one of the fastest 100-mile races *anyone* has ever run. "I never expected to lead the race."

Be that as it may, you can't help but be fascinated with the scene here, 53 miles into the challenge and halfway up 12,600-foot Hope Pass. Take a deep breath, check your watch. When they've passed, you realize she has picked up another 3 minutes. She is inching farther into the lead. You trot down the trail to the car and head for the next checkpoint. There, you wonder, another 20 miles down the path, will she still be leading? And if so, by how much?

It is essentially a test of humans against the distance, this or any 100-mile run. And yet from the beginning, the 1994 Leadville Trail 100 has also hinted at just the sort of epic race that will finally unfold, something more like a movie script than a hardscrabble footrace.

Ann Trason, a seasoned, scrappy 33-year-old from the San Francisco Bay Area, has been nipping the heels of front-running male runners on virtually every North American trail run since discovering the sport in 1985. Or, more often in recent years, letting them bark in frustration at *her* heels. Along with holding women's world records at 100K, 50 miles and 100 miles, Trason has a habit of winning ultras overall. She often finishes with no men in sight.

In June's prestigious Western States 100-Mile in California, eventual winner Tim Twietmeyer reportedly entered an aid station at 93 miles with one big question on his mind: "Where is she?" Everyone knew who "she" was, and she was a mere 10 minutes behind.

Trason eventually finished second at Western States, well behind Twietmeyer but beating her own course record by 37 minutes. As Leadville beckoned, then, no woman had won a major 100-mile race outright.

Not yet.

In Trason's mind, though, that was not the issue. "It's hard to imagine, but because I'm female and running in the women's race, it wasn't this competition thing that people made it out to be."

Fair enough. For Trason, this would be a chance to show how fast women can run. No male-bashing here, just advocacy. But for those of us watching, the possibility that female athletic excellence might eclipse male on this day kept us scuttling along the trail, measuring the possibility. Could she stay ahead, or would another fascinating character, or characters, steal the show? Juan Herrera and Martimano Cervantes would eventually emerge as the two leading challengers, but it was all seven Tarahumara Indians who teased the imagination.

Their people call themselves the Raramuri, or foot-runners. Legends of their long distance exploits in the mountainous areas of northwest Mexico's Copper Canyon have drifted north for ages, becoming yarns passed from one gringo runner to the next. The Tarahumara are said to travel up to 70 miles a day, 170 miles without stopping, 500 miles a week carrying 40 pounds of mail. Competitions between villages, in which runners kick a wooden ball along a trail for days on end, can cover over 100 miles before someone finally gives up. Just imagine, the legend went, how well these Native American Spartans would do in a footrace outside their own territory.

Imagine, indeed. With the exception of brief appearances in the 1928 and 1968 Olympics, though, it wasn't until 1992 that the Tarahumara first showed up to run outside their native environs. That was when wilderness guide Rick Fisher and ultrarunner Kitty Williams first brought some of them to Leadville.

Amid much speculation, the experiment went bust. The problem, it turned out, was an unfamiliarity with the trail and the strange ways of the North. The Indians stood shyly at aid stations, waiting to be offered food. They held their flashlights pointed skyward, unaware that these torches needed to be aimed to illuminate. And so on. All five Tarahumara dropped out before the halfway point.

The explanations seemed far-fetched, the legend tarnished. Until, that is, the 1993 Leadville race, when Tarahumaras — this time well-versed in ultrarunning practices, strategies and local topography — captured first, second and fifth. The legend, freshly polished, was back on its sandaled feet.

Every one of the 316 starters of the 1994 Leadville race knew the story, just as they knew the legacy of Ann Trason. They would get two chances to see the main characters: one at the start, one on the trail. The out-and-back course would allow everyone to see everyone at least once along the way.

Still, with 100 miles staring you in the face, who could have much fundamental interest in anything other than one's own survival?

At the prerace briefing the day before the run, Ken Chlouber, founder of this event and a veteran of nine, had asked for anyone who had failed to finish at least one Leadville run to stand. Dozens did. Then he asked for anyone who had failed to finish two or more to stand, and so on. By the time he asked for a show of how many had failed at least four times, it began to seem like he was picking on the handful of people still on their feet.

"The point is," said Chlouber, clarifying his intent, "there are some twisted minds out there."

Twisted indeed. And appreciative of other bent minds, so they applauded wildly when Chlouber introduced Laurel Myers, who had ten unsuccessful attempts — and was about to add number eleven. This may be the only sport on Earth where there is as much appreciation for those who fail but keep coming back again as for those who battle for the lead.

Saturday morning presented clear, still weather, a respite from weeks of soaking storms. Running 100 miles in the rain is no great treat, so this was greeted with enthusiasm. A full moon hung overhead, promising at least a dry start.

The clear weather was even more appreciated by crew members, who would be feeding, clothing and tending the destitute travelers for the next thirty hours. For an event that celebrates individual grit in the face of lonely struggle, there is a palpable sense of a wider community of support, an extended family of provisioners, well-wishers, spirit-boosters. Stories of runners in the final throes of exhaustion, when muscles turn to stone, faces droop below the knees, and personalities degenerate diabolically, are part of ultrarunning lore. Relief is spelled C-R-E-W.

"You know what 'crew' stands for, don't you?" asked Scott Mills, a

43-year-old entrant from Virginia. "Cranky runners, endless waiting."

Knowing this, runners at the start were genial. Best to enjoy one's normal nature before it gets reduced to shreds and shards. Best to bathe in camaraderie before the hounds of one's hellish bad self are loosed, somewhere around the 60-mile mark.

At the starting line, runners posed with friends and family members, while harsh television lights and the loudspeaker created a surreal mood. Perhaps, here on the highest Main Street in the country, one was simply living out a strange dream.

At 4 a.m., the dream got legs. Three hundred and sixteen runners dashed into the darkness, much too fast, it seemed.

"Good luck on your 30-hour journey," boomed an amplified voice at the runners' backs as they disappeared in the blackness. "We'll be here when you get back."

A half-mile later, at the top of a hill just outside town, those runners would be able to squint into the moonlit distance and see nearly the entire flank of the mountains they would be traversing. With a little imagination, you could almost make out the sharp-toothed, predatory grin of the Rockies.

There are only a handful of places along the Leadville trail where support crews and spectators come in contact with the runners. From a non-entrant's perspective, then, the journey becomes a series of vignettes, separated by large gaps of time filled with waiting, wondering, worrying.

The first scene was at the Tabor boat launch at about seven miles. There, like a crowd awaiting an alien encounter, dozens of people stood in the dark near Turquoise Lake, staring into the distance. To the right, the moon, about to dip below the peaks, sent a shimmering column of light across the lake. To the left, the stars in Orion's belt hung low in the sky. Straight ahead, across the water, the first points of light began dancing through the woods.

Just after 5 a.m., when those points of flashlight beams had spread flickering all along the shoreline, the first runner passed. Then another, then two more.

It was too dark to be sure who was who, so those of us watching simply passed on our good-lucks and looking-goods.

"Thanks," came the replies, followed by the soft padding of footsteps through the trees.

Six miles farther along the trail, we watched first Johnny Sandoval of Gypsum, Colorado, then Ann Trason, then Mark Tarr of Columbia Falls, Montana, enter and leave the May Queen aid station. Dawn was imminent, mist rose from the lake, and bagpipes played from somewhere in the distance. Like the rest of the field, the leaders used this station to discard or exchange items of clothing.

A race like Leadville is not so much a single race of 100 miles as a series of chunks — six, seven, 10 miles — that runners approach individually. Seeing friends, refueling and changing clothes all help regenerate.

"It makes such a difference," noted one runner. "It's like starting over."

Each of the Tarahumara used this opportunity to switch out of shoes provided by the sponsoring Rockport company and into the footwear they know best: sandals made from old tires, strapped on with leather cords. The perfect shoe, it seemed, for the next 87 miles of rocks, roots and rough terrain.

At the starting line, I had seen an elderly woman holding a sign that read: "Go, Glen, Go. Wisconsin Family Supporters." At May Queen I saw her again and asked about her son, Glen Vaassen. As it turned out, this was his first attempt at 100 miles, and his mother, father, three sisters and two nephews were here for moral support. Two years ago, she said, her son had a dream in which he finished his first 100-mile race, and his family was at the end to greet him.

"Doesn't that give you the creeps?" she said.

Creeps or clairvoyance, Vaassen would finish his first 100-mile race the next day in 28 hours, 53 minutes and 21 seconds. Feet swollen, tears welling up, family cheering his final, dog-tired steps.

When we saw the leaders again, Sandoval was still leading, but two Tarahumaras, Juan Herrera and Martimano Cervantes, had edged ahead of Trason. All were within 4 minutes of each other as they left the Outward Bound aid station at 23.5 miles.

In the full light of morning, these two Indians, dressed in an odd mixture of traditional and modern garb — breechcloths, bandannas, sandals, Rockport caps and shirts — were emerging as favorites.

Trason, meanwhile, exuding both strength and lightness, represented a kind of modern cultural icon, the exceptional female athlete. As it turned out, though, at this point she was less interested in what she represented than in where the hell her support crew was. Husband Carl Andersen finally showed up, taking full blame for upsetting his wife's focus.

"I just waited too long and missed her," he confessed later.

Missing your support crew is like having the transmission drop out of your car. Shaken by the experience, Trason pushed on.

During the 16 miles from Outward Bound to the next access point at Twin Lakes, the course climbs nearly 1,000 feet and then descends over 1,000 feet to the 39.5 mile mark. This was plenty of time and territory for a major overturn in fortunes.

When the first runner reached us, it was Trason. Herrera and Cervantes were a few minutes behind, while Sandoval had begun dropping back, and would eventually finish thirty-fourth.

Afterwards, Trason described the exchange of places before Twin Lakes as both odd and not totally pleasant. Earlier, Herrera and Cervantes had accelerated past her on downhill sections of the course, only to decelerate, turn and stare, then accelerate again. Not quite sure what to think of this, Trason threw in a downhill surge of her own, passing the two.

"Herrera took off when I passed him," noted Trason, "then stopped right in the middle of the trail and just looked at me."

To Trason, it seemed a sign from Herrera that he could outrun her whenever he chose, that he would not be beaten by a woman. And to the Tarahumara? After the race, third-place finisher Cervantes was reported to have expressed "the greatest admiration" for Trason during the race. One can only dimly imagine the full range of thoughts and emotions a native runner from an isolated village in Mexico must have felt, racing a woman through the mountains of Colorado.

Fifty miles into the Leadville 100 is the ghost town of Winfield. There, at the end of a hot, dusty road, volunteers had set up what looked like a mobile medical facility.

What must that point have felt like? To have run up and down trails since four in the morning, battling dehydration, thin air, weary legs and despair. To have climbed over a 12,600-foot mountain pass and ached down the other side. To have shuffled down a dusty dirt road to the aid station, with the sun retiring toward the horizon. To sit down for a moment for some food and drink.

Congratulations, you're halfway done.

And to know that almost the first thing you've got to face now is that same 12,600-foot mountain pass on the return. Somehow they all seemed to manage it, or at least they managed to begin it.

And still the question of who was going to finish first intrigued entrants, crews and spectators. Heading up the long climb to Hope Pass on the return trip, her husband Carl now along as pacer, Trason climbed steadily through the aspens and rock slides to the rarefied air above treeline. She was now 7 minutes ahead of Herrera.

And so it continued, for another 20 miles and two more mountain passes, past repeated words of encouragement from those still on their way to Winfield, runners who must have relished the chance to ignore their own discomfort long enough to wish this woman well. By the 72-mile mark, Trason's lead had extended to 18 minutes.

"I was heading up Hope Pass, and she just blew by me — voo-o-o-om!" remembered Glen Vaassen afterwards. "She was cruisin'."

It is the arrogance, or at least ignorance, of the spectator to assume to know the outcome of an event that isn't over. Knowing that Trason was beginning to shown signs of raggedness but impressed by the minutes she had gained, most of us watching were ready to call it a lock. What could possibly happen in those final 28 miles?

Leaving the Outward Bound aid station at 4:32 p.m., Trason wiped her brow with a bandanna and slowly jogged down the road, well ahead of both Herrera and the men's course record.

In the unobserved spaces between checkpoints, muscles stiffen, stomachs churn, spirits rise and fall, and ultra legends are born. Thus it was in the 1994 Leadville Trail 100, when word of Juan Herrera's dash up Sugarloaf and past Ann Trason began reaching the aid station at May Queen even before he did. Herrera arrived 6 minutes in the lead, then tore off around Turquoise Lake for the final 13 miles at what looked like 7-minute pace.

When Trason arrived at the aid station, the fire was washed out of her eyes, the result of an extended battle with nausea on the trail, and not for the first time in her ultrarunning career. "I'm trying to figure out why it happens," she confessed later. "It's sort of my limiting factor."

Pacer Carl later admitted to having had a hard time coaxing her to the finish, in spite of Trason's remarkable performance of 18:06:24, one that would break the women's course record by a spectacular 2 hours, 37 minutes.

"Oh, I knew that guy was going to catch me," Trason would say. She would also wonder, though, about the odd sensation of feeling as if she'd let people down, failing to do something she didn't set out to accomplish in the first place, to beat all the men.

Herrera, meanwhile, heading down those final 13 miles, scrambled into the darkness toward Leadville as the sky darkened, the moon rose, and stars began to dot the firmament. It must have seemed a kind of heavenly welcoming committee for the light-footed, tired-eyed Tarahumara, a familiar evening countenance for a man far away from home. Herrera reached the line in 17:30:42, the fastest time in the event's twelve-year history.

And, finally, headed to bed, which is more than can be said, yet, for the other 300 entrants of this race. They will continue to run through the night, under a sky ruled by what appears to be the planet Saturn.

"Saturnine," reads the dictionary. "Having or showing a sluggish, gloomy temperament. Suffering from lead poisoning." Yes, it *has* to be Saturn.

Several runners, like 39-year-old Thomas Taylor of Michigan, will feel themselves turning so sluggish on the final trek that they'll turn off their flashlights so runners behind won't realize they're walking.

"We got to the finish," Taylor will laugh later, after holding on for eighth place, "and found out the guys right ahead of us had done the same thing."

Others, those whose legs or feet or stomachs simply won't operate for a full 100 miles, will drop out and wait for another year. Over half of the starters will not finish, and will have to suffer sleep interrupted by the loudspeaker announcing those who did.

"That's the aggravating thing about this race," says one unlucky runner, Bill Barker of Princeton, Iowa, who ran out of steam at 60 miles. "You hear that thing all night long."

Still others will walk through the darkness, relying on their flashlights and those internal lights, too, holding on to the goal of finishing before the 34 closing time.

Founder Ken Chlouber will complete his tenth Leadville in 27:21:30. So will Harry Deupree in 28:21:45, while Bill Finkbeiner and Al Binder will each finish their eleventh. Nico Solomos, 56, will run 24:53:12, the forty-second and last finisher to win a gold-and-silver trophy buckle for finishing under 25 hours.

For almost all finishers, dim eyes will seem even more prominent than dead legs. But pride, a shared sense of achievement, will clearly shine behind those dim windows to the soul, uniting everyone who finishes and everyone who watches.

Of course what real difference does it make that anyone —

Tarahumara, woman, common citizen — finishes in front of anyone else, or that they have successfully wrestled their way through a 100-mile opponent in less than 30 hours?

"Car-ul! Car-ul! Car-ul!" the crowd shouts at the finish, as 66-year-old Carl Yates shuffles up the red carpet to become the 156th and last runner to reach the line, earning the final silver buckle of the day.

No difference, really.

September 1995

BLOOMS

*I pushed to the front, took the lead and knew
Shorter, among others, had me in his sights. But I
wanted to enjoy that first Bloomsday for as long as
I could at the front of the pack. The very fact of this
event seemed miraculous, and I wanted to savor it.*

EVEN BEFORE THAT FIRST-AID STATION, I knew I was in
trouble. I had beaten Frank Shorter before, but never while shouldering
organizational duties. Never before had I approached a water stop more
worried about whether the table and drinks were properly positioned
for the next thousand runners than about whether I could grab a cup of
water before my opponent did.

"Move up!" I shouted at the aid station volunteers as I ran past.
"You're too far off the road!" Somewhere up the street, Shorter was
getting away. I wouldn't see him again until the finish.

This edginess about logistical details was a new feeling. This
inaugural Lilac Bloomsday Run in 1977 was my first blush with race
organizing, and I had found it intensely distracting. I was a school
teacher and a competitor, not an event manager, but I still felt
responsible for the run's fate. I had suggested this thing in the first place.
Now, even though plenty of volunteers were in place and oversight of
the event was in someone else's court, I couldn't help but be distracted,
wondering if things were going according to plan.

In reality, though, by the time Frank Shorter began surging with conviction into his personal bubble of excellence ahead of the first Bloomsday pack, the success of the event was all but guaranteed. Over a thousand people had entered, many times more than we had anticipated. The entry form read "limited to the first 500 runners," because we cringed at the organizational challenges beyond that number. But as entries poured in, we realized it was easier to scramble to accommodate everyone than it was to figure out how to turn down anyone.

Spokane's Bloomsday Run was not alone in the explosive growth it was experiencing. In the late 1970s, every road race of every distance in every part of the country was growing like sci-fi protoplasm. People were wild about running and eager to have a race T-shirt to prove it.

No one knew where interest would peak. Wallowing in hyperbole, prognosticators jokingly forecast races with 50,000 entrants. Runners everywhere laughed giddily. A few years later we had one — in Spokane, a city of 180,000. Nothing in life has surprised me as much as that.

Nothing.

By the end of the 1980s, reflecting on the numbers, I crunched a few bits and bytes regarding the 53,155 finishers in the 1988 race. In *Bloomsday: A City In Motion*, I wrote: "During the race, that throng took an estimated 597,993,750 steps and lost 88,237 gallons of sweat. That's enough perspiration to fill a backyard swimming pool measuring 50 feet by 30 feet by 8 feet."

I loved that image. And for the weight watchers in the crowd, I added this one: "That same group expended 39,866,250 calories (KCal), the equivalent of 11,390 pounds of fat. Don't ask where it went, by the way, just be pleased that it's gone."

And finally, getting all those caloric units pointed in the same direction (and with a little analytical help from some engineering friends), I noted that the energy was "enough to lift the Space Shuttle (4 1/2 million pounds) 18 seconds into its trip, to a height of 5,200 feet. No roar of rocket engines either, just a big UMMPPHH! from the crowd, and there it goes, a mile high..."

Imagine that. Imagine the Shuttle in the middle of a big blanket, held tightly by 50,000 citizens in shorts, like Eskimos about to toss one of their comrades into the air for fun and a better view of the landscape.

UMMPPHH! People working together can do amazing things.

It doesn't surprise me any more to see 60,000 runners, joggers and walkers converging on downtown Spokane. But it did shock me to see 1,000 runners sitting on the steps outside the Opera House in 1977. Where had they all come from?

For reasons I can no longer recollect, we had decided to use the steps as a staging area, and then to march everyone to the starting line. I stood on the stage looking around for Shorter so I could introduce him to the crowd, but Frank was out jogging somewhere. Eventually he showed up, a puzzled look on his face.

"Doesn't anyone around here warm up?" he asked. It was a good question.

The field included many of the best runners in the state, as well as Shorter and Joan Ullyot of San Francisco — a doctor, writer, speaker and our top invited female. We all endured a short, informal parade to the starting line on Spokane Falls Boulevard near the Opera House. At 1:30 — a starting time chosen for maximum public visibility and, as it turned out, maximum chance of heatstroke — we were off, quickly zig-zagging up to Riverside Avenue.

As we headed through the downtown canyon, I remember feeling the exhilaration I've now come to expect at the start of every Bloomsday, a combination of freedom and adrenaline. I pushed to the front, took the lead and knew Shorter, among others, had me in his sights. But I wanted to enjoy that first Bloomsday for as long as I could at the front of the pack.

The very fact of this event seemed miraculous, and I wanted to savor it. In 1977, urban running was a new phenomenon, pioneered by events like the Peachtree Road Race and the New York City Marathon, which in turn were inspired by the venerable, though musty, Boston Marathon. Spurred by a national interest in urban renewal, powered by a growing allegiance to aerobic fitness, and sprinkled with a dash of rebellion from the 60s, road races were popping up in major cities across the United States.

In Spokane, we had recently enjoyed a world's fair and reconstructive surgery on the entire downtown core. The Spokane River gorge and falls were no longer criss-crossed with railroad tracks and asphalt, but instead enjoyed a position of prominence in the newly christened

Riverfront Park. An event that took advantage of all this seemed pre-ordained.

Or maybe it just looks that way two decades later, karma revealed. The reality was more a loose connection of chance encounters and offhanded remarks than solid links. I was interviewed after a fun run a few weeks after returning from the Montreal Olympics, and I told the reporter I thought the growing interest in running should be channeled into a downtown road race. I was quoted in the newspaper. A few days later, I happened to get on an elevator with then-Mayor David Rodgers.

"You're that Olympic runner, aren't you?" he asked.

Yes I was.

"Well, I read what you said in the newspaper, and I think it's a great idea."

A friend with the Spokane Jaycees overheard. When the elevator stopped, he suggested the Jaycees help organize the race.

The Lilac Bloomsday Run was born.

Well, not quite. There were still a bazillion details to work out, and at least one major hurdle: an approved course. Traffic engineers and police were reluctant to close Monroe Street, a major north-south corridor about a half mile from the finish. We, in turn, couldn't accept a course that ended short of Riverfront Park. Neither side would budge.

We managed to get a meeting together with police and city officials. We stated our conviction that Monroe had to be closed. The other side expressed their equally strong judgment that it was impossible. That exchange of viewpoints lasted about five minutes. Then Mayor Rodgers spoke up.

"You know," he said, "I remember growing up in Boston, and going down the block every spring with my mom and dad to watch the marathoners go by."

He got misty-eyed.

"I think this would be a great event for this city."

The meeting ended. We had our course.

The route we had chosen, by the way, was also meant to reflect James Joyce's novel *Ulysses*. The name "Bloomsday" is derived from the book, which is a bit of trivia I dredge up once or twice a year to entertain a few people. A poster in the Bloomsday office from Dublin, Ireland, explains the name this way: "The novel *Ulysses* treats the full spectrum of human experience in a detailed fictional account of ordinary events and ordinary people on a single day in Dublin, Thursday 16 June 1904. The wanderings of myriad characters through Dublin city on that day are meticulously recorded, principally that man about town Leopold Bloom — hence the name Bloomsday..."

But why — if Joyce's Bloomsday was June 16 — was ours the first Sunday of May? Well, that would put the event in synch with the blooming of lilacs, Spokane's official flower. The city's annual Lilac Festival is in May, and this would tie into it.

And what does Spokane have to do with Dublin? Well, Joyce once said, "If I can get to the heart of Dublin I can get to the heart of every city in the world. In the particular is contained the universal." So be it.

So when a friend and I designed the course, we looked for parallels to Bloom's Dublin journey, which was in turn a parallel journey to that of Ulysses in Homer's Odyssey. Joyce had fun with the parallels; so did we. There are miles to travel, obstacles to overcome, monsters to subdue — for Greek heroes and their modern equivalents — in the Mediterranean, in Ireland, in Spokane.

A few years later, another friend of mine wrote a letter to the James Joyce Foundation explaining the fun I had with all this: "He even designed the course with *Ulysses* in mind. For instance, running past McDonald's corresponded to 'Oxen of the Sun,' across a bridge where an island housing a goat could be seen corresponded to 'Eumaeus,' past the well-known spot where dope was peddled in town corresponded to 'Lotus Eaters,' etc. Of course, when he tried to explain all of this to local reporters, they were totally confused."

Yes, and so were the Spokane Jaycees when I first announced the name — The Lilac Bloomsday Run. Ta-daaa!

Dead silence.

Punning ends when running begins, and you are left with your own resources. That original Bloomsday route went across the Maple Street Toll Bridge, and I could tell by the time I hit the on-ramp a little over a mile into the race that I was faltering. I could sense that, organizational exhaustion or just a foolishly fast early pace, my minutes in the lead were numbered. I had only one goal left at that point: to be the first Bloomie — a name soon to enter the local lexicon — ever to pass through the Maple Street Bridge toll booth.

I surged, I cruised, and in a minute I passed the collection basket, the first runner in history to squeeze past without dropping a dime. Nearby, toll-takers stood smiling, enjoying this bizarre respite from the normal numb of coin collection. Heading uphill immediately afterward, Shorter caught me, challenged for the lead, and I began to worry about aid station placement.

Most of the race after that was uneventful. Another runner and Club Northwest teammate of mine, Herm Atkins, took over second place. I reached the finish line next to the clock tower in third. Later, I watched a dozen runners writhing on the ground with heatstroke under the Washington-Stevens couplet, and those organizational questions began haunting me again.

Like race organizers everywhere in the country who were trying to come to terms with mega-race logistics, we made some big changes to Bloomsday over the next few years. We moved the race earlier in the day, provided more water on the course, and gave detailed instructions to volunteers on how to get fluids to runners. We eliminated the parade. We changed the course, bypassing the toll booth. We moved the finish line out of Riverfront Park. We watched the event grow, and grow, and grow.

Now, about to celebrate our twentieth year, we're spending a fair amount of time remembering our roots and trying to nourish them. People working together can do amazing things, and everyone involved with the event wants to continue to generate amazement. Doing that requires thousands of hours of work by thousands of volunteers. It involves adjustments, realignments and a few major overhauls now and then.

Some things, though, never seem to change for me. I still get that great rush as the community stampedes down Riverside ... and Main and Sprague. And I still spend an awful lot of time after that wondering why I started so fast and why I'm feeling tired so early in the race. And that's about when, every year, my thoughts drift one more time from race-day competition to improved organizational strategies.

Still, organization aside, there is always that part of me — the once-swift Olympic runner — that can't wait to get back for another go at it. Next year, I tell myself, I will run smarter, worry less, run faster.

Yes I will. Yes.

October 1995

EPILOGUE

*I don't know. I see mist in the crystal ball. So,
looking down the pike, I choose not to predict, but
to dream — of good health, good companionship,
and deep breaths of fresh air in my lungs.*

HERE ON THE EDGE OF WINTER IN SPOKANE, I'm enjoying
what the next twelve months promise to bring. A twentieth chance to
run fast through downtown Spokane. The Atlanta Olympics. The
hundredth running of the Boston Marathon. More running adventures,
yet to be dreamed.

This much should be obvious: I want to run a 100-mile race. I can't
stop thinking about it. If I finally manage 100 miles at one sitting, it will
make no difference. But there it will be, done.

But let's talk about shorter quests. Since you made it all the way
through this book, I feel you've earned an update on some of the events
and individuals covered in these pages:

• The Ultimate Runner is no longer contested in Jackson, Michigan.
One or two similar events have sprung up around the country, including
one in Spokane. Mike McGlynn, the organizer of the original,
occasionally calls to discuss other wacko events he's been dreaming up.

• The Jim Hershberger MVP tournament moved into the annals of
history when its founder moved to prison. Hershberger was sent to
Leavenworth in 1990 for defrauding investors and filing false financial
statements relative to his oil business. As far as I've been able to
determine, he is the only person to have made it onto the front of a

Wheaties box and behind bars. Though the MVP had little to do with his crimes, an article in the Kansas City Times reported that "a former business associate contended Hershberger unfairly had another competitor disqualified [in the MVP] so that he could claim the $20,000 first prize." No comment on misdirecting cross country runners over a railroad bridge.

• The Summer Biathlon series, on the other hand, is alive and thriving, a near victim of its own success. I tried my trigger finger at this event one other time, and I failed just as miserably as the first. I'm considering a third try, but so far I've set no target date.

• Masters competition thrives. Bill Rodgers and Frank Shorter have raced each other dozens of times since turning 40 (Bill always wins). A little over a year ago, Eamonn Coughlin became the first human over age 40 to dip under 4 minutes for the mile.

• I've not had a rematch yet with my favorite librarian, Janet. That series stands 1-0 in my favor.

• This fall, the Carcross 10 reassembled under a new name — Who's Next? — and raced along the Klondike Trail once again. The Smokin' Old Geezers nailed our hides to the birch again.

• Johnny Kelley no longer runs the entire Boston Marathon. His streak ended in 1992, though he still manages to shuffle over the final 10 kilometers of the race every year. Not bad for a man in his late 80s.

• Likewise, the Arkansas Pikes Peak Marathon Society still manages to shuffle more than its share of Hawgs to the roof of the Rockies every August, while the most famous Hawg of all, Bill Clinton, shuffles around the Mall in Washington, D.C., earning fast food.

• The Empire State Building Run Up still lures its yearly lobby-full of runners with large calf muscles.

• The Dipsea hurtles happily toward its 100th year.

• The Ho Chi Minh City Marathon continues to attract U.S. veterans to its sweaty embrace, with less obstructions now that diplomatic relations with Vietnam have been restored.

Most running events, in fact, those I have covered in this book, are prospering. The Peachtree Road Race and the New York City Marathon turned 25 last year, and each was inundated with aerobic celebrants, not to mention a handful of stunned old-timers, scruffy human relics from those preboom years when a hundred runners was a *lot*.

Then, too, the impending 100th Boston has generated renewed interest in the marathon distance this year. Races across the country are jam-packed. The Atlanta Olympic marathons are sure to highlight new stars, heroes able to withstand heat, humidity and hills.

In spite of overall good health for the sport, though, there has also been considerable angst in the running community in recent years. Where lies the future of the sport, and what can we do to help? Summits have been held, task forces formed, papers issued, organizations restructured.

Last year, running lost two of its grandest figures — doctor-philosopher George Sheehan and New York City Marathon impresario Fred Lebow — two personalities impossible to replace.

There have also been new studies published recently on the relationship of running to health. One, by Dr. Peter Wood of Stanford, shows that higher mileage produces healthier blood profiles. Another, by Dr. Kenneth Cooper, warns that high mileage may weaken the immune system by releasing free radicals into the bloodstream. The last free radical I was aware of — Carlos the Jackal — was captured about a year ago, and my blood profile looks dandy, so I'm ignoring all the science and just trying to enjoy my sport in the midst of more immediate concerns — snow, rain, wind, heat, muscle pulls, Achilles tears, schedule conflicts, motivational lapses — that keep me from my appointed rounds.

In fact, looking forward to the next ten years, it's the small issues, the personal ones, that really pique my interest:

Will injuries disrupt my training?

Will my training partners remain constant?

Will I continue to enjoy 2-hour runs in the woods?

Will I find the wherewithal to stumble through a 100-mile run?

I don't know. I see mist in the crystal ball. So, looking down the pike, I choose not to predict, but to dream — of good health, good companionship, and deep breaths of fresh air in my lungs.

And one more dream while I'm at it. Ten years hence. New Year's Eve, 2005. Cold, clear night. Dark sky, crackling stars. I forsake the traditional Auld Lang Syne approach in favor of a night at home with my family.

At 11:30 p.m., I zip up my training suit, lace up my shoes, and am just heading out the door into the still, freezing air. Suddenly, my daughters Kaitlin and Catherine, 20 and 22 years old, dash into the room.

"Dad," they beg, "can we come?"

About the author

Don Kardong was the fourth-place finisher in the 1976 Olympic marathon. He lives with his wife and two daughters in Spokane, Washington, where he founded one of the nation's largest running events, the Lilac Bloomsday Run. Don is a senior writer for *Runner's World* and former contributor to *Running Times*, *The Runner* and other magazines. He is also the author of *Thirty Phone Booths to Boston: Tales of a Wayward Runner* (Macmillan Publishing Company, 1985) and co-author of *Bloomsday: A City in Motion* (Cowles Publishing Co., 1989).

To order more copies of

HILLS, HAWGS & HO CHI MINH

Send $14.95 per copy ordered, plus $3 shipping per order, to:

> Keokee Co. Publishing, Inc.
> P.O. Box 722
> Sandpoint, ID 83864

Visa or Mastercard orders by phone accepted toll-free at: 1-800-880-3573 from 8:30 a.m. to 5 p.m., Monday through Friday (Pacific Time). For orders by phone, please have at hand your credit card number and expiration date.